Studia Fennica
Litteraria 7

The Finnish Literature Society (Sks) was founded in 1831 and has, from the very beginning, engaged in publishing operations. It nowadays publishes literature in the fields of ethnology and folkloristics, linguistics, literary research and cultural history.

The first volume of the Studia Fennica series appeared in 1933. Since 1992, the series has been divided into three thematic subseries: Ethnologica, Folkloristica and Linguistica. Two additional subseries were formed in 2002, Historica and Litteraria. The subseries Anthropologica was formed in 2007.

In addition to its publishing activities, the Finnish Literature Society maintains research activities and infrastructures, an archive containing folklore and literary collections, a research library and promotes Finnish literature abroad.

Studia fennica editorial board
Markku Haakana, lecturer, University of Helsinki, Finland
Timo Kaartinen, lecturer, University of Helsinki, Finland
Kimmo Rentola, professor, University of Turku, Finland
Riikka Rossi, docent, University of Helsinki, Finland
Hanna Snellman, professor, University of Helsinki, Finland
Lotte Tarkka, professor, University of Helsinki, Finland
Tuomas M. S. Lehtonen, Secretary General, Dr. Phil., Finnish Literature Society, Finland
Pauliina Rihto, secretary of the board, M. A., Finnish Literature Society, Finland

oa.finlit.fi

Editorial Office
SKS
P.O. Box 259
FI-00171 Helsinki
www.finlit.fi

Studia Fennica Litteraria 7

The publication has undergone a peer review.

The open access publication of this volume has received part funding via Helsinki University Library.

© 2013 Anna Kuismin, M. J. Driscoll and SKS
License CC-BY-NC-ND 4.0 International.

A digital edition of a printed book first published in 2013 by the Finnish Literature Society.
Cover Design: Timo Numminen
EPUB: eLibris Media Oy

ISBN 978-952-222-444-6 (Print)
ISBN 978-952-222-749-2 (PDF)
ISBN 978-952-222-492-7 (EPUB)

ISSN 0085-6835 (Studia Fennica)
ISSN 1458-5278 (Studia Fennica Litteraria)

DOI: https://doi.org/10.21435/sflit.7

This work is licensed under a Creative Commons CC-BY-NC-ND 4.0 International License. To view a copy of the license, please visit http://creativecommons.org/licenses/by-nc-nd/4.0/

A free open access version of the book is available at https://doi.org/10.21435/sflit.7 or by scanning this QR code with your mobile device.

White Field, Black Seeds

Nordic Literacy Practices in the Long Nineteenth Century

Edited by Anna Kuismin & M. J. Driscoll

Finnish Literature Society · SKS · Helsinki

Contents

ANNA KUISMIN & M. J. DRISCOLL
Preface
Exploring the Processes and Practices of Literacy in the Nordic Countries 7

MARTYN LYONS
A New History from Below?
The Writing Culture of European Peasants, c. 1850 – c.1920 14

BRITT LILJEWALL
Recollections of Reading and Writing
Another Picture of Swedish Literacy 30

DAVIÐ ÓLAFSSON
Scribal Communities in Iceland
The Case of Sighvatur Grímsson 40

M. J. DRISCOLL
The Long and Winding Road
Manuscript Culture in Late Pre-Modern Iceland 50

SIGURÐUR GYLFI MAGNÚSSON
Living by the Book
Form, Text and Life Experience in Iceland 64

KIRSTI SALMI-NIKLANDER
Monologic, Dialogic, Collective
The Modes of Writing in Hand-Written Newspapers in 19th- and Early 20th-Century Finland 76

ANN-CATRINE EDLUND
A Country Maid and her Diary
Methodological Reflections on Historical Literacy Practices 89

ANNA KUISMIN
From Family Inscriptions to Autobiographical Novels
Motives for Writing in Grassroots Life Stories in 19th-Century Finland 101

KAISA KAURANEN
Odd Man Out?
The Self-Educated Philosopher and his Social Analyses of 19th-Century Finland   120

GUÐNÝ HALLGRÍMSDÓTTIR
Material without Value?
The Recollections of Guðrún Ketilsdóttir   134

KATI MIKKOLA
Self-Taught Collectors of Folklore and their Challenge to Archival Authority   146

PETRI LAUERMA
Finnish Revivalist Movements and the Development of Literary Finnish   158

LEA LAITINEN & TARU NORDLUND
Language from Below?
Indexing Identities in the Writings of Common People in 19th-Century Finland   169

Bibliography   190

Index of Names   209

Anna Kuismin & M. J. Driscoll

Preface
Exploring the Processes and Practices of Literacy in the Nordic Countries

> Valkia pelto,
> siemenet mustat.
> Kylvää ken taitaa?
>
> (White field,
> black seeds;
> who can sow?)[1]

Although the riddle quoted here – of which there are over 250 variants in the Folklore Archives of the Finnish Literature Society – comes out of oral tradition, the question it poses points to another realm: the white field is paper, the black seeds ink, and so sowing refers to the act of writing. At the time the riddle was first recorded, in the mid-19th century, the majority of Finland's rural population was not able to put their thoughts down on paper. From the 18th century to the early 20th, reading and writing were regarded as separate skills in Lutheran Finland, and the latter seen as unnecessary for much of the population. The situation was similar in Sweden and Norway, too: above all, mass literacy concerned the ability to read religious texts. Yet there were a number of ordinary people with no access to formal schooling who nevertheless learnt to write and subsequently used their skill to produce texts of many different kinds – writings which open up fascinating vistas for multi-disciplinary research.

The scene was rather different in Iceland, a country widely known for its exceptionally strong medieval literary tradition, first and foremost the many vellum manuscripts containing sagas and poetry of various kinds, chronicles, learned and religious works and so on – nearly all written in the vernacular. What is less well known is the fact that the literary culture of the following centuries was also largely practised via hand-written media, despite the arrival of the printing press in Iceland in the 1530s. In addition to the well-known body of medieval texts, there exists a rich corpus of literary material from the post-medieval period, a large proportion of which was commissioned, copied, read and/or owned by ordinary farmers, fisherman and labourers. As in Finland, there has in recent years been an upsurge in interest in these texts among Icelandic scholars involved in what may be called "Post-Gutenberg" manuscript studies, i.e. research into the structure and mechanisms of chirographic transmission in the age of print and how the two cultures existed side by side, for far longer, and far more dynamically, than has hitherto been appreciated.

The present collection of articles has its origin in interaction between Finnish and Icelandic scholars interested in the processes and practices of literacy among the common people. Anna Kuismin's multi-disciplinary research network focusing on literacy practices in 19th-century Finland (Kansanihmiset ja kirjallistuminen 1800-luvun Suomessa) has organised campaigns for collecting manuscripts and compiling catalogues of archival material, arranged seminars and conferences and produced both scholarly and popular publications. A team of researchers active in this Finnish network joined forces with their Icelandic colleagues from the Reykjavík Academy, a centre for independent scholars in the humanities and social sciences, and sought out scholars working on similar topics from other Nordic countries too. The result was a series of explorative workshops, The common people and the processes of literacy in the Nordic countries: Excursions into scribal and print cultures in 18th- and 19th-centuries, led by Professor Lea Laitinen from the University of Helsinki and financed by a grant from the Joint Committee for Nordic Research Councils for the Humanities and the Social Sciences in 2009.

These workshops brought together scholars from Finnish and Scandinavian languages, literature, history and folklore, social history, the history of ideas and book history to explore the practices and processes through which Nordic societies became more and more permeated by writing during "the long 19th century" (roughly from the French Revolution to the First World War). The first workshop was held at Kiljavanranta, Finland, and the second at the Arnamagnæan Institute, University of Copenhagen. In all, 23 participants from Finland, Denmark, Iceland, Norway and Sweden took part. In addition, keynote lectures were given by Wim Vandenbussche, Professor of Dutch linguistics at the Vrije Universiteit Brussel, and Martyn Lyons, Professor of History at the University of New South Wales, Australia.

The workshops in turn resulted in the research project Reading and writing from below: Toward a new social history of literacy in the Nordic sphere during the long 19th century, funded by a NORDCORP grant from 2011 to 2014 and led by Taru Nordlund and Anna Kuismin from the University of Helsinki, M. J. Driscoll from the University of Copenhagen, Ann-Catrine Edlund from Umeå University and Davíð Ólafsson from the Reykjavik Academy. This project involves researchers from several disciplines and seeks to contribute to the study of the social and cultural history of literacy in the Nordic countries by focusing on the roles played by the written word in the everyday lives of ordinary people, i.e. those with little or no formal education from the lower strata of society, and in this way challenging both traditional dichotomies such as manuscript vs. print, oral vs. written and centre vs. periphery and the ways in which the processes of literacy education, acquisition and appropriation have previously been understood.

The overall aim of the present volume is to throw light on various aspects of literacy in Finland, Iceland and Sweden[2] from the late 18th to the early 20th century. Although a number of different approaches are represented, what unites the contributions are the emphasis on socio-cultural contexts and the notion that literacy is not just the ability to read and write but rather the totality of the processes and practices involved in the production, dissemination and reception of written texts, thus providing insights into cultural diversity different from dominant spheres. In addition, the contributions have in common a focus on non-privileged people, their experiences and points of view. The writers naturally draw from research done outside the Nordic countries too, e.g. British new literacy studies.

Although the articles in this collection focus on specific historical periods and contexts, comparable developments are currently taking place within linguistic communities which are in the process of constructing their own cultures of literacy, and our project is thus of potential relevance to these emerging literate cultures, not least in examining the processes of knowledge acquisition on a grassroots level and their significance for democracy. There is also an interesting parallel between developments in the 19th century and the contemporary literacy practices which the current revolution in information technology has brought about in the lives of ordinary people.

In the first article, Martyn Lyons characterises the tenets of the "new history from below", which sees common people as active agents rather than passive recipients; it is based on writings from the grassroots and focuses on individual experiences of historical change. Cultural history today has two main intellectual ancestors, argues Lyons: one is the Annales School and the other is the British neo-Marxist social history of the 1960s. Both have given us a brand of "history from below", but they have seen this chiefly in terms of collective mentalities or movements. Lyons argues that the history of popular writing practices currently represents a new history from below, in that it emphasises individual rather than collective experience, and relies on what ordinary people actually wrote for themselves.

Literacy Acquisition and Scribal Cultures

The law for general education was passed in Denmark as early as 1814, whereas in Sweden it was passed in 1842, in Norway 1848, in 1907 in Iceland and in Finland not until 1921. In Sweden, research on the history of literacy has been conducted by social historian Egil Johansson from Umeå University. Using parish registers and their examination records to determine the literacy rates in the whole country, Johansson discovered that Swedish people learnt to read from the late 17th century onwards, whereas the ability to write was much rarer. In her article, Britt Liljewall employs a qualitative approach, using autobiographical narratives as her source material. She analyses different stages in reaching functional reading and writing competence and pays attention to the roles of gender and social status in the acquisition of literacy, finding an interesting connection between the long-cherished view of Sweden as a leader in the literacy sweepstakes and the notion of Sweden as a *folkhemmet* ("home of the people"), the cornerstone of national identity.

Like Liljewall, Davíð Ólafsson explores the acquisition of reading and writing skills outside the institutional literacy practices provided by the Church. The old written culture of Iceland, combined with the lack of access to the medium of print, gave rise to a scribal culture parallel to the culture of print. According to Davíð Ólafsson, self- (or self-initiated) education was one of the driving forces behind vernacular literacy practices. Both printed and hand-written texts were read aloud at winter-evening gatherings (*kvöldvökur*, sing. *kvöldvaka*), when people did handicrafts and passed the time in company. The case of Sighvatur Grímsson Borgfirðingur (1840–1930), from south-western Iceland, presents the phases in self-education needed for a fully-fledged scribe. An important part of the education of this "wordmonger", as the author likes to refer to his subject, was provided in the literary milieu of Akranes, where there was an active interest in the production and circulation of manuscripts. In addition to his copying activities, Sighvatur Grímsson wrote an autobiography, complied genealogies and produced other texts of various kinds.

After briefly sketching the history of manuscript culture in Iceland, M. J. Driscoll looks at another of the great "late" copyists, Magnús Jónsson í Tjaldanesi (1835–1922), an ordinary farmer with no formal education in whose hand are preserved copies, generally more than one, of nearly 200 sagas – essentially everything that was in circulation in Iceland at the time. Magnús was unusual among copyists in detailing in prefaces to his manuscripts how he had got hold of his exemplars and whether he had seen other versions of the texts he copied, providing a wealth of information on the mechanisms of chirographic transmission in late 19th- and early 20th-century Iceland, mechanisms which even as he wrote were rapidly becoming irrelevant as the *kvöldvaka* lost its importance as a social and cultural institution.

The tradition of *kvöldvaka* also figures in Sigurður Gylfi Magnússon's article on Icelandic autobiographies. The article claims that the ancient sagas – traditionally read aloud at gatherings but increasingly as time went on read silently in private – have had a profound impact on popular thought in Iceland well into the 20th century. The centrality of the sagas in Icelandic culture has left its mark as recurring motifs and on the reticent way feelings and emotions are described in life stories. The sagas taught Icelanders to fulfil their roles with stoicism and accept whatever circumstance threw at them, and they provided people with modes of living, thinking and shaping their memories. According to Sigurður Gylfi Magnússon, this could not have happened without the high degree of cultural homogeneity found in Iceland.

While there was a strong oral element in Icelandic scribal culture – since texts were most often written to be read aloud – Finland has had a lively tradition of producing hand-written newspapers. In her article, Kirsti Salmi-Niklander analyses the socio-cultural functions of this practice in 19th- and early 20th-century Finland, drawing attention to the social, ideological and emotional needs of those who contributed to and edited hand-written newspapers as a part of the activities in youth or workers' associations. Salmi-Niklander distinguishes three modes of writing in these papers: the monological mode, which provides possibilities for mediating ideological messages, the dialogical mode, which allow for the expression and processes of hidden tensions in small groups and communities, and the collective mode, which opens up ways of expressing emotions and experiences. These modes can be found in the hand-written newspapers of a single community and in the authorial strategies of individual writers. As Salmi-Niklander shows, however, their impact varies in different communities and at different historical periods.

Genres and Case Studies

The concepts developed in the New Literacy Studies and actor-network theory form the basis for Ann-Catrine Edlund's theoretical and methodological reflections on the study of diaries. Edlund also employs an ethnographic approach in her case study of the diary of Linnéa Johansson, a country maid in northern Sweden. Before starting to keep a diary, Johansson was involved in another literacy practice: writing down songs in a notebook. Edlund examines the functions of Johansson's diary keeping, the writer's representation of herself in her diary as well the ways in which her thoughts and feelings are expressed. There is a significant change which takes place in Johansson's diary: after having recorded events in the households at which she served, the diarist begins to create a space of her own on the pages of her notebook and becomes a subject in the narrative which is unfolding in her diary.

Anna Kuismin (formerly Makkonen) introduces a corpus of some sixty autobiographical texts penned by Finnish common people, drawn from several archives and from printed sources. The focus of her article is on the writers' motives and audiences. The earliest Finnish life stories drew generic traits from family inscriptions, devotional books and oral poetry, while some of the latest ones took their form from the first-person novel. Many kinds of reasons motivated people to write about the course of their lives: some wanted to pass information on for future generations, others to educate their peers. There were also those who were motivated by a need to apologise, take revenge or confess. Stories of conversion include both religious autobiographies and narratives focusing on the awakening to nation-building and public enlightenment.

Whereas the Icelandic farmer, fisherman and scribe Sighvatur Grímsson Borgfirðingur could enjoy the support of his network of like-minded people, the protagonist of Kaisa Kauranen's research, crofter Kustaa Brask, was more of an outsider in his surroundings. Brask was an indefatigable writer who sent thousands of hand-written pages to the Finnish Literature Society over several decades, writings which offer interesting perspectives into life in rural Finland – class relations, customs, ways of thinking and prevailing mentalities. Kauranen's article deals with these topics through an examination of a range of texts by Brask, including historical and societal writings, with an emphasis on those concerned with literacy and public enlightenment. His relationship with the Finnish Literature Society and the owners of the croft on which he lived provided constraints on the ways in which he could express his views on social inequality.

A New Look at the Archives

The articles of Guðný Hallgrímsdóttir and Kati Mikkola place emphasis on the awareness of the ways in which the collecting and classification of archival material have been practised and the kinds of ideologies that lie behind these practices. As Guðný Hallgrímsdóttir shows in her article, women's manuscripts and texts about women are not always easily found in library and archival catalogues, as they are frequently catalogued under the names of their husbands, fathers or brothers, which has naturally had consequences for scholars' selection of sources and resulted in a marginalisation of women in research. For example, the story of the servant woman Guðrún Ketilsdóttir (1759–1842) from northern Iceland, written down from her oral delivery, has been categorised as a story of a foolish person in Páll Eggert Ólason's catalogue of manuscripts in the National Library. When the text in its three manuscript versions is analysed and connected to the historical and cultural background of Guðrún Ketilsdóttir, a fascinating story emerges of an Icelandic woman from below.

Recording folklore was a vital part of both Icelandic and Finnish nation building, practised by scholars and amateur collectors alike. In her article Kati Mikkola analyses the relationship between the academic experts of the Finnish Literature Society and those lay collectors who came from the lower ranks of society. Analysing the correspondence and contributions of the two collectors Vilho Itkonen (1872–1918), a working-class man with theosophical leanings, and Ulla Mannonen (1895–1958), a Karelian evacuee, Mikkola shows how they challenged the authority of the archival authorities and points out how the once questionable and even controversial contributions contested the hegemonic concepts and roles offered by the collecting organisation. The work done by Mannonen and Itkonen underscores the dimension of variability added to the archives with the passage of time: once deemed worthless, they have now acquired new value.

Language

Petri Lauerma shows in his article how the revivalist movements contributed to the development of Finnish literary language in three separate, though partially overlapping, waves. The first wave of Pietism was felt in westernmost Finland as early as the 18th century, but it made only a superficial impact on Old Literary Finnish. The second wave is analysed through the cases of Henrik Renqvist (1789–1866) and Paavo Ruotsalainen (1777–1852). According to Lauerma, revivalism activated the use and knowledge of western-based Old Literary Finnish in eastern Finland, but it also guaranteed that the old literary language began to change. The third wave came when the "awakenist" type of revivalism spread into southern and northern Ostrobothnia (from the 1830s on). In general, the influence of northern dialects filtered away many features of eastern Finnish type, but it also made sure the Finnish language did not split into two literary languages during the 19th century.

Lea Laitinen and Taru Nordlund apply linguistic approaches to texts written by common people in 19th-century Finland. From the interactional point of view of contemporary historical sociolinguistics and linguistic anthropology, they focus on context dependent meanings of expressions referring to the participation in a communicative event: belonging to a group, membership and identity in a speech community, as well as its ideological implications. The authors analyse certain syntactic alternatives of Finnish personal forms that the self-educated writers used as a resource for creating their own linguistic practices and styles as members of local and global communities they identified with. Interestingly, the texts reveal that the writers have exploited resources from three different linguistic varieties shared in their social community: the old Biblical Finnish, the new Standard Finnish and their own dialect.

Laitinen and Nordlund draw the conclusion that the process of creating new stylistic practices cannot be described as either from above or from below but from a common ground. They also discuss theoretical concepts used in linguistic research on texts by self-educated writers. The authors point out that in the analysis of the texts, the notion intended standard is directly related to another key notion, audience design. As for concepts stylistic rupture and intended standard, they turn in actual practice easily to represent the ideology of from above. In this case, the yardstick of the text is, for instance, stylistic purity, the ideal of the standard language, instead of looking it into from the own meaning making of the text.

NOTES

1 Elias Lönnrot, "Suomalaisia Arvoituksia", in Z. Topelius, *Maamme-kirja*, 81.
2 There has been some research from below on the practices and processes of literacy in Norway and Denmark. Jostein Fet's *Skrivande bønder* is a valuable work, focusing on the northern Vestlandet from 1600 to1850 (Fet 2003). One can also mention Arne Apelseth's doctoral dissertation, *Den låge danniga*, from the University of Bergen in 2004, and the articles of Bjarne Stoklund, Bjørn Poulsen and Tine Damsholt on Danish peasant diaries in *Writing Peasants* (Lorenzen-Schmidt & Poulsen 2002).

Martyn Lyons

A New History from Below?

The Writing Culture of European Peasants, c. 1850 – c.1920

In Philippe Poirrier's recent book on the current state of cultural history, two great traditions stand out for the influence they have exerted worldwide over this domain: first, the tradition of the French Annales school, and second, the British neo-Marxist school (Poirrier 2008, 189). I would like to discuss them both very briefly, as part of the "old" history from below, in order to bring into relief what is new and different about the work being carried out today by historians of scribal culture and ordinary writings in Spain, Italy, France and the Nordic countries. What I call the "new history from below" is distinctive because it is based on writings from the grassroots, and because it focuses on individual experiences of historical change. The problem of reconciling the individual with the general remains, and we need to avoid producing a history of isolated fragments, in a gallery of fascinating but exceptional proletarian authors. In the second half of this chapter, I would like to illustrate some generalising themes and contextual problems in my own work which help me to resolve this difficulty.

The Old History from Below

First of all, then, I would like to offer some comments on the "old" history from below and on the difficulties it presents to the historian. For a long time, a history of the lower classes seemed unreachable, an impossible dream. The Annales School – the first great historiographical family to be considered in Poirrier's survey – believed, in its middle phase, that the lives of the anonymous poor could only be investigated on a collective basis, through long statistical series of demographic data, data on literacy rates or the price of bread. According to François Furet, a quantitative analysis was the only way to incorporate the lower classes into the general historical narrative, through "number and anonymity" (cited in Kaye 1984, 225). As a result, the subordinate classes remained a silent and disincarnated mass without any personal identity. In the Braudelian tradition, the regional histories for which the Annales School became famous concentrated on the interaction between the geographical environment and human society. Thus in LeRoy Ladurie's *The Peasants of Languedoc*, a chapter on the local vegetation and crops seemed literally to prioritise the vegetable grassroots over the human inhabitants of south-western France (LeRoy Ladurie 1966).

One of the hallmarks of the Annales paradigm was the development of the history of mentalities, as promoted by the founding fathers Marc Bloch and Lucien Febvre. Here again, the "history from below" focused on "collective mentalities" – a debatable concept since it did not sufficiently differentiate on grounds of class or gender. Both Bloch and Febvre, in different ways, sought to reconstruct the intellectual coherence of an entire age, assuming that coherence and unity underpinned every past culture (Burguière 2009). This was in clear contrast to Marxist approaches, which emphasised the material bases of cultural phenomena and stressed class conflict rather than cultural consensus. Febvre's own *Rabelais* was an illustration of this. Febvre argued strongly against psychological anachronism, because in his view to consider the scabrous poet an atheist was to impose a 20th-century idea on a 16th-century mind, for whom modern atheism was not conceivable (Febvre 1982). This study of one eminent writer, however, did not take into account the possibility that men and women, lords, merchants and peasants might each have their own mental horizons, viewed with conceptual tools that were not only different from each other, but perhaps mutually antagonistic.

In its later phase, when the Annales School as such was disintegrating, its historians turned to case-histories, and the vogue for quantification and "serial history" (the examination of long series of homogeneous data) declined. LeRoy Ladurie himself gave up counting illiterate conscripts and calculating the dates of the wine harvest as indicators of long-term climate change; in the 1970s he reconstructed himself as the author of the bestselling *Montaillou*, a micro-history of a medieval Pyrenean village full of real-life characters – a "history from below" from which we can today draw inspiration (LeRoy Ladurie 1972 & 1980). Natalie Zemon Davis's studies of individuals like Martin Guerre and Leo Africanus may also be considered in this category (Davis 1983 & 2007).

The Annales tradition influenced the historical discipline worldwide, which is why I have devoted attention to it here. Other forms of history from below have certainly presented valuable elements of originality, such as *microstoria* in Italy, *Alltagsgeschichte* in Germany or subaltern studies in India, but none of these had the same resonance outside the history of their own country. The Annales rejected traditional political narrative, and preferred the history of the popular classes to the history of elites, but it produced the "old history from below" – a history which remained collective and largely impersonal.

The British neo-Marxist school represents the second great tradition, and inspired the new wave of social history of the 1960s. Like the Annales, the British Marxists revolved around a journal – *Past and Present* – which, under editors like Philip Abrams, published left-leaning, cutting-edge research with a strong sociological flavour. Theirs was a very open and British form of Marxism, by which I mean it was undogmatic, unhampered by ideological rigidity, and it welcomed debate (Kaye 1984, 222–232). Its stars were the great English historians "from below" Christopher Hill (on the English Revolution of the 17th century), Eric Hobsbawm (in several well-known studies and, until his death last year, still producing), E. P. Thompson (on the British working classes) and George Rudé (on the crowd in the French Revolution), among others. Their studies revealed the working classes in the process of formation, in their political actions, with agendas and ideologies which differed from those of revolutionary leaders and were often antagonistic towards them. In studying workers' and revolutionary movements, these historians redefined "history from below" as the history of the politically conscious subordinate classes, and of the collective movements which advanced workers' struggles.

Of course, there were some partial exceptions to this picture, notably the micro-studies inspired by Raphael Samuel at Ruskin College, Oxford (Samuel 1975 & 1977), as well as the work of Richard Cobb on French Revolutionary history, which tended to focus on the anarchic, the criminal and the marginalised (Cobb 1972). But the generalisation still holds good. This was an "old" history from below in the sense that it focused on collective activism, political movements and the development of organised labour. Its protagonists analysed history based on class relationships and emerging class consciousness. Although they restored a sense of power and agency to the working-classes, they were primarily interested in public action rather than private lives. The actual members of the lower classes remained an anonymous mass and the personalisation of History from Below was yet to come. Since ordinary individuals rarely, if ever, spoke for themselves in this history, Antonio Gibelli has provocatively asked whether we have ever really had a "history from below" at all (Gibelli 2000).

The old history from below, then, was a collective and anonymous history, in which the true voices of ordinary people were rarely heard. The new history from below is in contrast more individualised, and more sensitive to the voices of the poor. We now know that the problem with ordinary writings is not that they are scarce and ephemeral, but that there is such an abundance of them that the historian hardly knows where to begin.

The New History from Below

I owe the phrase to Tim Hitchcock, who dropped it quite casually into his review of Sokoll's *Essex Pauper Letters* (Hitchcock 2004). I think he was on to something. The new history from below is new for four main reasons:
 1. It re-evaluates individual experience;
 2. It searches for the personal and private voices of *la gente comune*, however they
    may be mediated through institutional or other channels;
 3. It modifies the direction taken by the linguistic turn,
    against which it is in some
    sense a reaction; and
 4. It considers ordinary readers and writers as active agents in
    the shaping of their own lives and cultures.

I should like to comment on these four points in turn.

Re-evaluating Individual Experience

In re-evaluating individual experience, we have absorbed something from micro-history, represented by Carlo Ginzburg's *The Cheese and the Worms*, a source of inspiration but at the same time of some problems. In Ginzburg's account, Domenico Scandella, known as Menocchio, was a miller from Friuli in north-eastern Italy who was interrogated and eventually executed in 1600 by the Inquisition for his heretical beliefs (Ginzburg 1980). In Menocchio's original cosmogony, the earth was not a divine creation, but evolved out of chaos. Our planet was originally a huge soft cheese, through which crawled the angels, in the form of worms. How had Menocchio acquired these notions? Not, apparently, from the Anabaptists or other Protestants, with whom no contact can be found. Nor can his singular views be directly connected to his reading of the Koran, the *Decameron*, Mandeville's *Travels* or the medieval chronicles which came briefly into his possession. For Ginzburg, his unpredictable views were the result of a coming together of popular and learned sources. On one hand, there was the contribution of an archaic, oral tradition of peasant protest, rooted in a dim pagan past. On the other hand, Menocchio had selected and reworked information received from learned sources: the books which he told the Inquisition so much about. It was the mutual imbrication of the oral with the printed, the popular with the erudite, which produced his very personal heresy. Menocchio is a marginal case-study, a heretic who Ginzburg puzzlingly claimed was a "normal exception". In his micro-study of one individual, however, he gave a more authentic answer than did Febvre's *Rabelais* to the question of unbelief in the 16th century (Vovelle 1985). He also commented unforgettably on the history and theory of reading, the autonomy of the reader, the connections between the oral and the literate and the permeable nature of popular culture.

Ginzburg's analysis brings to mind literary treatments of the individual in history, such as Tolstoy's *War and Peace*. Tolstoy's fictional soldier, placed within the reconstruction of a real historical event, in this case a great Napoleonic battle, doesn't know he is part of History. He is a protagonist in a battle, but he cannot make sense of what is going on around him. He is an individual pawn with no view of the big picture. From the perspective of the individual soldier, it is almost impossible to tell who is advancing and who is retreating, who is winning and who is losing, he can see only his corner of the wood and the field, and the occasional skirmish which takes place there. He is a fragment of a great event and may be quite unaware that he is a participant in what historians may later decide to call "the battle of Austerlitz". So too with Menocchio and many of the subjects we are studying – they perceive disorder and confusion and are unable to situate their individual experience within any meaningful framework. The patterns of which they form a small part lie hidden from their view and may take a long time to emerge.

What can we make of a single case-study, whether of a man brazenly expounding his ideas to the Inquisition, or of authors of the autobiographical writings with which we are more familiar as historians of the modern period? This is history from below, and on a micro-historical scale. Menocchio was clearly unique, and so are many of the obscure authors (and readers) whom we study. But how can we use them?

Menocchio was, in Ginzburg's enigmatic phrase, a "normal exception": he was certainly an exception in the sense that his ideas were bizarre, and because he attracted the attention of the Inquisition and so entered the historical archive. He was exceptional, then, because he challenged orthodoxy and because unlike millions of others, he left traces which were recorded. At the same time, Ginzburg argues, he was normal because, however bizarrely, he condensed a number of popular beliefs, which were egalitarian, anticlerical and even pre-Christian (Serna & Pons 2000, Muir 1991).

Not all ordinary writers or readers wrote or read entirely in isolation. We must allow for instances of collaborative writing, as in the hand-written newspapers produced by young Finnish workers and studied by Kirsti Salmi-Niklander (Salmi-Niklander 2007, and in the present volume). The *libri di famiglia*, too, in which writers of varying social status recorded harvest yields, historical events and their own genealogical history, were multi-authored works, added to repeatedly by generations of the same family (Mordenti 2001). Such examples, however, do not remove the problem of balancing the individual (or the small group) against the broader history of social and cultural change. We study individuals, we assemble fragments: in so doing we give a human dimension to significant historical issues. Archaeologists, too, uncover fragments, but to give them meaning they must be located within a whole. So, too, our own fragments of popular writing, like the story Menocchio told the Inquisition, must be contextualised.

Common Folk (la Gente Comune) Write for Themselves

For untutored writers, pen and paper were unfamiliar and the task of composing (for example) a letter was often laborious and painful. And yet, in the late 19th and early 20th centuries, we encounter some extraordinary lower-class authors who, for the first time and often in exceptional circumstances, felt a desperate need to write. Matteo Russo, a Sicilian soldier in the First World War, sent over 80 letters to his wife even though he was almost completely illiterate (Russo 1993). Anselma Ongari and her husband Guerrino Botteri, both from peasant backgrounds although Guerrino became an elementary schoolteacher, bequeathed their children an *epistolario* of over 1300 love-letters written between 1914 and 1920 (Dondeynaz 1992). Pedro Jado Agüero, a small rural proprietor from Santander in northern Spain, saw several family members emigrate overseas and decided to keep, copy and record the entire family's correspondence, both in-coming and out-going (Blasco Martínez & Rubalcaba Pérez 2003). For intimate and familial reasons, writing was central to the existence and identity of writers of humble origins and with little formal education.

Clelia Marchi was another such writer. Clelia, if I may call her by her first name, was a peasant woman from a village near Mantua, born in 1912. She met her future husband Anteo threshing corn when she was 14. Within two years she was expecting the first of their eight children, of whom four died young. For 46 years, she and her husband shared a life of hard agricultural work. When Anteo died in a road accident in 1972, Clelia experienced a personal crisis.

Emotionally bereft, suffering from loneliness and insomnia, she took stock of her past life:

> "I feel empty," she wrote, "finished, useless I spend my days crying, I would never have thought that after 50 years of married life we would be separated like that; all my sadness I write it out at night, because I sleep little; like a human being when it is in sorrow." (Marchi 1992, 55).

In writing, she found a new reason to live. She took a black drawing-pen (*pennarello*) and wrote her autobiography on what came to hand – a large bed-sheet. As she explained:

> One night I had no more paper left. My teacher Angiolina Martini had explained to me that the "Truscans" had wrapped up a dead body in a piece of cloth with writing on it. I thought that if they did that, I can do it too. I could not wear out the sheets with my husband any more and so I thought of putting them to use for writing. (Marchi 1992, back dust cover).

Clelia Marchi wrote to fill her sleepless nights and to express her solitary anguish. Her sheet was less a tribute to her husband than a memorial to their long united life. She signed it with both of their names. She was not ready to give up, and writing was a reason to go on living.

Like many lower-class autobiographers, Clelia apologised for her poor handwriting and grammar and her lack of education, telling us that her formal education had never gone further than the second year of primary school. Her writing was characteristic of the ordinary writings of the semi-literate. It was improvised, it incorporated elements of local dialect, and her grammar and spelling were not always correct. The sheet itself was a *matrimoniale* – a double-bed-sheet that symbolised the conjugal life which had shaped and given meaning to her previous existence. Clelia called it her *Libro-Lenzuolo* – her sheet-book. It is preserved today in the Archivio Diaristico Nazionale in Pieve Santo Stefano, where it is exhibited once a year, and where the text has been transcribed.

Until quite recently, only the writings of educated people attracted the serious attention of cultural historians. Scholars have often expressed difficulty in searching for the unmediated voices of the poor and uneducated. Alain Corbin found predictable problems when he undertook his experiment to write the life of a nobody, the completely unknown 19th-century peasant clog-maker Louis-François Pinagot (Corbin 1998). There were very few documentary sources about Pinagot, most of them emanating from official records. The unknown peasant does not express himself in the archives, and Corbin can only conjecture and imagine his feelings and opinions. Pinagot is a virtual individual, and his story can only be told at second hand, through the records of the police, the clergy, the folklorists or others with their own agendas who are not from the peasantry itself.

Historians like Corbin have usually relied on indirect sources to reveal something about the culture of the silent masses. They will continue to do so, even if those sources are generated by institutions which attempted (usually in vain) to discipline the excesses of popular culture, expurgate its immoralities, mould peasants and workers into republican citizens or instil into them some kind of national consciousness. This oblique approach to the lives of the poor, as Peter Burke called it, often neglects the writings of the poor themselves (Burke 1978). The American historian Eugen Weber was guilty of this charge in his important book on the nationalisation of the French peasantry under the Third French Republic. In his view, the 19th-century masses were illiterate and inarticulate, and so peasant life was best studied through the lens of various cultural manifestations, ritual practices, religious ceremonies and customs, usually described by others (Weber 1976, xiii–xv). How could historians who have shown enormous sympathy with the culture of ordinary people in the past have been so unaware of popular writings and their value? Why did distinguished historians like Weber neglect the rich subterranean world of ordinary writings? Perhaps because of a lack of imagination on their part, or perhaps – dare I suggest? – out of sheer intellectual laziness.

Beyond the Linguistic Turn

Post-modernist influences on historiography, which we loosely call the "linguistic turn", have forced us to re-consider the history we write. We now recognise that the texts we ourselves compose obey certain rules and conventions and adopt certain strategies. Our own history-writing has a literary aspect, in the sense that it constructs a narrative and deploys certain rhetorical strategies to persuade the reader. The history we write is never a transparent account; it is a text, an artefact which refers to other texts, can only be understood in conjunction with other texts and uses literary devices to sway and convince.

On the other hand, the "linguistic turn" has bequeathed us a legacy which now appears in a much less positive light, especially for our own project on the scribal culture of the subordinate classes. The protagonists of the "linguistic turn" were intent on deconstructing dominant discourses, showing how they were formed and the functions they were designed to perform. In concentrating on discourse formation, however, historians neglected to consider how such dominant discourses were actually consumed. We now need a greater focus on the *reception* of official discourses, and it is time to direct the techniques of deconstruction and discourse analysis towards the texts, however fragmentary and inarticulate, of the subordinate classes. This need is especially applicable in the study of "national identity from below".

One significant general theme in the study of ordinary writings from the 19th century onwards is the question of the acculturation of the masses to the national priorities and values being promoted by the nation-state. Hitherto, national identity formation has often been interpreted as a priority of the dominant bourgeoisie, concerned to incorporate the masses through a range of nationalising institutions like primary schools, the army and the newspaper press. It is not always clear, however, that the masses internalised national priorities without questioning and resistance. We need to study how nationalist discourses were consumed as well as how they were constructed and disseminated, and how the masses responded with their own alternative views of the world. Through the examination of ordinary writings, we may be able to understand a little better the lower-class assimilation of national myths, languages and beliefs. In studying the interaction between the lower classes and those who rule over them, we must analyse not only the official transcript of the relationship, which tends to give us only the self-portrait of an elite, but also, as James Scott called it, the "hidden transcript of the poor" (Scott 1990).

Giving Agency to Ordinary Writers

Following this point to its logical conclusion, the new history from below recognises the autonomy of lower-class writers (and readers), and refuses to regard them as passive receptacles for information and ideologies produced by someone else. One very good example is the study of the writings of emigrants from Spain to the Americas in the early 20th century. The study of individual and family correspondence throws new light on the subjective experience of emigration – a field hitherto dominated by sociologists and specialists in the international labour market.

Emigration was not simply determined by macro-economic factors, nor can its motivation be reduced to an analysis of so-called "push" and "pull" factors. There were also personal and family decisions involved. The problem with the socio-economic approach is that it treats emigrants as people responding passively to impersonal changes like industrialisation and fluctuations in the labour market. It deprives them of any independent choice. In Spain, some official sources for migration history in the 19th century denounced it as a social disease which was weakening and depopulating the nation. They attacked recruitment agencies which allegedly exploited the poverty and gullibility of desperate young men – a version of the story which deprived the emigrants of independent choice. Other official sources did the opposite: they provided a mythical picture of America as a great adventure. The personal writings of emigrants, however, reveal the expectations and emotions involved in the emigration process. For the migrants, leaving home was neither a disease nor an adventure, but simply a family necessity.

Laura Martínez's study of the 121 letters of the Moldes family, covering half a century and sent mainly between the Asturias and Chile, reveals the complex relationship between individual choice and family strategy. The letters show, from a micro-historical angle, the attempt of distant males to exert family control through correspondence, and they illustrate the strategies and work ethic necessary for individual success (Martínez Martín 2006). Individual writings, although never representative, re-evaluate the subjective element in history. The decision to emigrate, in the words of Croci and Bonfiglio,

> [...] was not the automatic consequence of prevailing conditions in the places of departure and arrival, but rather a strategy based on a choice of options made by a few people, individually or in groups, within specific family or community contexts, according to the needs, aims and values of the social group to which they belonged. (Croci & Bonfiglio 2002, 12, 24–25).

Soldiers' Writing in World War One

Two momentous events made a fundamental impact on the cultural lives of ordinary people in the late 19th and early 20th centuries. These were, firstly, the beginning of mass emigration across the oceans, particularly to the Americas, and secondly, the First World War. Quite apart from the enormous social and economic repercussions of these events, they both generated a seismic cultural shift: they produced a massive outpouring of letter-writing amongst people who were barely literate and totally unaccustomed to handling a pen. The prolonged and painful separation of loved ones and family members caused by the extraordinary circumstances of war and emigration made writing essential. Writing was needed to hold families together and manage their collective affairs. Through writing, individuals worked from a distance to sustain their social identities as members of a family group. Besides personal correspondence, they wrote family books, notebooks, diaries, song books, recipe books and home-made encyclopaedias. They wrote profusely, and in unfamiliar and "non-literary" genres.

My own work on soldiers' writings in the Great War dips into a vast ocean of correspondence. The First World War produced a flood of letter-writing, by peasants whose literary capacity has often been underestimated. In 1915, the French military post was handling 4 million letters daily (Bacconnier et al. 1985, 29). Jean Robin, a soldier from Nice, spent 104 days at the front in 1915. In this period, he sent 390 letters or cards, and received 256. In other words, every day, Robin sent three or four letters and got two or three replies (Bacconnier et al. 1985, 19). Italy, during three and a half years of war, produced 4,000 million postal items, in spite of the fact that 35 % of Italians were officially illiterate on the eve of the war (Gibelli 2002, 197). France produced about 10,000 million postal items, and Germany at least 30,000 million during the First World War. The years of 1914–1918 engendered "a sudden and irrepressible bulimia" of letter-writing (Lyons 2003). The war spawned an enormous and unique corpus of popular literature which could not be contained in spite of the efforts of postal censors and administrators. What now, in the present state of scholarship, are the general ideas and organising themes with which we can analyse this mass of individual testimonies?

Formulaic Writing

Soldiers' letters followed standard ritualistic formulas, giving and asking for news about health, discussing letters and postcards sent and received, sending greetings to many relatives and neighbours. As a result, their writing leaves us with an overwhelming sense of banality. The letters of the Savoyard soldier Delphin Quey are a good example of the emptiness and silences of soldiers' correspondence. They offer a nearly complete set of family exchanges during the war years. Delphin's letters always opened with a standard report on the state of his health, and went on to discuss letters received from home, postal delays, parcels received and parcels desired. He would repeat the same formulas over and over again: "I am in good health as ever I hope all the family is the same", or to close: "Nothing more of interest at present. Your son who is thinking of you." There are no intimacies, and few expressions of feeling, even though Delphin's elder brother Joseph had been killed in action in 1914. The main concerns expressed in Delphin Quey's letters are personal health and the price of mules, goats, sheep and horses (Lovie 1981).

Perhaps the censor's presence, and the threat of a week or two in confinement as punishment for epistolary indiscretions, may have restrained some French soldiers. Yet this does not adequately explain the "laconic" nature of most of the correspondence. There were other forces at work which imposed reticence. Ephraïm Grenadou explained in his memoirs:

> On leave I used to get letters from my friends from time to time, saying "Have fun while you can. Here things are going badly". I didn't like that kind of mail; I was afraid my parents might read it. When I used to write to them, I never told them things were going badly. (Grenadou 1980, 136).

There were things one preferred not to write, in order to maintain the consoling and comforting nature of the letter from the front.

The letters such men wrote and received contained absolutely essential platitudes. Marie F. thus wrote to her husband in 1915: "I am writing not very interesting things to you, but I wanted to write to you and, well, I must put something" (Bacconnier et al. 1985, 43). Anything would do. *Quelques lignes seulement* ran another typical letter, "Just a few lines, to give you a sign of life" (Bacconnier et al. 1985, 43). They wrote, and expected to receive, comforting repetitions of laconic formulas, which conveyed very little of their experience. Rosa Roumiguières invited her correspondent to dispense with words altogether. "I'd be happy with a single line, a single word," she wrote in August 1914, "even with just an envelope with nothing inside, but write to me often" (Bacconnier 1985, 44).

Certainly, as Antonio Gibelli has insisted, there were exceptions to the sameness of soldiers' letters (Gibelli in Croci 1992, xi). Usually they were most formal and also most reticent when writing to parents. As a sign of respect, Italian soldiers would write *Madre*, *Padre* and perhaps *Sposa* with capital letters. They might break the pattern when addressing a wife or lover, or a privileged confidant such as the local priest. Occasionally their emotional reaction to the death of a comrade or brother is evident, and the writer's own fear and desperation stand out in spite of their formulaic writing.

The Oral in the Text

Although writers rarely wrote in their local dialect, their phrases and their spelling were strongly influenced by dialectical forms. Oral culture was important for ordinary writers, and their writing was close to everyday speech. According to Emilio Franzina, "oral writing" is characterised by its openness and inherent extroversion, as when soldiers' letters address a wide group of relatives and try to include them all (Franzina 1987, 29). Oral writing uses fixed formulas and is full of redundancies and repetitions. Many letters from Italian troops finish with the question *hai capito?* (do you understand?), as if a verbal conversation were in progress. Recurring phrases like *ho sentito la tua lettera* (I heard your letter) and *vi dico queste due righe* (I tell you these two lines) also suggest the presence in the text of verbal forms of communication (Gibelli 1991, 54). The primacy of oral forms explains many of the misspellings and deviations from formal Italian occurring in workers' and peasants' letters. The writing of the war produced texts which reflected oral speech patterns, peppered with spellings and occasional words from the rich lexicon of regional dialect.

The linguistic test of national unity was fundamental, and the correspondence of French soldiers was overwhelmingly and significantly written in French. There are a few letters in patois or regional languages. There are some illiterate letters, composed by third parties, or read to the addressees by third parties at their destination (Cochet 1985, 21). Considering the linguistic diversity of French society a mere half-century before this, however, their number is not significant. There were letters in bizarre French which linguists believe were literal translations of Occitan or Catalan expressions, a sign that writers were still thinking in their native language as they struggled to compose in French (Bacconnier et al. 1985, 20, 49, 52–53). Government schools had apparently produced a hybrid or counterfeit French, in which expressions in local languages still surfaced. When southerners wanted to express strong emotions, they might revert completely to their spoken tongue.

This is not the whole story, however. Although almost all correspondents wrote in the national language, they could produce a highly individualised form of written French. There were letters, for example, both from the front and from home, composed in wildly aberrant grammar and spelling, betraying authors who had little or no familiarity with the act of writing. There were many examples of untutored phonetic spelling, in which for example *dysenterie* became "descenterie", and some writers imaginatively invented the new psychological condition of *anxiétude* ("anxiosity") (Bacconnier et al. 1985, 64). Louis Lemaire's wife wrote a stream of invective quite oblivious of spelling conventions and almost completely liberated from the burden of punctuation:

> Vraiment il faut que ceux qu'il fond durée la guerre [= ceux qui font durer la guerre] que ce sois des vrais bourreaux […] c'est féneant la c'est buveur de sang bande de cochon de salop ci il serait dans les tranchées va cela la guerre finiré plus vite je ne comprend même pas comment les hommes y reste encore [for this phrase the letter was confiscated] […]. Je m'ennuie à mourir quelle putain guerre. (SHAT 16 N 1551, Louise to Louis Lemaire, 1.2.1916).

> The ones who are stretching this war out are real executioners […] it's slack it's bloodthirsty bunch of pigs load of trash if they were in the trenches then the war would finish sooner I can't understand how people can still be there […] I am sick to death what a motherfucking war.

Louise wrote entirely phonetically, but she had absorbed the talk of the trenches and was quoting doses of it back to her husband.

National Identity from Below

As I have suggested above, the study of soldiers' writings from the trenches leads us into the important theme of national identity. It allows us a glimpse into the extent to which the rank-and-file of the army had absorbed the nationalist ideologies which justified (French or Italian) participation in the war. It is abundantly clear that the ordinary soldier identified first and foremost with his family, and secondly with his village. This is not necessarily inconsistent with patriotism, but the nation, if it was present in the soldier's consciousness at all, was a low priority.

THE *PAESE*

For Italian soldiers, loyalty to the *paese* was particularly marked. Soldiers at the front would send greetings to their local mayor, the barber and the village schoolteacher. But writing to one's local priest was an even surer method of connecting with one's local community. Letters from the front might be published in fortnightly diocesan letters. Some soldiers asked for their letters to be read to the congregation during the sermon; a few foresaw this eventuality and requested that the priest should respect their anonymity. Either way, the soldier's letter belonged to the village (Stiaccini 2005, 10, 26–27). About 100 soldiers from the commune of Fara Novarese, a small community of about 2,700 inhabitants, wrote to the village priest, Don Gaudenzio Manuelli, and the corpus of letters he received has been studied by Carlo Stiaccini. The soldiers wrote to the priest for moral support and consolation, and they often sent a letter as a remote way of making their regular confession (Stiaccini 2005, 27). Sometimes there was a very practical reason for enlisting Don Manuelli's sympathy: his official support was needed in applications for special leave or transfers away from the front lines. Above all, however, the priest was a vital link with their community and a channel for local news. Almost all the soldiers who left Fara Novarese wrote to him at least once, and they would remember the main religious festivals including the priest's own name day and the day of the village's patron, Saint Damian (Stiaccini 2005, 22).

To identify with one's village was to love its church and its bells. When Emilio Barbieri wrote to his brother Nicola in 1916, he asked him to pass on his greetings to the *campanile* and the bells of their native Montebruno, in the Genoese hinterland (ALSP Epistolario Barbieri, Emilio to Nicola, September 1916, exact date unknown). In a sentimental letter of October 1915, Giuseppe Mossetti wrote nostalgically to Don Manuelli:

> From the windows of this billet I look out from time to time in the direction where I know our beloved village lies, and I seem to see our bell-tower from which the bells are ringing out inviting the faithful to mass [...] (Stiaccini 2005, 53).

Campanilismo was not just a metaphor for localism, it denoted a literal attachment to the village. Local saints and shrines were worshipped and respected. The soldiers of Fara Novarese invoked St Damian, rather than Jesus or the Madonna (Stiaccini 2005, 34), while the Genoese placed *ex-votos* for a soldier's safe return at the shrine of Madonna della Guardia or Madonna del Carmine. Their religious practices were close to folk tradition and had an intensely local focus.

It was painful to be separated from one's village. According to Jay Winter, some soldiers from the Abruzzi kept with them a little bag of earth from their native village, or dust gathered from a local shrine (Caffarena 2001, 38). Bernardo Maurizio, a prisoner in Sigmundsherberg, near Vienna, wrote of the comforting presence of his fellow Ligurians in his otherwise alienating environment:

> when we have finished work at six o'clock we go almost every evening to take a stroll around the fence at our factory which is very big, and we swap happy and sad memories of times past in our dear villages; this way time passes reasonably well. What is really good is that we can speak in dialect, and we all dream of our sweet Liguria [...]. (ALSP Epistolario Maurizio, 21.5.1918).

Compared to the strong emotional connections with family and *paese*, national consciousness was extremely weak. I have found collections of soldiers' letters including dozens and even hundreds of letters and cards sent from the front in which mention of the nation is completely absent. Nor did ordinary soldiers usually discuss the purpose of the war, and one suspects that most *fanti-contadini* (the peasant infantry) had extremely feeble perceptions of what that purpose was. Occasionally, we find starkly anti-patriotic sentiments expressed, and this is usually in a letter that was intercepted by the censor. As one soldier wrote home to Cattolica (Forlì province) in 1916: "I will never give my right arm for the motherland but rather I will give it to save myself and my comrades" (Procacci 2000, 415). This letter had been blocked and sent to the Supreme Military Tribunal. Like other censored letters it survived in the Archivio centrale dello Stato in Rome.

Such language is rare. Soldiers certainly spoke of the war sometimes as a scourge (*castigo*), as disgusting (*schifoso*), but their most common reaction in their correspondence was fatalistic resignation. *Bisogna avere pasiensa*, Emilio Barbieri urged his father, *anche di fronte alla morte* (You have to have patience, even in face of death) (ALSP Epistolario Barbieri, date not given). Giovanni Panattaro told his uncle *pensiamo soltanto che finiscie presto questa musica* (We are thinking this music has to end soon) (ALSP Epistolario Panattaro, 15.8.1916). The war was to be endured, not resisted, and not understood.

Perceptions of "Italy"

For many soldiers, Italy itself had only the haziest existence. For some of them, "Italy" signified the war zone. Luigi Barbieri reported in 1917 to his sister and father: "we went to Villa Vicentina which is nearly in Italy" (ALSP Epistolario Barbieri, 23.10.1917). Luigi Secchi, too, understood Italy to mean the area opposite contested territory, referring to "these two months that I have been in Italy" (ALSP Epistolario Secchi, 3.3.1917). Damiano Dessilani wrote of being *in itaglia*, when he was at Palmanova, a transport centre 25 kilometres south of Udine (Stiaccini 2005, 142). Arriving in this *Itaglia* could be extremely disorienting, since people spoke a different language there. Emanuele Calosso told his mother that people using the dialect of the Veneto were talking *mezzo austriaco* (half Austrian) (cited in Caffarena 2001, 57–58).

Even if soldiers did identify with Italy as a place, they never identified with the state and its institutions. This was especially true of the prisoners of war, abandoned by their own government as presumed deserters and left to starve in Austrian prisons (Procacci 2000). Unlike the case of the French *poilus*, the Italian soldiers' correspondence I have read never mentioned a single national politician. Whereas French soldiers occasionally discussed the international scope of the war, for instance lamenting the defection of Russia in 1917 which they saw as disastrous for France, Italian soldiers never had such broad horizons. Their attention was focused on survival, their family and their village. Nevertheless, the war was a reality and death was ever-present. The state had organised it and the state would punish them if they did not conform. From here on, the nation had a violent presence in their lives that they could not ignore.

Nevertheless, an enormous distance separated the world-view of educated officers from the peasant infantry. Their loyalties remained above all to family and neighbours, and they had a weak and uncertain grasp of the nation as an idea. Patriotic slogans surface from time to time in their correspondence, but this was the inevitable result of exposure to official and clerical propaganda; it did not necessarily signify anything but a cursory acquaintance with national priorities or the Risorgimento myth. The psychologist Antonio Gemelli summed up popular attitudes thus in 1917:

> Soldiers talk little of the motherland; basically they don't know what it is; but if anyone, by just studying a few expressions, decided that our soldier has no love for his country, he would be mistaken. The motherland for him is the little village, the little field, the church bell-tower, the cemetery, his old mother [...] (Gemelli 1917, 67).

National identity looks very different when viewed "from below". National solidarity and the formation of a national memory encountered continuous refusal and evasion. In 1918, there was a move in the village of Fara Novarese to erect a war memorial, a monument to the dead. The patriotic idea was supported by the local elite, the mayor, the doctor as well as the local priest, Don Manuelli, to whom many dead soldiers had written during the war. But the war memorial project had to be abandoned for lack of local support. According to Don Manuelli, "the inhabitants, especially the families of the dead, did not want any memorial to the fallen" (Stiaccini, 2005, 17). Historians have devoted much time and effort to the study of how the Great

War was memorialised and mythologised in various national contexts. Fara Novarese is a very small example, but it is worth sometimes recalling all those who have dropped out of sight because they refused to memorialise the experience or subscribe to alien national myths.

The General Context

Broader questions do not disappear in the minutiae of individual lives. On the contrary, the writings of the individuals concerned help us to address some significant issues. Their personal disorientation as a result of war or emigration must be seen in the broad context of social and economic change. The long-term rural exodus of peasants from the countryside to the city and beyond irrevocably changed the traditional dynamics and cohesion of village communities. In the First World War, the modern world erupted violently into the lives of ordinary people, forcing them to confront the trauma of mass industrialised warfare, and the new power of the state to organise it. Industrialisation and modernity challenged the social identities of peasants and workers. Just at the moment when social evolution made them feel like anonymous parts in an impersonal machine, they started to write, in order to re-assert their individuality in a changing and unstable world. Theirs was a writing of absence and desire – the desire to return to one's loved ones, to familiar surroundings and to the stable co-ordinates of a world which was irretrievably disappearing. In the First World War, it was also a writing of survival – "writing to stay alive" (*scrivere per non morire*) was how the Italian soldier Francesco Ferrari put it (Croci 1992). Writing was synonymous with existence itself. Individual stories thus have a general context in the advent of modernity, and the development both of national identity and personal identity.

The First World War represented the explosive irruption of modernity into the peasant world. Peasants' social lives were dislocated, their goods and livestock requisitioned and they were called on to sacrifice their lives by a state which had hitherto scarcely impinged on their existence. They were fascinated by the novelty of trains and aeroplanes, their sense of time and their normal work patterns were disrupted, and they came face to face for the first time with the traumatic realities of mass industrialised warfare. They became anonymous parts of a huge machine, submerging their individuality in a vast industrial enterprise whose ultimate purpose was unclear to them. Writing home, in this context, was a means to preserve some continuity with the life they had known, to connect themselves with the previously stable values of the family, the land and the village community. Writing was a way to protect something of their individual identity. The spread of writing practices is often seen as an expression of modernity; but we might equally interpret it as a form of personal resistance *against* modernisation rather than a symptom of its advance (Gibelli 1987, 13).

Archival Sources

ALSP (Archivio Ligure della Scrittura Popolare):
ALSP, Epistolario Barbieri.
ALSP, Epistolario Maurizio.
ALSP, Epistolario Panattaro.
ALSP, Epistolario Secchi.
SHAT (Service historique de l'Armée de Terre):
16 N 1551, *Lettres Saisies*.

Britt Liljewall

Recollections of Reading and Writing

Another Picture of Swedish Literacy

> My father was illiterate. He had never learnt to write or to read handwritten text. Without real understanding he had practised writing his name for ceremonial events. Sometimes it looked like a fence with uneven poles. Sometimes it looked like a dog. […] He never learnt to read a text written by hand. He could not even read what he had written himself. (Ivar Lo Johansson, *Analfabeten*, published in 1951).[1]

The 1960s saw a growing interest in the history of alphabetisation in the Western world, fostered by engagement with so-called "underdeveloped countries" (e.g. Lerner 1963, Goody 1968, Schofield 1968, Stone 1969). Scholars discovered striking parallels between pre-industrial Europe and the developing countries, and literacy was seen as one of the most important prerequisites for modernisation. It was argued that historical understanding of alphabetisation in Europe would help the developing countries in their pursuit of progress.[2]

In Sweden research on the history of alphabetisation started with the studies of the social historian Egil Johansson from Umeå.[3] Working with parish registers, Johansson used these documents to determine how Swedish – and Finnish – people learnt to read well before other European nations, despite the fact that Sweden became industrialised some hundred years later than was the norm for more developed parts of Europe. Johansson claimed that the campaigns organised by the state and the church in late 17th and early 18th centuries were successful, and that about 90 percent of the adult population could read at the turn of the 19th century. He did not find many differences between social classes and genders, nor between town and country. This discrepancy between the high rates of reading skills, the scarcity of schools and late modernisation has been characterised as the "Swedish anomaly" (e.g. Lindmark 1990, 6).

Egil Johansson was also one of the pioneers in the study of the other aspect of literacy, the ability to write.[4] Here the results were very different. Sweden could not boast of having had large numbers of people who knew how to write at the turn of the 19th century. This gap between reading and writing skills existed up to the end of the century. The studies showed that in writing there were great differences between social groups, men and women, and different regions, as well as between townspeople and country dwellers.

The gap in time between reading and writing has also been seen as a part of the Swedish anomaly.

During the 1970s, when the results of this early research were presented and spread internationally, this pattern was characterised as "Swedish literacy".[5] The delay in the ability to write and the wide gap between the acquisition of the skills of reading and writing were not much discussed in connections to the concept of literacy at that time, and the meaning of what these skills actually consisted of was hardly touched upon. Thus Sweden – and the rest of the Nordic countries – stood out as the clear winner in the European championship in literacy.

This positive view of Swedish literacy has persisted as part of common knowledge. The historian Birgitta Odén presented thought-provoking criticism of the quantitative methods and the tendencies in the source material of literacy research already in 1975, but it had no significant effect on the over-all picture. Among other things, she pointed out that the registers the Lutheran pastors kept on their parishioners' ability to read cannot be taken at face value. People talking about literacy did not pay enough attention on the fact that the concept of literacy, according to UNESCO's definition, includes both reading and writing. Another problem Odén saw was connected with the relationship between the priest as an official authority and the common people. Egil Johansson used the perspective of consensus, whereas Birgitta Odén took the perspective of confrontation. Neither did the main tenets of the picture drastically change as a result of the discussions of "the second generation" of Swedish literacy research in which Johansson also took part. This discussion focused on the functions, the social contexts and the psychology of literacy.

The main data Egil Johansson used in his early research consisted of examination registers kept in Swedish parishes. The figures for literate people in the registers do not only represent the pastor's interpretation of his parishioners' reading skills, however, one has also to take the clergyman's reputation into account. The registers were inspected by the bishop on his official visits, and on these occasions the pastor's position was at stake, as he was the one responsible for organising the teaching of reading in his parish. One could suspect that some pastors chose to improve the figures to present a more flattering picture of their parishioners' skills.

Autobiographical Narratives – an Alternative Source Material

I have chosen to study the acquisition of literacy skills from another perspective and on the basis of another source. My data consists of 38 autobiographical narratives which include recollections of learning to read and write, all but two written by men born before 1840, at a time when primary school attendance was not the right of every citizen in Sweden – in fact, the majority of the autobiographers did not attend any school of any kind during their childhood. The writers came from the broad category of "common people" (*allmogen* in Swedish). About half of them were children of farmers who owned their land, while the other half were children whose parents were crofters, carpenters or soldiers.[6]

These old autobiographies written by common people – in total I have collected 265 such documents for my book *Självskrivna liv* (Liljewall 2001) – are usually short and addressed to the writer's own children. The majority of the manuscripts are preserved at the homes of the writer's descendents or – in the original or as a copy – at local folklore societies. Many have subsequently been published by the descendents or archives. A few of the texts were even published by the writers themselves, and in these cases the intended readers included a wider range of people, not just the members of the author's own family.

Naturally, source criticism is needed also when dealing with this kind of material. As with autobiographies in general, the life stories in my corpus were mostly written when the authors were advanced in age. The narratives are retrospective, with the greatest amount of space given to things and events distant in time and "exotic" from the point of view of the writer's present day, such as childhood in a more traditional society. One can see that the writers tend to dramatise and even exaggerate the differences between now and then.7

There are other problems in using autobiographical narratives as sources for the study of literacy. One has to keep in mind that the texts were written by exceptional people, who cannot be regarded as representatives of the majority of the population in terms of their skills and attitudes towards literacy; quite the contrary. First of all, these narratives signify a successful road to literacy. The ability to read and write can be seen as a crucial factor in the self-images of these more or less self-taught writers in 19th-century Sweden.

When analysing people's recollections of learning to read and write it is also important to distinguish two levels of time in autobiographical narratives. In my data, the time of the events depicted in the stories is usually the early 19th century, while the time of writing is the end of the century. It is more likely that the attitudes expressed in the texts, for example towards reading and writing, reflect the time of writing rather than the time of the events. Some autobiographers in the corpus used in this study rose socially, and literacy skills played an important role in this process.

The descriptions of the matter-of-fact things – how the teaching of reading and writing was arranged, who was involved in it, etc. – are probably more reliable for the time of the event than the recollections concerning one's motives and progress in learning. And since the gap between the event described and the time of writing is usually wide, there is a risk that the often-told story has become petrified and that stereotypical ways of telling about learning to read and write have acted as a kind of a screen over the memories.

In spite of these problems, life stories of common people provide valuable material for understanding literacy before the era of general education, because they provide perspectives and knowledge from inside and from below, e.g. from the point of view of the individuals in question, rather than marks in a church register. Furthermore, as will be discussed below, these recollections reveal important qualitative differences in understanding the concept of literacy which have not been sufficiently taken into account in the widespread notion of advanced Swedish literacy.

What kinds of attitudes were there toward reading and writing among the common people in 19th-century Sweden? Which qualities of reading and writing were supported or opposed by the families involved? What was the relationship between the acquisition of literary skills and gender and social stratification? What does Swedish literacy look like when studied using another type of data than the parish registers?

Recollections of *Elementary Reading*

The autobiographies offer new possibilities for assessing the level of reading ability among the common people. From their literate activities later in life it is obvious that the writers themselves can be characterised as advanced readers. In telling about their own process of learning to read they make a clear distinction between the acquisition of formal (elementary, passive) and functional (advanced, active) reading skills. In the narratives, reading by heart, reciting by rote and reading already known texts, principally of a religious nature, characterise formal reading ability, while silent reading, reflections on the text and the desire also to read "worldly" texts stand out as factors of the functional skill.

The acquisition of formal reading ability is seen in positive light in the life stories. Positive support was strong and training took place within the family, most often with the mother as a teacher. The skill was examined by the clergymen at the catechetical meetings held in each village. The aim of literacy teaching was to know by heart some passages of the Bible and the Psalter as well as the Catechism with Luther's commentary. Sometimes reading from the book instead of knowing the text by heart even seemed to be a negative thing: "I still remember a humble young clergyman who conducted the examination. He walked about, the catechism in hand, asking questions. This, I thought, lowered his standing in my eyes, because he did not know the book by heart." (Pehr Sjöbring, b. 1776, written 1840.)[8]

In only a few of the stories – five out of the 38 – problems encountered in the teaching of elementary reading are mentioned. In these exceptional cases there were practical difficulties connected to the child's social situation, for example when children had parents who were dependant workers or children who had to work outside the family at an early age. When the writers, in spite of these problems, found ways to overcome these obstacles and learn to read they were able to stand out as "winners":

> When I moved away from my parents' house I could only spell the texts in the ABC-book.   During the three years I herded sheep I worked reading the Catechism; nobody wanted to   teach me anything, and I trained myself a little bit. (Anders Petter Andersson in Marstorp, b. 1817, written in the 1880s).[9]

Recollections of *Advanced Reading*

When the autobiographers describe the process of acquiring functional reading ability – characterised by silent reading, reflections on the text, an inclination toward reading and the use of unknown and secular texts – the recollections they narrate are different from those concerning the acquisition of elementary reading skills. At least half the writers dealing with this theme relate difficulties they encountered. First of all, functional reading was something that not all parents could master themselves. If one wanted to expand one's skills, it was necessary to find support from outside. Many parents – and sometimes also the others around them – did not or could not help their children to pursue learning beyond their own elementary level, the level required by the church. Above all, functional reading was resisted at the lowest level of society.

Magnus Persson Turk, a soldier's son born in 1772 who was called "Läsarenasse" ("Reading Piggy"), describes a scolding he got when he did not put his book away in the evening – the reason was obviously not just the expense of lighting. Similar incidents, related to a child's desire, even a passion to read, are narrated in other stories. Johannes Nilsson, a crofter's son born in 1796, was prevented from reading a book called *Örtagårdssällskap* ("The herb garden society" by Johann Qvirsfeld), despite its religious content. Gustaf Fredrik Lagerström, born in 1816, the son of a teacher (!), was allowed to read only because his body was "small and delicate".

Several autobiographers mention the difficulties in acquiring reading material other than the Bible and the Hymnal. Even when they could, such "worldly" books were difficult for them to read, being mostly printed in the modern Roman type ("Latin") instead of the familiar Gothic ("German" or "Swedish"). Parents were often not capable of teaching their children to read "Latin", so the children were cut off from what could be called the "news". The family training method could keep up established knowledge, but had difficulties in making knowledge change and grow.

> As for reading, I was taught by my mother … as she according to the knowledge of the time was seen as skilful in reading, but she didn't know "Latin", and therefore I was ignorant in this until I myself over the years worked to learn that art, which I thought was quite big and important, as I was very fond of reading history books and novels and found them mostly printed in "Latin" […] (Karl Stenholm, b. 1824, written c. 1880.)[10]

On the one hand, many autobiographers reveal that their parents doubted children's, especially girls', need to proceed beyond the elementary reading. On the other hand, there are about an equal number of descriptions of the support parents gave to their children in their pursuit of further learning. How representative are these narrative in terms of the situation in early 19th-century Sweden? There are naturally certain tendencies in this kind of data. One of them concerns positive selection: it is probable that those children who were talented in reading (as autobiographers probably must have been) got more support in developing their reading skills than average children. This leads to a hypothesis that a greater proportion of the common people than is the case in this study ought to have met resistance in more developed training.

One can also suspect another kind of tendency in autobiographical material, however. At the time of writing, the authors may have exaggerated the degree of opposition they once met with in order to make their own efforts seem greater. In describing their road to functional reading as filled with obstacles, their personal strength and ambition stand out. Conflicts also make the story of their lives more dramatic.

What can be concluded is that the picture of reading at the beginning of the 19th century in Sweden looks different based on my data than the one we get from parish records. Autobiographical narratives reveal that formal reading ability was common, while functional ability was rarer.

Recollections of *Writing*

In addition to acquiring functional reading skill, recollections of learning to write are also included in the autobiographies. At least in their old age the writers were skilled enough to write about their lives, and had thus achieved functional writing ability. Those of the writers who talk about the problems in trying to improve their reading ability above the formal level also describe obstacles encountered in learning to write. These were generally connected with the social position of their parents.

First of all, in order to practise writing, one needed a pencil or a pen, ink and paper. These were difficult to obtain for many children from the lower classes, as anything that involved spending money was problematic in a society that was more or less self-subsistent. The 14-year-old Olof Andersson, son of a farmer, wrote in his diary in 1842: "It is shit not to have a real pen."[11]

Another obstacle was that handwritten texts that could serve as models for the budding writer were a commodity in short supply. In addition, there were two different styles of handwriting, as well as in printing, the older "Swedish" and the more modern "Latin". If one wanted to learn to write, help had to be sought from outside the family, as common people usually did not possess the skill themselves. Autobiographers often describe their parents' negative attitudes toward writing:

> So I was toying with the idea of learning to write, but my father was against it because, he said, it is of no use to poor people like us. We remain poor workers anyhow. But my insistence had an effect and he bought me a sheet of paper from a rag-and-bone man and some ink from the chemist's shop. Then Maja Stina Ringberg wrote down the first alphabet for me, and then Nils Ringberg the second one. And so I wrote between the lines again and again till there was no more room left for a letter. (Jonas Stolt, b. 1812 as son of a crofter, written ca. 1880.)[12]

In narratives of learning to write, gender plays even a bigger role than social status. Among farmers, only boys were encouraged to learn to write. In Jonas Runbäck's family the eldest brother was sent for some weeks to a schoolteacher to learn to write and count. Then he taught the skills to his younger brothers, but not to his sisters. Anders Pers relates that his mother, born in 1826 into a farmer's family, would have liked to learn to write, but that this was denied her: "Such a thing was man's work."[13] In the light of these examples it is easy to understand why it is so hard to find autobiographies written by common women in the 19th century.

Summary and Discussion

In the recollections of their childhood around the turn of the 19th century, the writers emphasise a clear border between the elementary or formal ability to read and the more qualified or functional reading. The former was not called into question either socially or by gender, while the latter, along with functional writing ability, met with considerable opposition. There were differences in attitudes depending on social strata and gender. According to the narratives I have studied, these two skills seem to have grown parallel and within the same temporal and social contexts. The great time gap between reading and writing in the old picture of Swedish literacy must, if one considers functional skills, be questioned.

The "Swedish anomaly" fades away in the light of this autobiographical material. It seems that it was mostly boys from the upper strata of the common people – but not the boys from the lower strata, or the girls at all – who got the opportunity to acquire qualified literacy as early as in the beginning of the 19th century. It is likely that "modern" masculinity, but not femininity, was connected to functional literacy well to the end of the 19th century.

If literacy is defined – as it generally is internationally – as including both reading and writing and also emphasising the functionality of the skills, literacy in Sweden must have been limited around 1800. When the literacy of the common people is studied from inside, one can argue that it was relatively late and unequal both socially and between the sexes. This situation did not change until the second half of the 19th century. Thus Sweden did not take the lead in developing literacy, but was more or less at the same level as most other European countries.

As mentioned above, early research on literacy was motivated by an interest in social reformation: literacy on the one hand and "modern" societies on the other. Statistics on literacy were used as a criterion in assessing the level of development of the country. But scholars, including Egil Johansson, realised that the relation between literacy and social development was far more complex. First of all, one needed to discuss literary skills in qualitative terms. It became common among social scientists to stress the identity forming force of literacy behind social development. Researchers had insights about reading and writing as a tool to growing and independent reflection both on self and on society. But to reach this, the skills must of course be functional, because they were agents in enhancing the capabilities of abstracting, categorising and reflecting.

Consequently, the distinction between the literate and the illiterate has been toned down and instead the border drawn, as in the life stories used in this article, between formal and functional abilities. A similar border can be drawn between "archive skill", characterised by formal but at the same time passive ability, and "communicative skill", where usefulness, activity and quality are stressed (Olson 1980). If literacy is to change society, it has to be communicative and active.

One can also argue that alphabetisation, in the sense of widespread but formal reading ability, could act as a hindrance to modernisation, that it could be seen as a tool for traditionalism and even backwardness and oppression.[14] My data seem to support this view. That it was enough to be able to know a set of Christian texts by heart is a view many writers recollect from their childhood, an attitude which hardly suggests the potential for social change. The strong connection to traditional church culture, rather than to growing secularisation, becomes evident in an antagonism toward secular literature – and to Roman type. It is obvious that the church had greater interest in controlling information than in the circulation of ideas.

In short: the early and widespread formal ability to read did not necessarily signify social change. After all, there was a wide gap between the advent of formal reading ability and the relative late modernisation in Sweden. Perhaps one could even claim that modernisation was delayed in Sweden because of the common people's ability to read based on the home training method. This could be, and was, used as an argument against establishing schools and professionalised education.

In the light of the evidence from the common people's life stories, the "Swedish anomaly" fades away. As mentioned above, Birgitta Odén expressed this view already in the 1970s. In the second generation of literacy studies there were displacements in the same direction. Why then has the old notion survived for so long? And why do I think it is possible to change it now?

One explanation can be found in the connection to the Swedish Folkhemmet ("Home of the people", folk home") identity. In both the "traditional" picture of Swedish literacy and the notion of the folkhemmet we find the same elements: the emphasis on early modernisation, the feeling of having had a history different from other countries and having found the exemplary models for others to follow. These cornerstones of modern national identity have not been seriously challenged until the 2000s. Nowadays, however, we Swedes seem to build our identity on similarities rather than differences, complications rather than simplifications, and problems rather than solutions. We have started to think of ourselves as Europeans. Sweden, like most other countries, has had a violent history. Swedes have also traded slaves, conquered colonies and been racists. We have imprisoned political opponents and sterilised those who did not fit in.[15] And now I present a picture of Swedish literacy without the unique patterns and more or less like all the others. Perhaps I am contributing toward the building a new myth, one of similarity instead of singularity.

So let me end with a compromise: even though the early Swedish reading ability was formal and mainly functioned as a tool of control, the same skill could be fairly easily developed into a communicative and progressive type of literacy. Perhaps this "Janus-face of literacy" (e.g. Lindmark 1990, 22) can explain the relative rapidity of the process of modernisation Sweden went through at the turn of the 20th century.

And, if nothing else, the different pictures of Swedish literacy discussed here can teach us something about how time-bound the use of history can be.

Notes

1 *Min far var analfabet. Han hade aldrig lärt sig skriva eller läsa skrivet. Han hade på gehör övat in ett slags namnteckning att ha vid högtidliga tillfällen. Den liknade ibland en gärdsgård med omaka störpar. Ibland liknade den en hund. (...) Han lärde sig aldrig läsa skrivet. Han kunde inte ens läsa vad han själv skrivit.*
2 Among other things, the connection between modernisation and widespread literacy is based on the assumption that a literate culture is more capable of storing information than an oral one. Literacy also enhances participation in official discussion, which is a perquisite for democracy. Moreover, it can be a tool to break down old social hierarchies; new groups taking possession of vital information can be a powerful force. On a more private level, literacy can promote self-reflection, characteristic for a modern individual (see e.g. Ong 1982, Graff 1987).
3 A bibliography of Egil Johansson's works is presented in Lindmark 1998.
4 Johansson 1977, 55–60. For later studies of writing ability in Sweden see also Lindmark (above all 1994), Nilsson & Pettersson 1992, Nilsson & Svärd 1994.
5 In 1975 an international symposium on literacy took place in Iran. Here Egil Johansson presented his on-going studies, see Johansson 1976. Compare also Johansson 1977, 5–6, where he discusses the concept of literacy and chose to adjust it to fit the reading tradition in Sweden and Finland. See also Johansson 1981.
6 See Liljewall 2001, Chapter 4, where the 38 autobiographies dealing with literacy are presented in more detail. For those explicitly referred to in this article, see also under "Bibliography".
7 For a more detailed discussion of common people's life stories as historical sources see Liljewall 2001, particularly chapters 1–3.
8 *Jag tycker mig ännu se där en ung, oansenlig prest förrätta förhöret, och gå på golfvet och fråga ur cathchesen, den han höll i handen och således icke sjelf kunde den utan till. Detta mindskade hans anseende hos mig.*
9 *Då jag flyttade ifrån mina föräldrar kunde jag blott stafva i Abc-boken. Under de tre åren jag vallade fåren, jag med min läsning i Katekesboken arbetade, ingen menniska vill lära mig något, jag öfvade mig något häri.*
10 *Vad det anbeträffade med läsning det lärde mig min moder [...] ty efter den tidens bildning ansågs hon som skicklig i läsning, men latin kunde hon ej, varföre jag blef olärd deri tills jag skälf under årens lopp tillkämpade mig den konsten, som jag tyckte vara ganska stor och viktig, ty jag var mycket begifven på historie och romanläsning och fan till min stora bedröfvelse, storsta delen sådana böcker tryckta med latin [...].*
11 *Rektig pänna är skit att icke hafa.* Olof Andersson's diary is analysed in Liljewall 1995.
12 *Så föll mig i hågen att få lära mig skrifva, men därtill tyktes far vara trög, ty han sade, att det tjänar oss fattige till ingen ting, ty vi bli ändå icke annat än fattiga arbetare. Men min enträgenhet verkade likväl på honom, så att han af en lumpsamlare köpte åt mig ett ark papper och skaffade lite bläck från apoteket. Så skref Maja Stina Ringberg för mig det första alfabetet, och sedan Nils Ringberg det andra, och så skref jag emellan raderna och åter emellan, så länge det fans rum för en bokstaf.*
13 *Sådant var karlgöra.*
14 E.g. Lockridge 1974, Odén 1975, Loftur Guttormsson 1981, Gawthrop & Straus 1984.
15 On the Swedish slave-trade see e.g. Harrison 2007; on colonialism Fur 2006; on racism e.g. Blomqvist 2006; on political prisoners e.g. Köll 2005; on eugenics e.g. Runcis 1998.

LIFE STORIES REFERRED TO IN THE ARTICLE

A.P. Andersson på Bohyttan (b. 1813), written and published in 1893 as *Minnen och hågkomser*.
Anders Petter Andersson i Marstorp (b. 1817), written and published in 1887 as *En sjuttioårig Gäsenedmans Lefnadsöden*
Olof Andersson i Tränghult (b. 1827), *Dagbok för 1842*, unpublished, Borås stadsmuseum.
Lars Johan Angelin (b. 1852), written and published in 1902 as *Min självbiografi tillägnad doctor Åke Belfrage*.
Anna Carlström (b. 1780), written and published in 1841 as *En modig kvinnas händelserika levnad*.
Gustaf Fredrik Lagerström (b. 1816), written in the 1890s, published in 1966 as *Minnen. Kulturhistoriska anteckningar från 1800-talet*.
Ivar Lo Johansson (b. 1901), *Analfabeten. En berättelse från min ungdom,* 1951.
Johannes Nilsson (b. 1796), written in 1850, published in 1987 as *Laggaren Johannes Nilssons levernesbeskrivning*, in Vadsbobygden.
Jonas Runbäck (b. c. 1830), written in 1902, *Aftonbetraktelser. Skildring öfver min 70 åriga tillvaro tillägnad mina Syskonbarn*, unpublished, in Nordiska museet, EU 10726.
Pehr Sjöbring (b. 1776), written in 1840, published in 1993 as *Från Bringebäck till Fyris. Anteckningar ur min levnad*.
Karl Stenholm (b. 1824), written c. 1880, published in 1961 as *Bygdesnickaren och spelmannen Karl Stenholms minnen*.
Johas Stolt (b. 1812), written in 1880, published in 1892 as B*yskomakaren Jonas Stolts minnen från 1820-talet*.
Magnus Persson Turk (b. 1772), written c. 1850, published in 1956 as *Magnus Turk. En självbiografi belysande folkfromheten i Kalmar län under förra hälften av 1800-talet*, in Kalmar län.
Anders Pers (b. 1860), written and published in 1948 as Lärare, bonde, tidningsman.

Davið Ólafsson

Scribal Communities in Iceland

The Case of Sighvatur Grímsson

Introduction

A distinction between *vernacular* and *institutional literacy* has been among the key tenets of the approach of the so-called New Literacy Studies (NLS) since the 1980s (e.g. Heath 1993, Street 1984, Barton & Hamilton 1998). In their monograph *Local Literacies*, Barton and Hamilton argue that *vernacular literacy practices* are not regulated by the formal rules and procedures of dominant social institutions but rather have their origins in everyday life. Learnt informally, they are not systematised by any outside authority. In this way vernacular literacy practices differ from *dominant literacy practices*, which are associated with schools or other institutions of learning. Vernacular literacy is rooted in the home; it is integrated into other everyday activities and can rarely be separated from its use (Barton & Hamilton 1998, 247–252). This division is one of two analytical starting points for the account presented here of everyday literacy in 19th-century Iceland.

The other concept pertinent here is *scribal culture*, which is where vernacular literacy practices are rooted and exercised. Scribal culture refers to the production, dissemination and consumption of hand-written texts, practices which persisted alongside the ascending print culture in pre-modern Iceland, as elsewhere in Europe (e.g. Love 1993, Ezell 1999). According to numerous studies in cultural, literary and book history over the last quarter century, the scribal medium continued to play a considerable role in pre-modern societies after the introduction of printing. The French cultural historian Roger Chartier has summarised this turn in the following way:

> With the work dedicated to manuscript production in England, Spain and France over the past decade, no one today would argue that "this" (the printing press) killed "that" (the manuscripts). Numerous kinds of texts (poetry anthologies, political libels or tracts, aristocratic books of conduct, newsletters, libertine and unorthodox texts, music scores, etc.) enjoyed a wide circulation through manuscript copies. […] In short, it is now recognized that printing, at least in the four centuries of its existence, did not lead to the disappearance of hand-written communication or manuscript publication. (Chartier 2007, 393).

In the present article, the concepts of *scribal culture* and *vernacular literacies* are used to explore the procedures of primary instruction in reading and writing as well as the opportunities people had for furthering their education beyond the minimal level required by the authorities at the time. I approach these questions through the study of a man who came from a humble background but left behind him an enormous quantity of written material: personal writings, literary and historical texts and transcriptions, now preserved in the Manuscript Department of the National and University Library of Iceland (NULI). Sighvatur Grímsson Borgfirðingur (1840–1930) spent most of his life with a pen in his hand, even though he earned his livelihood principally as a farm hand, crofter and fisherman. My aim is to examine three aspects of education and scribal culture as they appear in texts describing Sighvatur's early life. The first of these concerns the primary instruction he received and the second the literary milieu of his hometown, Akranes. The third aspect deals with Sighvatur's endeavours in self-education during his adolescent years.

Literacies in Pre-Modern Iceland

As a necessary backdrop to the analysis of scribal culture in 19th-century Iceland and its vernacular educational processes, two points must be stressed here which highlight the disproportion between vernacular and institutional literacy. Firstly, the fact that there was little secular print material and no operative local book market to speak of in Iceland until well into the second half of the 19th century, despite the relatively early arrival of the printing press in Iceland around 1530. Controlled by the church, the printing press was intended primarily to supply households with religious literature. This meant that only a handful of secular books in Icelandic were printed until the second half of the 19th century. The lack of the kinds of cultural institutions usually associated with print – presses, publishing houses, booksellers, public libraries etc. – meant that secular literature had to find other paths of dissemination.

Secondly, what few primary schools there were were unattainable for a large proportion of the population. At the end of the 19th century there were only a handful of primary schools, mostly in fishing villages and larger towns. Youngsters in rural areas were at best educated by ambulatory teachers or during short stays at the local pastor's house (Loftur Guttormsson 2008, 21–35). Household instruction was the dominant form of primary education. After 1880, when a new law was passed, ambulatory schooling became common: a self-taught schoolmaster or a formally trained teacher spent a short period of time at each farm. This custom-made schooling suited the social structure of the time and lasted well into the 20th century in many rural areas, despite a new law in 1907 which decreed four years of mandatory education for every child (Loftur Guttormsson 1992, 207–222).

According to Lutheran doctrine, every individual was to approach the word of God directly, rather than through a priest or other mediator. Being able to read was therefore a prerequisite, along with the availability of pious texts in the vernacular. In this way, literacy came as a by-product of religious instruction. The so-called "Act of Household Discipline", issued in 1746, decreed that every child should learn to read before his or her confirmation. In the terms used by Barton and Hamilton, the required level of *institutional literacy* for the ordinary people of Iceland was thus to know and to be able to read Luther's *Small Catechism* on one's confirmation day. The literacy campaigns of the mid-18th century were aimed only at spreading the capacity to read, while the ability to write was not considered essential for people's salvation.

Primary reading instruction was mostly executed at home and supervised by the pastors. Lessons were usually started when children were five or six years old, and the process was concluded with the rite of confirmation around the age of thirteen. This system resulted in nearly universal literacy in Iceland by the turn of the 19th century, but, as was said, it only applied to the ability to read. It was not until the education act of 1880 that writing became a mandatory part of basic instruction (Loftur Guttormsson 1989, 127–128, 136–137). There were, however, many ordinary Icelanders who acquired the skill of writing and employed it for various purposes. This was achieved without much institutional input and had a significant impact on everyday Icelandic culture. The vernacular tradition of auto-didacticism was to a great extent propelled by scribal production and the circulation of handwritten reading material.

First-hand accounts of self-taught writers often deal with the problems with which the autodidact was faced, such as the lack of primary schools and competent teachers. Parents and guardians could provide only the minimum level of instruction; they often lacked interest in literary matters and, in some cases, were even openly hostile towards such endeavours. Then there was the aforementioned lack of printed secular reading material. The case histories of many self-taught writers emphasise the importance of informal education and the availability of hand-written reading material. They reveal the shortcomings of the educational system, the conflicting attitudes towards learning in society and the strength of individuals' pursuit of knowledge and entertainment. The texts reveal that the world of *vernacular literacy* was much broader and more variegated than the narrow output of printed material would suggest. It was through manuscripts that knowledge was chiefly produced, gathered and mediated within the context of everyday cultural practices and without formal authoritative command.

Formal and Informal Schooling in Akranes

Sighvatur Grímsson was born and raised in the seaside village of Akranes in the county of Borgarfjarðarsýsla in south-western Iceland, the youngest of four siblings. At that time his parents were crofters who made their living primarily from fishing. They were extremely poor during these years, and the family was subjected to frequent relocation. Documents suggest that his parents were separated at times, before the death of Sighvatur´s father in 1851.

In his regional history of Borgarfjarðarsýsla, Kristleifur Þorsteinsson (1861–1952) gives an account of the state of literacy in the district, basing it partly on his own experiences (Kristleifur Þorsteinsson 1935–1938, 364.) It is consistent with many first-hand narratives from 19th-century Iceland which relate that before the 1870s it was rare for children to be able to write at the time of their confirmation. Some boys had started their pursuit toward the skill of writing, however, armed with quills or old pens, raven's blood or homemade ink, or simply by scribbling with a stick on ice or other suitable surface. Some obtained model alphabets from scribes while others copied old letters and envelopes, often resulting in somewhat inconsistent calligraphy. According to the account of the local clergyman, Jón Sveinsson, basic instruction mostly took place at home, but from 1850 to 1880, a fisherman called Sigurður Lynge (d. 1881) took a good number of children for tutoring and instructed them in reading and Christianity as well as a bit of writing and arithmetic (Jón Sveinsson 1913, 68, see also Kristleifur Kristjánsson 1989, 14–16). Sigurður Lynge also served his community by writing and transcribing texts, his extant manuscripts reflecting extensive study and scholarly work. Nothing, however, suggests that Sighvatur Grímsson ever attended Sigurður Lynge's school, although it is evident from his diaries that he was acquainted with Lynge family. It is likely that the fee was an obstacle for Sighvatur's parents.

In his short autobiography, written in his early fifties, Sighvatur describes – using the third person singular – his primary education and early literacy practices. At the age of seven he learnt from his mother to recognise the letters of the alphabet and to connect them into syllables and words. First he was shown the letters of the old *Sjöorðabók* by Bishop Jón Vídalín (1666–1720) and could read the book fluently after a fortnight. This was just before Christmas 1847. At the time Sighvatur was growing up, there were two typefaces to be found in Icelandic books, Gothic or blackletter type (*Fraktur*), then going out of fashion, and the more modern Roman type (*Antiqua*).[1] Sighvatur's mother, born at the turn of the 19th century and accustomed to the older typeface, was unable to read Roman type and so taught her son to read the *Fraktur* typescript that was generally used in religious publications.

This description reveals several interesting aspects of the procedures and priorities of household education at the time. Firstly, Sighvatur was primarily taught to recognise and read the typeface used in religious publications. The choice of *Sjöorðabók*, an 18th-century compilation of Christian sermons, similarly points to institutional, religious literacy, i.e. the ability to read through a familiar (religious) text (Loftur Guttormsson 1998, 8, Munck 2004, 275–276).[2] Secondly, the passage reveals how the progress of Sighvatur's learning was at first limited by the available literacy skills within the household.

The next step in Sighvatur's self-education was for him to learn to read Roman type on his own initiative. The boy got hold of one sheet from *Alþingistíðindi* in Roman type and started to compare the letters with his *Sjöorðabók*, which was printed, as was said, in blackletter. In this way he was able to guess the identity of the letters for which he found no match in the older text, and by springtime he could read Roman type fluently (NULI,

Lbs 3623 8vo, [1–2]). Now he could also read secular books, but there was a shortage of them, at least in print. Instead, there were hand-written books, but to read them, one had to acquire yet another literacy skill – a challenge even more demanding than the previous one. The quality and age of manuscripts varied a great deal, the types of script changed with time and personal handwriting styles varied from one writer to the next. Mastering all these aspects of literacy was crucial for anyone seeking access to the world of secular literature in mid-19th-century Iceland. In his autobiography, Sighvatur describes the process of learning to read hand-written texts in the following way:

> The following winter he got the *Rímur af Eiríki víðförla*, transcribed by the poet Lýður Jónsson, and then he used the same approach of comparing it with the printed version, and made good progress. Using that method, he took every hand-written book he could lay his hands on, and by the time he was eleven years old there was no manuscript, however cryptic and opaque, that he could not read without hesitation. (NULI, Lbs 3623 8vo, [2]).[3]

Sighvatur's ability to read fluently different kinds of texts earned him the position of the "household reader" and gave him the opportunity to become acquainted with a wide range of reading material. After having learnt to read both Gothic and Roman typefaces Sighvatur wanted also to learn to write. He notes in his autobiography that nobody in his household was able to instruct him, however (NULI, Lbs 3623 8vo, [2]). Writing utensils were also hard to obtain, but Sighvatur began collecting scrap paper and quills as well as used and blunt steel pens which he sharpened. He managed to get hold of, among other things, an alphabet of capital letters from the teacher and scribe Sigurður Lynge, mentioned above. However, since he fashioned his letters using a wide assortment of models and entirely without instruction, his handwriting became rather incoherent and imperfect, according to his own account (NULI, Lbs 3623 8vo, [2–3]).

Sighvatur's description of his progress in learning to read and write is somewhat paradoxical. On the one hand he maintains that no one was willing or able to teach him to write, but at the same time it seems to have been relatively easy for him to obtain handwritten material, to teach himself to read different handwriting styles by comparing them with printed texts and, finally, to teach himself to write. All of Sighvatur's efforts at acquiring literacy in this poor fishing and farming community were marked by these two conflicting conditions: on the one hand the community and his family were unable to provide more than the mere basics of reading and Christian knowledge, while Iceland's formal educational system was still centred on home schooling under the supervision of the parish priest; on the other hand, it is evident from Sighvatur's narrative, and other sources, that there were other, informal routes to knowledge through vernacular literary – and predominately hand-written – culture. These contradictions in Sighvatur Grímsson's youth are, to some extent, a fair description of the cultural landscape of the society as a whole in the 19th century and are echoed by numerous other contemporary narratives, as well as the extant scribal material. As the institutional literacy practices – household-based education and the very limited supply of secular printed books – failed to fulfil the increasing demand for reading material, there developed a vernacular system based on scribal communications.

The Scribal Community of Akranes

Sighvatur Grímsson's description of his early autodidactic literacy practices gives an insight into several aspects of scribal culture: the availability of handwritten texts, their roles in people's lives and, naturally, the copying, reading and dissemination of manuscripts in a local setting. In practicing the reading of a hand-written text Sighvatur used a manuscript of *Rímur af Eiríki víðförla*, composed by the 17th-century poet Guðmundur Bergþórsson (1657–1705), one of the most productive and best-known literary figures of the early modern period in Iceland. To him are attributed at least thirteen *rímur*-cycles,[4] including the longest extant work in the genre, *Olgeirs rímur danska* (Finnur Sigmundsson 1966a, 75–87), in addition to occasional poetry and a lengthy account in verse of the lives of various renowned philosophers called *Heimspekingaskóli* ("School of Philosophers"). During his own lifetime, and for some time thereafter, Guðmundur Bergþórsson's poetry circulated entirely orally and in hand-written form. There are some 400 manuscripts containing his poetry in the National Library, among them 70 transcripts of *Heimspekingaskóli*, dating from both before and after its original publication in print in 1785.

The work Sighvatur read, *Rímur af Eiríki víðförla*, exists in 35 copies. The copy that Sighvatur practised his reading on had been made by Lýður Jónsson (1800–1876), a poet and scribe who spent most of his life in the village of Akranes. He seems to have been both well known and widely read in his time: 20 *rímur*-cycles are attributed to him, most of them short and composed as contemporary lampoons rather than lengthy heroic or fantastic narratives in the traditional style (Finnur Sigmundsson 1966b, 102). Lýður Jónsson was one of the hundreds of popular poets whose work circulated almost entirely through scribal and oral transmission. At least extent 80 manuscripts are associated with his name in one way or another – autographs, transcripts of his works as well some transcripts by him of other peoples' work.

Both Guðmundur Bergþórsson and Lýður Jónsson appear to have made an impact on Sighvatur Grímsson, as he continued to collect and copy their poems throughout his life. This is especially apparent in an annotation on Sighvatur's transcript (from the early 1890s) of Lýður Jónsson's lampoon *Álfhildar ríma* from 1857 (NULI, Lbs 2289 4to). Sighvatur made his transcript from an autograph which was missing its first page, but he was nevertheless able to reconstruct the first ten stanzas of the poem from memory. Another example of transmission between oral and scribal media is seen in a manuscript compilation from the early 1890s: there is a verse by Lýður Jónsson which Sighvatur learnt directly from the poet as a young boy. In addition, there are several other poems by the same poet, copied from local transcripts and autograph manuscripts as well as poetry by others copied from manuscripts in Lýður's hand.

This manuscript compilation also includes other indicators of a vibrant scribal culture at Akranes four decades earlier and the importance of popular poetry in everyday life. In the compilation, Sighvatur revisits the cultural scenes of his childhood and adolescent years, his own early compositions and transcripts, his father's poetry, verses he learnt from his mother and uncle and some of the local poetry that formed the backdrop of daily life during his upbringing. Some of the poems in the collection were copied by Sighvatur from earlier transcripts which he made in his mid-teens based on oral recitations by his mother and his uncle, while others were copied from autographs. Yet another compilation that reflects the literary dynamism at Akranes in this period is a collection of *ljóðabréf* ("verse-letters") amassed by Sighvatur in the spring of 1890 from various older transcripts, including several items dating from mid-century (NULI, Lbs 2291 4to).

In 1865 Sighvatur Grímsson began to bring together his poetry in an orderly manner in an anthology he called *Syrpa* ("Medley"), which eventually comprised three volumes, altogether nearly 1000 pages of text (NULI, Lbs 2325 8vo). Its first section reveals how Sighvatur was, from his early teens on, an active participant in the tradition of everyday vernacular poetry characteristic of the period. The oldest text in the anthology, from 1853, when Sighvatur was in his twelfth year, is a letter written in verse to his friend Jón Stefánsson in the neighbouring county of Dalasýsla. From the spring of 1856 on, Sighvatur documented his life consistently in verse form, recording events trivial and remarkable alike.

A large portion of the poetry in Sighvatur's collection was composed for others, and in their name, on various occasions such as proposals in verse and verse-letters, which are indicative of Sighvatur's status as a communal "poet laureate", first in Akranes and later in other communities. All this indicates indisputably how Sighvatur, from an early age, drew upon a vibrant literary environment that was predominantly driven by oral and scribal transmission.

Adolescence and Self-Education

Sighvatur continued to live with his mother in Akranes after his father's death in 1851, occupied with wool work and other crafts. During the summers he was sent to the nearby county of Dalasýsla, where he served as a shepherd and later a farm hand involved in hay-making and other everyday farm work. During his later adolescent years Sighvatur worked as a fisherman in Akranes and thus became prepared for all the major aspects of labouring, and later being head of a household in the farming and fishing community. Simultaneously, his interest in literature and historical knowledge grew and in the evenings he read aloud sagas that he had procured for other members of the household, as was commonly the role of teenagers keen on books.

In a short and rather opaque paragraph in his autobiography, Sighvatur notes that during his time in Akranes he had begun to transcribe some family sagas for himself from old printed editions when he was able to borrow them (NULI, Lbs 3623 8vo, [3]). Here Sighvatur may be referring to some of the oldest items in his collection: a manuscript containing three sagas and one shorter tale (NULI, Lbs 2312 8vo). Unlike most of Sighvatur's later transcripts, this group includes no details about the originals, where he got them, or if they were in manuscript or print. None of these four sagas had then been printed in Iceland, but two had already appeared in Denmark. Though Sighvatur states that the sagas were hard to obtain, many of them were circulating in transcripts around the country. One of them, *Gunnars saga Keldugnúpsfífls,* is for example preserved in 43 copies in the National Library of Iceland, 22 of them from the 19th century, while another, *Finnboga saga ramma*, is found in 36 transcripts, 20 from the 19th century (Ólafsson 2002).

Transcripts by Sighvatur with earlier dates can be found in a miscellany of several *rímur* cycles and other writings from the mid-1850s (NULI, JS 435 8vo). Its first three *rímur* were composed by farmer and carpenter Magnús Jónsson (1763–1840) between 1811 and 1826, one of the most productive poets of his time and an industrious scribe. Magnús's poetry was primarily disseminated in handwritten form and/or orally, and manuscripts containing his poetry number a little short of 150. Following the three *rímur*-cycles is a transcript of the aforementioned 17th-century poem *Heimspekingaskóli* by Guðmundur Bergþórsson, concluded on 29 November 1858. This lengthy poem had by then appeared twice in print, in 1785 and 1845, but whether Sighvatur made his transcript from a printed or handwritten exemplar is not clear.

An even more impressive testimonial to the educational aspect of scribal culture in pre-modern Iceland is the last part of Sighvatur's adolescent miscellany, a section of just over 70 pages bearing a heading that translates "A book of knowledge, transcribed from a manuscript by the late Pastor Snorri Björnsson from Húsafell" (NULI, JS 435 8vo). Snorri's book, now preserved in the National Library, had in the 1850s been in the possession of a grandson of the scribe, Snorri Jakobsson, a farmer at Klettur in Borgarfjörður, not far from Akranes, and it is most likely that Sighvatur borrowed it from him (Sighvatur Grímsson 1962, 87). Despite the seemingly transparent heading of Sighvatur's transcript, it is in fact descriptive of only some parts of the section, as Sighvatur copied only selected parts of Snorri's book, combined it with texts from other manuscripts and rearranged the content to some degree.

The original creation of Snorri Björnsson's "book of knowledge" is itself another vivid example of how scribal reproduction of texts can be located somewhere between transcription and composition. This unique and discordant compilation drew its material from various sources, Icelandic and foreign, and offers a fascinating insight into the scribal library of the 18th century and the processes of scribal reproduction (Þórunn Valdimarsdóttir 1989, 295). Sighvatur Grímsson's transcription of Snorri Björnsson's manuscript was thus very much in the tradition of scribal transmission, a process which challenges modern(ist) views of authorship and fixed texts.

Sighvatur Grímsson left his birthplace in Akranes for good and became fully employed as a farmhand. After the first year as a servant, Sighvatur comments in his autobiography that he was never able to look inside a book during that time due to the demanding work (NULI, Lbs 3623 8vo, [3–4]). Later he gave this account of himself around that time:

> Now he owned nothing but a change of clothes for daily use and a few books, could write letters about as well as was then common with common people, had learnt to calculate almanacs in his twelfth year and knew it well, understood Danish well (spoken), which he had heard a lot at Akranes at springtime when merchants came to trade, and had also often been to Reykjavík. In addition to this he had obtained some of the Icelandic sagas, volumes 1–9 of the *Yearbooks*, and the complete *Sturlunga* chronicles, and had read a lot of other various materials. (NULI, Lbs 3623 8vo, [5]).[5]

During his childhood and adolescent years at Akranes, Sighvatur Grímsson had tried his utmost to acquire literacy skills and education within the cultural environment of his time. It is evident from the testimony of his autobiography as well as the extent manuscripts written in his hand from this period that scribal transmission was central in the local circulation of texts, and accordingly in Sighvatur Grímsson's acquisition of information and education. In the following years, first as a farmhand but later as a tenant farmer, Sighvatur continued to collect and transcribe literary and historical material and disseminate it among his neighbours in various communities around western Iceland.

Conclusion

The history of education in the advent of modernity in Iceland has two main features, a formal structure and ideology "from above" on the one hand, and, on the other, more or less autonomous channels of instruction and information which can be labelled with the term "vernacular education". The former was marked out and implemented in a joint effort of worldly and spiritual authorities in accordance with what they saw as the necessary level of literacy and its appropriate use. The second feature, however, rests upon the endurance and, in fact, intensification of scribal culture during the 19th century and the potential it offered a self-initiated quest for education and emancipated literacy practices.

Sighvatur Grímsson received his first tutoring at home from his parents, under the supervision of the parish minister, as was common among ordinary people throughout most of the 19th century. But Sighvatur was, from an early age, drawn to books and texts of a historical and literary nature, which at the time largely circulated in handwritten copies. Through self-education, young Sighvatur was able to amass greater and wider skills and knowledge than was expected or called for by the authorities or by society as a whole. In this manner, Sighvatur was by no means typical of young people of his status, but he was not an abnormal or isolated example either. He was, throughout his lifetime, firmly located within networks of like-minded people. His case, while extreme, illuminates the pathways of the informal educational system, which were closely intertwined with the pathways of scribal communication in 19th-century Iceland. The autodidactic element of scribal culture as a forum for self- (or self-initiated) education appears to have been one of the driving forces behind the vigorous literary culture of the era. The present paper deals mainly with Sighvatur's childhood and adolescent years, from his first lessons up to the time when he embarked on the active pursuit, processing and representation of knowledge, but it is clear that learning was not limited to the traditional time periods or settings of formal education, but was seen as a life-long endeavour.

NOTES

1   The transition was taking place in these years, and *Alþingistíðindi* ("the Parliamentary Minutes") was in fact the first publication to be produced fully in Roman type in Iceland, printed at the renovated and relocated *Landsprentsmiðjan* in Reykjavík in 1845. Icelandic texts in Roman typefaces printed in Copenhagen had been available since the early 19th century (Þorsteinn Þorsteinsson 1994, 507).
2   The book referred to as *Sjöorðabók* is Jón Vídalín's *Sio Predikaner wt af þeim Siø Ordvm Drottens Vors Jesu Christi, er han talade sijdarst a Krossenum* (Hólar, 1716). After this first edition, the book was reprinted four times, in 1731, 1745, 1753 and 1832.
3   *Veturinn eftir fékk hann Eiríks rímur víðförla með hönd Lýðs skálds Jónssonar, og hafði þá hið sama ráð, að bera saman við prentið, og vannst það vel. Þannig tók hann hverja skrifaða bók eftir aðra, sem hann á náði, og þegar hann var ellefu ára gamall, kom engin sú skrudda fyrir, hversu rammbundin og mórauð sem var, að hann ekki læsi viðstöðulaust [...].*
4   In Icelandic literature the word *rímur* or *rímur* cycle referes to a genre of epic poetry extremely popular throughout the pre-modern era.
5   *Hann átti nú ekkert til nema aðeins skiptaföt til daglegrar brúkunar og fáeinar bækur, gat skrifað sendibréf nokkurn veginn, eftir því sem þá gjörðist með alþýðu, hafði lært fingrarímið á tólfta árinu og kunni það ágætlega, skildi vel dönsku (talaða), sem hann hafði vanizt á Akranesi á vorin, þegar lausakaupmenn komu þar til verzlunar og hafði auk þess oft komið í Reykjavík. Þar með hafði hann eignast nokkuð af Íslendingasögum, Árbækurnar 1.–9. deild og Sturlungu alla og hafði lesið allmikið af ýmsu.*

ARCHIVAL SOURCES

Manuscript Department of the National and University Library of Iceland:

NULI, JS 435 8vo. *Rýmna bók Innihaldandi Rímur Eptir Íms Skáld; Nefnilega Magnús sál. Jónsson. Skrifuð árið 1856 af Sighvati Grímssyni* [name written in runes] *Á Akranesi Borgarfjarðar síslu.*
NULI, Lbs 1973 8vo. Sigurður Lynge's diaries.
NULI, Lbs 2289 4to. *Hít*. Miscellany written in the hand of Sighvatur Grímsson, 1891–1892.
NULI, Lbs 2291 4to. Poetry miscellany in the hand of Sighvatur Grímsson, 1890–1891.
NULI, Lbs 2312 8vo. Compilation of *sagas* and poetry in the hand of Sighvatur Grímsson, 1859–1865.
NULI, Lbs 2325 8vo. *Syrpa*, vol. 1–3. Poetry miscellany in the hand of Sighvatur Grímsson,
NULI, Lbs 3623 8vo. Sighvatur Grímsson's autobiography written in 1892. Autograph

M. J. Driscoll

The Long and Winding Road

Manuscript Culture in Late Pre-Modern Iceland

The extent and quality of manuscript production in Iceland during the middle ages – remarkable in view both of the small size and relative isolation of the country – is well known.[1] Less well known is the fact that manuscript culture continued to thrive in Iceland, long after the coming of print in the 16th century.[2] With paper quickly replacing the more expensive vellum and a steady increase in literacy among ordinary people throughout the period, manuscript transmission remained the norm, for many types of literature at least, throughout the pre-modern era.[3] The present article examines this phenomenon, with particular focus on Magnús Jónsson í Tjaldanesi,[4] an ordinary farmer with no formal education who was still copying manuscripts in the first decades of the 20th century, as James Joyce sat in Trieste and Zürich writing *Ulysses*.

The Medieval Background

The culture of the book first came to Iceland in the wake of Christianity, the earliest settlers, who came predominantly from Norway in the 9th and 10th centuries, having by and large been pagan and illiterate. It may be assumed that books in Latin were brought to Iceland in connexion with the conversion, in the year 999/1000, and then subsequently produced in Iceland for domestic use. It is unclear exactly when writing in the vernacular began, but Icelanders must certainly have been writing in their mother tongue by the year 1100 (Turville-Petre 1953, 74–80; Hreinn Benediktsson 1965, 13–18). The earliest extant vernacular manuscripts, few in number and nearly all fragmentary, date from the second half of the 12th century, however, and contain mostly translations of religious (homiletic and hagiographic) and learned (computational and historical-geographical) material. Although this can be no more than a small part of what was produced in Iceland at the time, we cannot know how representative a part it is, but it would not be entirely surprising if the first products of book culture in Iceland were texts of clerical provenance intended for the furtherance of the new religion.

Although it is the 13th century, during which the history of the kings of Norway known as *Heimskringla*, attributed to the chieftain Snorri Sturluson (1178/9–1241), and the major *Íslendingasögur*, or "Sagas of Icelanders", are thought to have been composed, which is regarded as the "golden age" of Icelandic literary production, relatively few manuscripts survive from this period. It is the following century, however, the 14th, which appears to have been the "golden age" of Icelandic manuscript production. Altogether about 300 manuscripts, nearly half of those that survive from the medieval period, are dated to the 14th century, including many of the largest and most impressive Icelandic medieval codices, such as *Flateyjarbók* (GkS 1005 fol.), written about 1387-94 (Guðvarður Már Gunnlaugsson 2005, 249).

This "golden age" came to an abrupt end in the beginning of the 15th century with the arrival of the Black Death (1402-03), which decimated the population and had severe consequences for book production in Iceland. The professionalism so evident in 14th-century manuscripts disappears, and there begins a long period of stagnation in palaeography and orthography. Literary works continued to be produced, however, now including translations of sermons, saints' lives and exempla from Danish, German and English sources, some presumably printed. In the 15th and early 16th centuries we also see an increasing number of manuscripts containing what were later to become Iceland's most popular prose genres, the romances or *riddarasögur*, both translated and indigenous,[5] and the mythical-heroic *fornaldarsögur*,[6] as well as metrical romances or *rímur*,[7] a genre which, alongside the prose romances, would come to dominate manuscript production in Iceland.

There are somewhere between 700 and 800 medieval Icelandic vernacular manuscripts extant, most of them defective or fragmentary (Stefán Karlsson 2002, 833; Guðvarður Már Gunnlaugsson 2005, 249). How large, or small, a percentage this represents of those produced is impossible to say, but it is unlikely to be greater than 15-20%, and perhaps as little as 6-7%.[8]

We know the names of only a handful of scribes from the medieval period, so it is difficult to say to what extent laymen were involved in manuscript culture in Iceland. For the earliest period, till about 1250, it is probably safe to assume that all scribes were clerics. But the larger monasteries appear early on to have produced books not only for their own use but also for members of the laity – as well as for export to Norway (Stefán Karlsson 1979). It seems also clear that prominent laymen themselves kept scribes in their employ. On the literacy of the laity in the middle ages there is little direct evidence, but there is a good deal of evidence from the 16th century onwards, all pointing to a very high degree of literacy among not just the richer classes of society but also, and increasingly, among ordinary people (Loftur Guttormsson 1989). To what extent this can be taken to represent the situation in the middle ages has been the subject of some debate, but there can be no question that the lay elite played an active role in the production and transmission of secular literature from the 13th century onwards, and that in the course of the middle ages direct involvement in literary production and dissemination spread to other layers of society (Stefán Karlsson 1970; Stefán Karlsson 2006).

Manuscript Culture in Post-Reformation Iceland

Several things happened in the course of the 16th century which were to change the nature of manuscript culture in Iceland. Firstly, and most obviously, there was the Reformation, complete in Iceland in 1550, which had a profound effect, as elsewhere in Northern Europe, on the intellectual life in the country. One direct result of the Reformation was that manuscripts of an overtly Catholic nature were destroyed or "recycled", i.e. cut up for use in book bindings or scraped clean and written on again, although just how many is hard to say. In general the production of manuscripts appears to have fallen off in the immediate aftermath of the Reformation, even in the case of the native saga literature; there are only a very few saga manuscripts which can be reliably dated to the first half of the century, and virtually none to the second half. The production of manuscripts did not stop altogether, however, and we have some impressive codices of the lawbook *Jónsbók* – despite the fact that it appeared in print in 1578 – as well as collections of religious and moralising poetry and *rímur*.

Concurrent with the Reformation, paper made its appearance, gradually replacing the more expensive and difficult to produce vellum; the oldest Icelandic paper manuscript now extant, AM 232 8vo, is in fact the *cartularium* (1540–48) of Gissur Einarsson, the first Protestant bishop of Iceland (at Skálholt). Vellum still tended to be preferred for certain types of manuscripts, legal codices for example, until well into the 17th century, but the number of paper manuscripts increased rapidly.

There was another major event in the 16th century: the arrival of print. The first printing press was set up at the bishop's see in Hólar sometime in the early 1530s. The effect this had on manuscript production in Iceland was limited, however, for the simple reason that for the two and a half centuries following its introduction, that is until the founding of the press at Hrappsey in 1773, printing in Iceland remained entirely in the hands of the Church, which, for the most part, did not consider secular literature, including the older saga literature, to be suitable for publication (Klemens Jónsson 1930, Steingrímur Jónsson 1989). Even once the church's monopoly had been broken, few secular literary works were printed, the chief concern of those who published books in Iceland being the dissemination of practical knowledge for the betterment of their countrymen. Most were therefore openly hostile to popular literary genres such as sagas and *rímur*, which they viewed as inimical to progress (Loftur Guttormsson 1987). While on the continent, in Britain and in much of the rest of Scandinavia, precisely this sort of thing had formed the basis for a booming book trade from the 16th century onwards, in Iceland this material continued to circulate almost entirely in manuscript.

Although the Reformation had no immediate effect on the spread of literacy in Iceland, it is clear that there came a general increase in popular literacy with the pietistic reforms of the 18th century, which saw to it that at least one person in every household could read. With the spread of literacy to all levels of society came an attendant increase in the number of people at the lower end of the social scale who were actively involved in the production and dissemination of manuscripts. And here we are in a better position to identify these people: from about the middle of the 17th century it became customary for scribes to identify themselves in colophons, often giving also the date and place of writing. Title-pages also began to appear, in imitation of printed books, which frequently provide information on the identity of the scribe and circumstances under which the manuscripts came into being or the use for which they were intended.

There was, as has been said, a general lull in the production of manuscripts in the 16th century, particularly those of a historical or pseudo-historical nature, i.e. sagas. In the 17th century there begins what is commonly identified as a revival in interest in the earlier saga literature, which came in the wake of humanist interest in the sagas as historical sources (Springborg 1977, Jakob Benediksson 1981, Haraldur Bernharðsson 1999). This revival was centred on the activities of the two bishops, Þorlákur Skúlason (1597–1656, bishop from 1628) at Hólar, in the north of Iceland, and Brynjólfur Sveinsson (1605–74, bishop from 1639) at Skálholt, in the south, who enlisted the services of a large number of copyists, both learned and lay, who were set to copying the more important works of the middle ages, in particular those felt to be of historical interest. Most prominent among the people who copied manuscripts for Bishop Þorlákur was Björn Jónsson á Skarðsá (1574–1655), who, although he had received no formal education, must be counted as among the most learned men of his age. And in fact, the majority of 17th-century copyists, those whose names are known, were not members of the clergy although many had spent time at the schools in Hólar or Skálholt or were the sons of clergymen.

One such was Magnús Jónsson (1637–1702), nicknamed *hinn digri* ("the stout"), who lived on the island Vigur in the fjord Ísafjarðardjúp, in north-western Iceland. Magnús was the son of a clergyman and had himself attended the school at Skálholt briefly, although he left without completing his education. He was a wealthy man by Icelandic standards and had a passionate interest in literature, assembling in the course of his lifetime a significant collection of manuscripts of all types, some of which he copied himself but most written for him by others. There are at least 20 manuscripts that were either written by Magnús or at his behest, and about as many again which were produced by the scribes who chiefly copied things for him and in which he may therefore have been involved (Jón Helgason 1955, 7–14; Jóhann Gunnar Ólafsson 1956, 122–24). The level of manuscript production under the auspices of Magnús í Vigur was unequalled anywhere in the country at the time. Many of Magnús's manuscripts have highly elaborate title-pages with florid titles, such as the following, from a manuscript now in the British Library:

> A collection of stories of foreign peoples, extremely enlightening concerning the inhabitants of various other countries, foreign emperors, kings, counts, dukes, earls, knights, lords, gentlemen, dignitaries, heroes, warriors, noteworthy, powerful and highborn men, who populated the various parts of the world in olden times, containing their genealogies and origins, their budding precociousness, wisdom and chivalrous endeavours in horsemanship, scholarly studies, duelling,

fearlessness and other developments in various kingdoms, which they conquered with bloodshed and battle. Carefully put together, revised and improved by the honourable and highborn nobleman Magnús Jónsson in Vigur, for the education and entertainment of those who wish to hear such stories. Written down at his request by Jón Þórðarson. Anno MDCXCVI.[9]

Magnús í Vigur typifies in many ways the kind of book-loving Icelander of whom there were hundreds in the ensuing centuries, men whose circumstances were perhaps less comfortable than Magnús's, but whose love of the written word was no less great. It was these men who came to dominate manuscript production in Iceland, for the most part ordinary people with little or no formal education, often the heads of large households, who spent the long winter months sedulously copying out texts.[10]

In many cases, these manuscripts were for private use, copied to be read aloud at the *kvöldvaka*, or "evening wake". In its broadest sense, the term *kvöldvaka* refers to the period of the day, in winter, during which the lamp was lit, i.e. from shortly after sunset until the time when the members of the household retired for the night. It is also commonly used to refer to the reading aloud of sagas and recitation of *rímur* and other poetry during this period, a practice dating apparently from the earliest times and surviving, in some places at least, until the beginning of the 20th century. A good deal has been written on this practice, especially with reference to the middle ages, for the light it may be able to throw on the origins of Icelandic saga-writing (Hermann Pálsson 1962; Mitchell 1991, 92–114; Driscoll 1997, 38–46). An understanding of the institution of the *kvöldvaka* is no less crucial to a study of manuscript production in post-medieval Iceland, however, as it provided the context for which – and in some cases clearly also in which – a large number of manuscripts were produced.[11] This link with the *kvöldvaka* is sometimes made explicit in the titles given to the manuscripts. The title-page of Lbs 2787 8vo, for example, reads: "An entertaining book containing a few sagas to pass the time in the evening at home and for the edification of those willing to listen, compiled and written by Finnur Gíslason in 1872".[12]

Some scribes were so prolific, producing far more manuscripts than they themselves could possibly have made use of, that they clearly had other concerns, and there are examples of crofters and labourers supplementing their incomes through copying texts. Some people, though not scribes themselves, had others copy manuscripts for them, and put together large collections, suffering from what Grímur M. Helgason, describing one such, Jón Jónsson í Simbakoti (1834–1912), called "an insatiable longing for books".[13] Jón í Simbakoti was also able to use this "longing for books" to supplement his income, lending his books and manuscripts out to the local farmers and fishermen for a small fee (Grímur M. Helgason 1988).

One of the more prolific scribes of the 19th century was Þorsteinn Þorsteinsson (1792–1863), who was born at Hamar í Fljótum in Skagafjörður, northern Iceland. His father, Þorsteinn Guðmundsson, had attended the cathedral school at Hólar, graduating in 1783 (he had not been a good student, and was not able to secure a living), but the younger Þorsteinn had no formal education. He spent most of the early part of his life at the farm Heiði í Sléttuhlíð and then later on the island Málmey, both also in Skagafjörður. Þorsteinn, despite having to farm and fish for a living, devoted himself to collecting and copying manuscripts and assembled a large library in the course of his lifetime, the bulk of which was acquired by the National Library (Landsbókasafn Íslands) in Reykjavík in 1893 (Sigurgeir Steingrímsson 1972, 48-50; Guðmundur Sigurður Jóhannsson et al., ed. 1981-99, VII, 295-97). There are about 60 manuscripts preserved in his hand, altogether about 16000 pages, the earliest of them dating from about 1810 and the latest from 1860. In terms of contents they are about equally divided between *rímur*, altogether some 200 different cycles, and prose sagas, all the major genres of which are represented, the translated and original *riddarasögur, konungasögur, Íslendingasögur* and various other things, for example a translation of the *Thousand and one nights*. There are also collections of poetry, various accounts of travel in the middle east (*reisubækur*) and texts on Roman and Greek mythology. Even during Þorsteinn's own lifetime it was recognised that his texts frequently contained errors and omissions, it was thought – perhaps over generously –owing to the poor quality of his exemplars (Finnur Sigmundsson ed. 1950-51, I, 149-50; cf. I, 360), and librarian and biographer Páll Eggert Ólason (1948-76, V, 205) comments tersely in *Íslenskar æviskrár* that "everything was very shoddy from his hand".[14]

Another of the more prolific scribes of this period was Jóhannes Jónsson (1798-1877). In the census for 1816 he is listed as a *vinnumaður*, i.e. common labourer, at the farm Stóra-Vatnshorn in Haukadalur, Dalasýsla, western Iceland, but he eventually became *bóndi*, i.e. a farmer who owns his own land, at Smyrlahóll, a medium-sized farm, also in Haukadalur. The number of manuscripts surviving in his hand is relatively small, only seven complete manuscripts plus a few bits and pieces, but we know that Jóhannes copied a large number of texts because he left behind a list of them, entitled "Register of the *rímur*, sagas, various poems, hymns, and prayers, along with other things, that have been copied by Jóhannes Jónsson, farmer at Smyrlahóll in Haukadalur, initially begun about the year 1818, to 1855-56", now JS 203 8vo.[15]

In addition to several hundred hymns and poems, Jóhannes lists 49 sets of *rímur* and 86 sagas. Only three saga manuscripts in his hand have survived. The oldest of these was begun in 1851 but completed in 1857, after the "Regystur" was compiled, and the other two post-date it entirely. These manuscripts contain texts of 70 sagas altogether, 48 of them not listed in the "Regystur", bringing Jóhannes's total output to 134 individual titles. Of these 70 survive, giving a survival rate of 52%. But this assumes Jóhannes only copied each saga once, which is clearly not the case, since a number of the sagas listed in the "Regystur" are found in manuscripts which post-date it and must therefore have been copied at least twice. It is impossible to know how many times Jóhannes might have copied a given saga. For comparison there is one set of *rímur*, the *Rímur af Reimari og Fal* by Hákon Hákonarson (c. 1793-1863), which Jóhannes says he copied over 20 times, and yet not a single copy survives in his hand. If, on average, he only copied every saga twice, the rate of survival is down to 30%; if he copied each one an average of ten times, which is perfectly possible, we are down to 6%, which is probably nearer the truth.

Like Magnús í Vigur (or the scribes who worked for him), Jóhannes was also fond of giving florid titles to his manuscripts. The oldest of the manuscripts surviving, still in private ownership, is entitled "A storybook of men of old, relating their ancestry and actions, strength and fortitude, temperament and physique, prowess and wisdom, their manly deeds and much else, now written and collected by Jóhannes Jónsson, farmer, from Smyrlahóll, during the years 1851–57",[16] while another, Lbs 1767 4to, has the equally colourful title: "Twenty-six sagas of emperors, kings, dukes, earls, barons, farmers, servants and slaves, good and evil; collected and copied by Jóhannes Jónsson".[17]

Magnús í Tjaldanesi

One of the very last, and certainly among the most prolific, scribes in Iceland was Magnús Jónsson (1835–1922), who was born nearly 200 years after his namesake in Vigur, and lived most of his life on the farm Tjaldanes in Dalasýsla, western Iceland (Jón Guðnason 1961–66, II, 375, Páll Eggert Ólason 1948–76, III, 439). An ordinary farmer with no formal education, Magnús devoted his long life to copying texts, the majority of which he collected under the general title "Fornmannasögur Norðurlanda", that is, "Sagas of the ancient men of the northern lands". In about a dozen cases, Magnús's texts are the only copies now extant.[18]

There are 43 manuscripts in Magnús's hand known to the present writer, 34 of them dated, the earliest to 1874, the latest to 1916; the nine remaining are undated but appear to be earlier than the dated volumes. They contain, in total, texts of 171 individual sagas.[19] Of over half of these there are two, three or even four copies, so that the total number of texts, as opposed to sagas, is 315, altogether some 28000 pages, or over 6 million words – impressive by any standards. But certainly there were many more manuscripts which have not been preserved, in all likelihood at least twice as many.[20]

Magnús's texts cover the full range of saga types, including essentially all the medieval *fornaldar-* and *riddarasögur*, both translated and indigenous, nearly 50 of the younger Icelandic prose romances sometimes referred to as *lygisögur* (lit. "lying sagas"), 28 of the younger "reconstituted" *fornaldarsögur*, i.e. works which were written after the Reformation, chiefly on the basis of Saxo's *Gesta Danorum* (Power 1984), 13 translations of German *Volksbücher*, which generally reached Iceland through Danish intermediaries (Seelow 1989), and 10 of the *Íslendingasögur*. Only one of these is found among the sagas in the volumes bearing the title "Fornmannasögur Norðurlanda"; the other nine are preserved in a volume of about the same size and with the same general layout as the "Fornmannasögur" volumes but entitled "Íslendíngasögur. Þriðja bindi" (Sagas of Icelanders, volume III). As no other volumes in this collection have survived, it is impossible to know how many there may have been, but one may safely assume another two. If they contained a similar number of texts, the total for the three volumes would have been around 30; if there had been a fourth, the collection would have comprised essentially all the sagas normally ascribed to this genre.

Four of the sagas classed by Magnús as "Fornmannasögur Norðurlanda" are what would at the time probably have been termed *æfintýri* (adventures, tales). These were literary works of the 17th or 18th century which had found their way, principally via Denmark, to Iceland, and circulated, recast in Icelandic prose, in manuscripts alongside the romances and mythical-heroic sagas. One of the works which comes under this heading is 'sagan af Skanderbeg', a biography of Georgius Castriotus (1405–68), the Albanian national hero, known as Iskander-Beg or Scanderbeg. The saga is a translation of a chapter in Ludvig Holberg's *Heltehistorier* (Copenhagen, 1739), itself based on Barletti's *Historia de vita et gestis Scanderbegi Epirotarum principis* (Rome, 1506–10). The saga became quite popular in Iceland and is found in about a dozen 19th-century manuscripts as well as a set of *rímur* (Driscoll 2007).

This may seem a rather curious ragbag of material, but in fact Magnús's scribal production is exceptionally homogeneous by 19th-century standards – just compare Þorsteinn Þorsteinsson and Jóhannes Jónsson. There are no *rímur*, or indeed any poetry of any kind, preserved in Magnús's hand; nor are there any of the genealogical works (*ættartölur*), biographies (*ævisögur*), annals and so forth with which 18th- and 19th-century Icelandic manuscripts abound. This dedication to a single genre – however amorphous or ill-defined it may appear to our modern sensibilities – is really quite remarkable.

About half the volumes in the "Fornmannasögur" collection contain prefaces. In these, Magnús typically discusses his exemplar, how he had got hold of it, by whom it had been written, when and where, and the nature of the text, frequently in relation to other copies he has seen. Magnús can only have got the idea of prefacing his saga texts with information of this kind from printed books – he even numbers the pages of his prefaces using lower-case Roman numerals – but the prefaces depict a world at a considerable remove from the world of print and provide a wealth of information on the scribal network in late 19th-century Iceland. Indeed, the structure and mechanisms of chirographic transmission depicted by Magnús in his prefaces appear, in their essentials, to be the same as at any time during the previous three or four centuries.

Magnús indicates in several of the prefaces that he began copying sagas at an early age. In the preface to *Huldar saga*, an 18th-century reconstruction of a lost medieval saga about a troll-woman, Magnús explains how he first developed this interest:

> Ever since my youth I have had the desire to read sagas and when I was grown up I began collecting sagas, first the sagas of Icelanders and not only them but also all the romances I could get hold of, and later I began making copies of them [...]. When I was a shepherd boy at Staður á Reykjanesi round about the age of confirmation there was a labourer there named Teitur, the brother of Ólafur Teitsson the farmer on Sviðnur in Breiðafjörður; he was a knowledgeable man. He owned a manuscript containing *Huldar saga* along with other sagas. I tried repeatedly to read this manuscript but with little success as it was tattered and worn and the script was bad. I had little idea then of the value of old books.[21]

It does not appear to have taken Magnús very long to develop an appreciation of "the value of old books", as it is clear from other prefaces that he must have began copying at about the same time. In his preface to *Hálfdánar saga Brönufóstra*, one of the *fornaldarsögur*, for instance, he says that that saga was one of several he copied around the age of confirmation. The circumstances under which he did so – at Ögur, one of the *verstöðvar*, or fishing stations, in the Westfjords, where men, principally farm-labourers, came together every year in the early spring to fish[22] – are described in several of the prefaces. Another place Magnús fished out of was Vigur – the home of his namesake and predecessor, Magnús *digri*.

A very clear picture emerges from the prefaces of a scribal network, concentrated on the area around Breiðafjörður in the west, but covering the whole of the country, and comprised for the most part of people like Magnús, ordinary, uneducated farmers who appreciated "the value of old books". Well over a hundred individuals are named in the prefaces as having provided Magnús with manuscripts, the better part of them well-known scribes themselves. One of Magnús's regular contacts was Guðbrandur Sturlaugsson á Hvítadal (1820–1897) (Jón Guðnason 1961–66, II, 454). Hvítidalur is not far from Tjaldanes, only about eight kilometres, and Guðbrandur, a slightly older contemporary of Magnús's, shared his enthusiasm for saga manuscripts. There are at least seventeen manuscripts preserved in Guðbrandur's hand, the majority still in private ownership, including three which have recently come to light in Sweden; all contain similar material to that found in Magnús's collection. Many of Magnús's texts came from or by way of Guðbrandur, where Guðbrandur had managed to get hold of manuscripts which they both then copied.

Magnús also makes frequent mention of Gísli Konráðsson (1787–1877), a well-known poet and lay scholar who lived for the last twenty-five years of his life on the island Flatey, which lies about 45 km to the west of Tjaldanes (Páll Eggert Ólason 1948–76, II, 66–67). Magnús appears to have known Gísli well, and several of his texts derive from Gísli's manuscripts. Magnús's copy of *Trójumanna saga* – a translation of a 17th-century Danish translation of Guido de Columnis's *Historia Troiana*, rather than the 13th-century compilation of the same name which was based chiefly on Darius Phrygius's *De Exicidio Troiæ* – is copied from a manuscript in Gísli Konráðsson's hand, he says, which had been given to him by Gísli's son Indriði (1822–1898). Curiously, one person Magnús must have known, given they both knew Gísli Konráðsson, but never mentions, is Sighvatur Grímsson Borgfirðingur (1840–1930) – a prolific scribe in his own right and Magnús's chief rival for the title of "last man standing" (Davíð Ólafsson 2008, 2010; see also Davíð Ólafsson's contribution to the present volume).

Many of Magnús's exemplars came from further afield, however, and there are numerous descriptions of the great lengths he was often forced to go to in order to get hold of a manuscript. The following, the preface to *Rígabals saga*, a romance ascribed to the poet and clergyman Jón Oddsson Hjaltalín (1749–1835) (Driscoll 1997, esp. 75–132), will serve as an example:

When I was young I copied this saga at Staður in Reykjanes from an old manuscript that Kristján Einarsson from Grónes got for me and was owned by his foster-father, Ólafur Guðmundsson from Grónes. Later I lost the copy I had made and was unable to get another one anywhere, no matter where I looked; I was told there were copies in this place or that, but whenever I tried to get hold of them they were not there or had been lost, and it was the same with the Grónes manuscript; when I tried to get hold of it again it was nowhere to be found and obviously destroyed long ago. Finally Guðbrandur á Hvítadal was able to get a copy in 1889 from Sigurður Árnason from Kirkjuhvammur, or rather through his agency, from up north in Fljót, he said, and then I borrowed it from Guðbrandur.[23]

Magnús sometimes also uses printed books as sources. A good many of his *fornaldarsaga* texts, for example, are said to have been copied from the printed edition, but Magnús generally adds something to the effect that he has previously copied or at least seen the sags in old manuscripts. And this seems to be his criterion: he will, in the absence of a manuscript copy, take the text from a printed edition, but only when he himself knows there to have been a manuscript copy of it. Where his text is based on a manuscript copy he generally also compares it with that of the printed edition. Sometimes he is prepared to admit that the printed text is better, as with *Ragnars saga loðbrókar*, which he has copied from a manuscript but then compared with the printed edition: "they are the same for the most part, but where they differ the printed text is probably the more correct".[24] But as often as not he prefers the manuscript copies. Regarding *Saga af Andra jarli og Högna Hjarandasyni*, one of the younger romances, which appeared in a popular printed edition in 1895, he says: "it seems to me that there is a great difference between the wording of this text and the printed one, but a small difference in the plot and yet some, but I find the written text fuller, and the narrative better organised, although the difference is not great".[25] Sometimes he seems content to regard them simply as different versions. His text of *Sagan af Kára Kárasyni*, another of the younger romances, is from Einar Þórðarson's popular printed edition from 1886, but Magnús says that he has another copy "which I copied from manuscripts, but the wording of that version is very different, although the plot is the same",[26] adding that that version was in no way inferior to the printed one. Regarding *Mírmanns saga*, an indigenous romance thought to have been composed in the 14th century, he says:

There is something strange about this saga; it has been found widely here in the west and I have copied it many times for various people, because its subject matter has been felt to be exceptional and the saga is lovely. But then came the version that was printed a few years ago which is so old-fashioned and unlike the other in wording that they have nothing in common apart from the name, although in both the story was essentially the same. The one I have copied here is taken verbatim from the printed version, but I have also the other one in another manuscript.[27]

Although Magnús says that he has copied the text of the printed edition "orðrétt" (verbatim), Desmond Slay has shown in his edition of *Mírmanns saga* that a great many changes have in fact been made, although mostly of a relatively minor nature (Slay, ed. 1997, cxv–cxxii). Magnús's texts of *Hrólfs saga kraka*, *Eiríks saga víðförla* and *Sturlaugs saga starfsama*, all *fornaldarsögur*, are similarly based on the printed editions but with a good many minor changes (Slay 1960, 94–97; Jensen, ed. 1983, clxxx–clxxxi; Zitzelsberger, ed. 1969, 334).

In general, Magnús's attitude toward the text appears to have been that so long as one didn't tamper with the plot, which he calls "efni" (substance, material), one could do pretty much whatever one saw fit with the actual words, which he refers to as "orðfæri" (wording), or "búningur" (clothing, attire). Magnús frequently comments in the prefaces that he has felt obliged to tidy up ("laga") the sagas he copies stylistically. *Sagan af Falentín og Urson*, a translation of a Dutch chapbook, he says, was "exceptionally poor in style, but I have tried to remedy this somewhat",[28] and of *Bevers saga*, one of the translated romances, he writes: "the wording of the saga was not good, and I have tried to put right what I considered most disagreeable, but have nowhere altered the story".[29]

This attitude is reminiscent of that of oral cultures, and the Swiss medievalist Paul Zumthor (1972, 68–74) argued that a fundamental fluidity – *mouvance* as he termed it – is also a feature of medieval written texts, which, like oral texts, never achieve a state conceived of as final. That this should still be the position taken in late 19th- and early 20th-century Iceland is, on the face of it, remarkable. But given that so many other aspects of literary transmission had remained essentially unchanged in Iceland for over half a millennium, it is perhaps not so remarkable after all: Magnús was arguably simply doing what copyists had always done.

Magnús was regarded during his lifetime as a highly learned man. The book-seller and publisher Sigfús Eymundsson (1837–1911), who brought out a popular edition of *Skáld-Helga saga* in 1897 based on a text provided by Magnús, notes in an afterword:

> All his life he has collected and searched for old manuscripts and copied all that he thought was in the least important and worthy of saving from oblivion. He now has 18 books of copies in 4to, each book of 800 pages, and here there are many rare sagas, which he has managed to get his hands on from various places and then copied. He is surely one of the most knowledgeable men now living in Iceland.[30]

It is also a measure of the respect afforded him that in 1909 Landsbókasafn Íslands bought a complete set, 20 volumes, of his collection "Fornmannasögur Norðurlanda", along with the single volume of *Íslendingasögur*, for which he was paid 250 kr. – roughly half of what the library had to spend on acquisitions in any given year. But times were changing, and the value of Magnús's life's work has not been appreciated by subsequent generations. His "editorial method", which, as noted above, consisted of him changing the texts he copied as he saw fit, was at odds with accepted scholarly practice, and the material he was so keen to save from oblivion – essentially what ordinary men and women read in Iceland in the second half of the 19th century – did not fit in with the new notions, defined and dictated by the national-romantic intellectuals in Reykjavík and Copenhagen, of what constituted "Íslensk menning" (Icelandic culture).

It seems clear that Magnús, toward the end of his life, was well aware that the world he inhabited was fast disappearing. "It is so strange" he says at one point, "that these old books disappear, so that no-one knows what has become of them".[31] The social changes that took place in Iceland in the first decades of the 20th century were greater than at any other time in the country's history, and led, among other things, to the end of the *kvöldvaka*, the practice that had kept manuscript culture alive in Iceland for so long; with the passing of that practice, the manuscripts no longer had any role to play.

Notes

1. On Icelandic manuscripts generally see Halldór Hermannsson 1929, Jón Helgason 1958, Ólafur Halldórsson 1989, Sverrir Tómasson 2002, Gísli Sigurðsson and Vésteinn Ólason 2004 and Guðvarður Már Gunnlaugsson 2005. Major manuscript collections are found in Reykjavík (Landsbókasafn Íslands and Stofnun Árna Magnússonar), Copenhagen (Den Arnamagnæanske Samling and Det kongelige Bibliotek) and Stockholm (Kungliga Biblioteket), for which the published catalogues are, respectively, Páll Eggert Ólason et al. 1918-1996, Kålund 1888-1894, Kålund 1900 and Gödel 1897-1900. Smaller but none the less significant collections of Icelandic manuscripts are also found in London (British Library), Oxford (Bodleian Library) and Uppsala (Universitetsbibliotek).
2. It has, over the last 20 years or so, gradually come to be recognised that the invention of the printing press did not lead to the immediate disappearance of handwritten communication, as has sometimes been claimed (see e.g. Chartier 2007); but manuscript culture arguably lasted longer, and played a greater role, in Iceland than anywhere else in Europe (see also Davíð Ólafsson's article in the present volume).
3. By "late pre-modern Iceland" I mean Iceland in the period from the Enlightenment (the effects of which began to be felt in the 1770s) to the First World War, roughly what is referred to in other contexts as "the long 19th century".
4. Traditionally, and still today, most Icelanders do not have surnames, but rather a patronym, ending in "-son" for men and "-dóttir" for women; as this is not really a name, but rather a description, Icelanders are normally referred to by their first names (and are indexed accordingly). It was also common, although it never had any official status, to refer to people by the place they lived, using the appropriate preposition and the name of the place in the dative: Magnús í Tjaldanesi.
5. The term *riddarasaga* (lit. "saga of knights"), is used both for the translations of French courtly literature which were produced in Norway in the course of the 13th century as well as for the original Icelandic works similar to them in theme and structure but not based directly on any continental models; on the former see Glauser 2005 and the latter Driscoll 2005.
6. For a definition of the genre see Torfi Tulinius 2005; for aspects of the history of the transmission of the *fornaldarsögur* see Driscoll 2003.
7. *Rímur* were arguably the most popular literary genre of late medieval and early-

8   modern Iceland, with over a thousand individual sets preserved from the late fourteenth-century onwards, the majority of them based on prose sources, in particular the romances; see Hughes 2005.
8   This would agree with estimates for Europe in general, cf. Jakobi-Mirwald 2004, 162.
9   *Sagna Flockur Wtlendskra þiöda Forkunar fródlegur Af Jmislegumm Annara Landa þiödumm framande Keisurum, Kongumm, greifunm, Hertogum, Jórlum, Riddurum, Junkiærum, herumm, höfdingium, hetiumm, kóppumm, merkelegum maktar & mikelshättar mónnumm, er ädur ä fyrre øldumm adskilianlegar hälfur heimsens byggdt hafa. Jnnehalldande þeirra Ættslöder & uppruna, blömlegan bradþroska, Vijsdöm & riddaralegar íþrötter, í Vtreidum, bökname, Einvijgum, äræde & ätektum ijmsra konga rijkja, er þeir med ofsa & orrustumm under sig laugdu. Kostgiæfelega Saman Hendtur, yfirsenn & endurbættur af Ehrurijkum & ættgófugum höfdings manne Magnuse Joonssyni ad Wigur, þeim til frödleiks & skiemmtunar, er þesshättar fornar fräsaugur heira vilia. Enn af hans forlage skrifadur af Joone Þördarsyni Anno MDCXCVI* (London, British Library, Add. 4859).
10 Manuscript production in the 18th and 19th centuries has thus far not been the subject of systematic investigation; see however, Grímur M. Helgason 1973, 1979 and 1988; McKinnell 1978-79, Driscoll 1997 and, most recently, Davíð Ólafsson 2008 and 2010.
11 Cf. the articles by Davíð Ólafsson and Sigurður Gylfi Magnússon in the present volume.
12 *Ein Skjemtileg Søgu Bók Innihalldandi nockrar Søgur til dægra stittjngar á kvøldumm j heima húsumm og fródleiks þeim sem eptir taka vilja Samann sett og Skrifud af Finni GyslaSini 1872.*
13 *óslökkvandi þrá eftir bókum.*
14 *allt er mjög óvandað frá hendi hans.* Tereza Lansing is currently conducting an investigation of Þorsteinn Þorsteinssons manuscripts as part of the "Reading and writing from below" project.
15 *Regystur, Jfir Rímna Flokka, Forn Søgur, Ýmisleg Kvædi, Sálma og Bæner, med fleiru, Hvad upphripad hefur Jóhannes JónsSon, Bóndi á Smirlahóli í Haukadal. upphaflega birjad hér umm bil árid 18.18 til ársins 18.55.-56.*
16 *Søgu-Bók Forn-manna, Sem Fráskírir þeirra Ættum og Atgjørfi, Hreisti og Hugprídi, Lunderni og Limaskøpun, Vopnfimi og Viturleík<,> Manndád og Mørgu Fleíru, Ad níu Skrifud og Samansøfnud í eitt af Bóndanum Jóhannesi Jónssyni á Smirla-hóli á Árunum 1851-52-53-54-55-56-7.*
17 *Tuttugu og sex FORN SØGUR af Keisurum, Konúngum, Hertugum, Greifum, barónum bændum, þjónum og þrælum, vænum og vondum. Samansafnaðar og ritaðar af Jóhannesi Jónssyni.*
18 Magnús and his manuscripts are discussed in greater detail in Driscoll 2012.
19 This figure does not include several short biographies of ancient Greek poets and philosophers translated or adapted from Latin sources by Jón Espólín (1769-1836), which Magnús uses as fillers in three of the manuscripts.
20 This is clear both from Magnús's own statements in the prefaces to many of the volumes, discussed further below, and from statements made about Magnús by others, including Magnús's grandson, Magnús Árnason, who said his grandfather's manuscripts had numbered around 100 (Einar Gunnar Pétursson, personal communication).
21 *Síðan á úngdóms árum mínum hefi ek haft löngun til at lesa sögr, ok þegar ek var kominn til fullorðins ára, fór ek at safna saman sögum, fyrst Íslendinga sögum, ok eigi ateins þeim heldr öllum riddarasögum sem ek gat náð til ok fengið, ok síðan fór ek at skrifa þær upp [...]. Þegar ek var smali á Stað á Reykjanesi um fermíngar aldr var þar vinnu maðr er Teitr hét bróðir Ólafs Teitssonar bónda í Sviðnum á Breiðafirði, hann var fróðleiksmaðr hann átti skrædu af Huldar sögu, ásamt fleyri sögum; ek var opt at*

reina at lesa þessa skræðu en geck þat illa því hón var rotin ok máð, & slæm skriptin. Þá hafði ek litla hugmynd um gildi gamalla bóka (Reykjavík, Landsbókasafn Íslands, Lbs 1501 4to).

22 The fact that sagas and *rímur* were read and copied at the fishing stations or *verstöðvar* has been noted, but never explored in any depth. There is a brief treatment of literary activity in the *verstöðvar* in the Lúðvík Kristjánsson 1980-86, IV, esp. pp. 238-55.

23 *Þessa sögu skrifaði ek úngr á Stað á Reykjanesi eptir söguskræðu sem Kristján Einarsson á Grónesi útvegaði mér, en fóstrfaðir hans Ólafr Guðmundsson á Grónesi mun hafa átt hana. Síðan glataði ek sögu þeirri sem ek skrifaði, ok gat hvergi fengit hana aptr hvar sem ek rýndi eptir, mér var sagt hón væri til í þessum ok hinum stað, en þegar ek lagði drög til at fá hana þá var hón ecki til eða glötuð, sama var um Grónes skræðuna þegar ek reyndi at fá hana aptr, þá var hón hvergi til, ok víst undir lok liðin fyrir löngu. Loks gat Guðbrandr á Hvítadal fengit hana átján hundrut áttatýgi ok nýu hjá Sigurði Árnasyni í Kirkjuhvammi eða fyrir Sigurðar milligöngu norðan úr Fljótum at hann sagði, og svo feck ek hana hjá Guðbrandi* (Reykjavík, Landsbókasafn Íslands, Lbs 4940 4to).

24 *ber þeim saman at mestu, en þat sem milli ber mun sú prentaða réttari* (Reykjavík, Landsbókasafn Íslands, Lbs 1491 4to).

25 *mér þykir æðimikill orðamunur þessarar & þeirrar prentuðu en lítill efnismunr ok þó nockr, en mér finnst þessi skrifaða orðfyllri, ok frásögnin skipulegri þó at þat muni ecki miklu* (Reykjavík, Landsbókasafn Íslands, Lbs 1498 4to).

26 *sem eg hefi skrifað eptir skræðum, en hún er mikið frábrugðin að orðfæri, en ekki að efni* (Reykjavík, Landsbókasafn Íslands, Lbs 1507 4to).

27 *Þat er nockut einkennilegt með þessa sögu hón hefir verit víða til hér á vestrlandi, og ek hefi skrifað hana mörgum sinnum fyrir ýmsa, því at efni hennar hefr þótt merkilegt, og sagan er falleg. En svo kom sú sem prentuð var fyrir nockrum árum, sem er svo forn og ólík hinni at orðfæri at þær eiga ecki saman nema nafnið, en þó er efnið beggja at mestu leiti hið sama. Þessi sem hér er skrifuð er skrifuð orðrétt eptir þeiri prentuðu en hina á ek líka til á annari bók. Saga þessi er merkileg og gömul, ok þykir ein sú bezta af riddarasögum* (Reykjavík, Landsbókasafn Íslands, Lbs 1494 4to).

28 *frábærlega bág at orðfæri en ek hefi reynt at laga þat nockut* (Reykjavík, Landsbókasafn Íslands, Lbs 1503 4to).

29 *orðfæri sögunnar var ecki gott, ok hefi ek reynt at laga þat sem mér þótti óviðfeldnast, en hvergi brjálað efninu* (Reykjavík, Landsbókasafn Íslands, Lbs 1501 4to).

30 *[H]ann hefir alla sína æfi safnað og leitað eptir gömlum handritum og afskrifað alt, sem honum hefir þótt eitthvað merkilegt eða þess vert að ekki týndist; hann á nú í afskriftum 18 bækur í 4o, hverja bók upp á 800 síður, og eru á þeim margar fágætar sögur, sem honum hefir lánast að ná í víðsvegar af landinu og síðan afskrifað; hann mun vera einn af sögufróðustu mönnum, er nú lifa á landi hér* (Sigfús Eymundsson, ed. 1897, 42).

31 *Þat er svo undarlegt at þessar gömlu bækr hverfa, svo at einginn veit hvat af þeim verðr* (Reykjavík, Landsbókasafn Íslands, Lbs 1503 4to).

Sigurður Gylfi Magnússon

Living by the Book

Form, Text and Life Experience in Iceland

Setting the Scene

There is a rich tradition of life-writing in Iceland during the long 19th century. A fair number of ordinary working men and women, particularly rural smallholders and tenant farmers, set down records of their lives in the form of autobiographies (see e.g. Sigurður Gylfi Magnússon and Davíð Ólafsson 2002, 175–209). The accounts found in these life stories demand our attention and raise questions about the general experience and modes of behaviour of poor people in Iceland, particularly in comparison with those more favourably placed in society. The fruits of the Icelandic life-writing tradition are to be found in published autobiographies (where the author is also the main character), semi-autobiographies or memoirs (where the author is not the main character) and conversational books (where the cooperation between the author and the main character is marked in the text with questions and answers). A database created a few years ago shows that from the latter part of the 19th century to 2004 there were 1089 books published in Iceland which can be categorised as life-writing. The greater part of them, approximately 85%, were written by men. The main characters in the books here under consideration – which represents 75% of the database – were all born in the second half of the 19th century or the beginning of the 20th.[1]

To this list of research material can be added a large body of other first-hand sources – diaries, letters and other personal testimony, much of it unpublished and hidden away in archives. Such sources have formed part of Icelandic popular culture for many centuries and can be characterised as "ego-documents". In these documents one is more likely to hear the voices of women, especially in collections of letters and in the ethnological database created by the National Museum of Iceland on the basis of questionnaires. The database contains information collected from respondents from 1960 and up to the present day dealing with all possible angles of human experience in Iceland. All these texts – the life-writing tradition and "ego-documents" – bear witness to lively literary activity and provide a rich source for the historian interested in investigating the relationship between personal writing and people's real life experience.[2]

The foundation that was laid in every home in the country for the shaping of the individual promoted the development of the autobiography and literature in general. The *kvöldvaka* (the winter-evening gathering or "wake") provided a powerful focal point for the cultural homogeneity that prevailed throughout the country: popular culture was available to all, in a remarkably similar form (Sigurður Gylfi Magnússon 1993). The very fact that literacy was general at all levels of society had a major impact on both written and spoken language. The education that reached to all levels of Icelandic society provided conditions that enabled people of all classes to feel confident about expressing themselves on current issues and preoccupations (Sigurður Gylfi Magnússon 2010, 85–98, see also Davíð Ólafsson in the present volume). Without this foundation the Icelandic tradition of life-writing would have stood on far shakier ground.[3]

The present article focuses on what was undoubtedly one of the main influences on how people in Iceland, and in particular those who chose to record their memories for posterity, viewed and interpreted their lives. In the Icelandic autobiographies one can sometimes sense that the author may not actually have a great deal to say but intends to tell his story nonetheless. The narrative follows the life course according to a fairly standardised pattern, taking on various shades and nuances from experience as it unfolds. So it seems natural to ask what it was that made people who had perhaps spent almost their entire lives within a narrow compass of experience feel impelled to produce formal written records of their memories? In this paper I shall suggest that the explanation is perhaps best found in deep-seated psychological longings among those who wrote their autobiographies, longings that manifested themselves also in these people's attempts to broaden their education through informal channels, often under very difficult circumstances. It will also be argued that the autobiographers felt themselves in a sense driven to "textualise" their lives, to interpret them in terms of particular forms of narrative, and in so doing to "recreate" them and "balance the books", so to speak.

Ancient Sagas and Living Tradition

The debt owed by the autobiographers of the 19th and early 20th century to the tradition of saga-reading during the winter-evening gatherings is considerable.[4] The sagas and other ancient writings exercised a considerable influence on children in their formative years. With their support young people were able to face up to and endure the hardships that were an ever-present part of rural life in Iceland (Sigurður Gylfi Magnússon 1995a, 295–323). The sagas provided children in farming communities with the models they lacked due to the heavy workloads placed on their parents and guardians. They taught them to fulfil their roles with stoicism and accept whatever circumstance threw at them, just as the ancient heroes had done (Sigurður Gylfi Magnússon 1995b, 57–72). But, as argued below, the sagas provided them with many other motifs that they were able to seize on and adapt to their personal needs.

According to the literary historian Vésteinn Ólason, the ancient literature fortified people in their struggles with daily life. Men needed courage as they ventured out to sea in open boats in deepest winter or across mountain tracks in uncertain weather, and endurance and tenacity were a ever-present necessity, even when not in the face of imminent mortal danger – heroes who show no fear and triumph over all the odds were naturally salutary models: "It was without doubt this more than almost anything that made the sagas dear to the farmers who chose them as material to read out to their households: they fostered courage in the menfolk and inculcated in the womenfolk an appropriate respect for their achievements"[5] (Vésteinn Ólason 1989, 216).[6]

Vésteinn Ólason's comments on the influence of the ancient literature on the conceptual world of people in post-medieval times (1550 to the present) and possibly earlier are fully in line with what comes out of the great majority of the autobiographies. From the autobiographies, however, we can cite much more direct evidence of the influence of the sagas on the mental world of children and, indeed, on all cultural life in the 19th century. The autobiographer Sæmundur Dúason (b. 1889), for example, has this to say about his childhood response to the ancient literature: "It might well be that all this reading and *rímur* poetry[7] shaped my character and attitudes to the present in various ways. This was at a time before people started casting doubt on the veracity of the sagas, though not everyone took the most flagrant exaggerations in them seriously. To me, at least much of what I read was unadorned reality"[8] (Sæmundur Dúason 1966, 69). Following on from this, Sæmundur then attempts to assess precisely how the sagas influenced him and what kinds of models they provided:

> There was no shortage of examples for anyone who wished to model himself on the conduct of the great men. Conversely, neither was there any dearth of bad examples to shun [...]. Though I do not recall attempting explicitly to ape the saga heroes, it is quite certain that I admired those heroes who displayed the greatest manliness in all they did. Similarly, I felt a deep aversion to those who were the meanest scoundrels and wretches, men you could never trust and who left a trail of mischief wherever they went. The ethics of the sagas were more often than not absolute and categorical. (Sæmundur Dúason 1966, 69)[9]

From this and many similar examples it is clear that the world of the sagas permeated the lives and attitudes of children and young people in the 19th century – and indeed of the vast majority of the common people of Iceland, as Vésteinn Ólason points out.

In his autobiography *Ljúfa vor* ("Sweet spring"), Magnús H. Árnason (b. 1891) gives a picturesque account of his quickening interest in the sagas as a child:

> I found learning to read fairly easy. But I was a bit lazy. I started reading the sagas when I was ten. And once I had managed to pick my way through *Egils saga* there was nothing I wanted to read more than the sagas. My father had *Víga-Glúms saga* in gothic lettering and I learned this script so as to be able to read the saga. When I had got hold of and read most of the sagas, there was still *Grettis saga* that

I had not read. I got word that Ólafur of Melgerði had a copy, but the story went that *Grettis saga* was such a favourite of his that he would not lend it to anyone. But I wanted that saga very much, because I had heard so much talked about Grettir. (Magnús H. Árnason 1961, 29–30)¹⁰

Magnús plucked up his courage and went to visit the farmer. "I broached the matter with some trepidation but Ólafur took my request well and said he felt he had to lend me the saga as I had gone to all the effort of coming out in a snowstorm to ask for it" (Magnús H. Árnason 1961, 30).¹¹ Children like Magnús appear to have been driven with an unquenchable desire to devour these ancient tales; as he himself tells us, he had grown up among animated discussions of the qualities of the principal characters.

We find a similar picture in the autobiography of Hafsteinn Sigurbjarnarson (b. 1895) where he describes the winter-evening gatherings on the farm where he lived as a child:

> When the light had been lit in the evening it was an established custom for sagas to be read the whole night until a half past eleven, excepting the time when people went to tend the cowsheds or to eat. This reading fell to the boys from Syðsta-Hvammur. The sagas went on loan from person to person and everything was read that could be obtained, often the same books winter after winter, the sagas and whatever else. (Hafsteinn Sigurbjarnarson 1974, 100)¹²

The sagas were discussed with animation and in fine detail in many households: "The reading was almost always followed with interest by young and old, and when there was a break in the reading the material was discussed. Very often opinions were divided," said a male respondent (b. 1861) from Austur-Húnavatnssýsla, interviewed by the Danish folk high school teacher Holger Kjær in 1930 on his journey round Iceland surveying attitudes to education. Kjær's informant went on:

> When talking about sagas, different men had different heroes. Some even pleaded extenuation for character defects and wrongdoings that turned up in the story and tried to argue that such and such had to be that way; others argued back and the discussions at times became quite heated. These discussions served to quicken and sharpen the understanding of us children of the characters of the people in the sagas and how they wove the thread of their fate to achieve fame and renown, prestige and success, or infamy and shame, downfall and disgrace, life or death. My heart often burned in my chest and my eyes filled with tears, either of happiness or sorrow.¹³ (Kjær 1, 5–6)¹⁴

The literary historian Viðar Hreinsson cites a similar example of impassioned empathetic involvement in the ancient sagas in the poetess Kristín Sigfúsdóttir's (b. 1876) description of a saga reading in a typical Icelandic household:

> An old woman told me that at one time in her childhood she had heard *Laxdæla saga* being read in the house where she lived. When they got to slaying of Kjartan,

an old man, half in tears, called in from out in the living room: "Oh, stop reading, stop reading. What a damned accursed villain that Bolli was to kill Kjartan!"

The man who was reading fell silent and put down the book. But after a little while another sound came from the same direction: "Oh well, maybe you can carry on just a bit further." And so the reading was taken up again.[15] (Viðar Hreinsson 1998)[16]

It is important now to consider to what extent and in what ways this influence of the ancient sagas was passed through to the writing of the autobiographies. It seems reasonable to hypothesise at this stage that the influence went deep, pervading all aspects of the writers' literary activities. If so, this has fundamental repercussions for our treatment of autobiographies as historical sources. We must therefore now turn in greater detail to the relationship between form and content in the autobiographies.

Literary Motifs

The fact that a single literary form can have so dominant a place within a culture as we find in Iceland can bring various problems of interpretation when sources such as life-writing or ego-documents are used in socio-historical analysis. The problems can affect both the literary and historical value of such sources. A chain reaction of mutual influence is liable to arise, leading to circular argumentation – "sites of memory" in the life course, such as was the case with confirmation in the 19th century, had a decisive effect on people's social formation; the values associated with them could result in those who looked back over their lives "reshaping" their experience in accordance with a predetermined structure in which the event itself had a specific place, assigned to it by the institution responsible. In the case of confirmation, it was of course the Church that determined how the event was interpreted. To take another example, when considering childhood, the autobiographers offer two principal interpretations: their younger years are seen either as a road that brought them eventually to happiness and fulfilment or as one that led to ruin and consigned them to the stony path of poverty and hardship.[17] The choice taken by individual writers when interpreting their own lives was determined by what the person in question believed to be the actual experience in his or her own particular case.

It rarely seems to occur to people to view the interpretative route they select as part of the process involved in each person's re-evaluation of his or her own self: it is regarded rather as a genuine reflection of that person's life as it actually unfolded. The way people present and explain the course of their lives is naturally based on their experiential observations of life as a whole, but it is also coloured by the narrative approaches on offer, by new insights into the self and by the very process of retelling personal experience. The narrative method thus creates a circle of mutual influence, taking in the individual, literary form, the environment and experience, all of them working together to determine how authors of autobiographical writings present their formation in written language.

It is worth asking what significance this has for the interrelationship of autobiographical literature and the shaping of memories. As I see it, there are two things in particular that need to be considered here. First, the influence of the sagas on children's upbringing and early experience of life, and the way in which the sagas continued to be a central part of people's lives throughout their adult years. These people had no problem putting themselves in the shoes of the saga heroes and many thus came to the conclusion that their own everyday lives were special and remarkable in the same way as those of the early settlers of Iceland.

Second, the unique regard in which the sagas were held – a status that still in a sense hangs over all cultural activity in Iceland and was until very recently instrumental in shaping people's modes of living and thinking – extending, unsurprisingly, to their literary form, making the sagas the obvious pattern against which most autobiographies were shaped until well into the 20th century. The dominance of the received forms, we can imagine, led people to see their own life experience, for instance from their childhood years, in terms of precepts and patterns found in these texts. We see this most obviously in the use of certain motifs. A striking case in point is the repeated occurrence of the "coal-biter", or "male Cinderella", motif, in which a person who shows no promise as a youth suddenly displays unexpected talents. This was a familiar motif to all Icelanders – from the Bible, in the story of Jacob and Esau, but especially from several of the sagas, notably those of Grettir and Þorvaldur the far-travelled. Motifs of this kind were a part of people's lives and could shape and colour how they interpreted the world and, by extension, how they remembered their own childhood experiences, and also how they came to present their lives in text. In this sense the sagas were a completely natural and integral part of the authors' relation of the events of their own lives.

In recent years Viðar Hreinsson has drawn attention to the prevalence of the coal-biter motif in Icelandic culture in a series of articles and lectures.[18] In relation to the poem *Fíflið* ("The idiot", 1895) by the Canadian-Icelandic poet Stephan G. Stephansson, for example, he notes:

> In the poem Stephan brings together the main features of this narrative motif. In his youth the coal-biter is a simpleton, a child who is generally on the outside but who enjoys the love and favour of his mother. He has scant regard for the conventional rules of social intercourse but turns out well in the end. This is originally a folktale motif, related to the Cinderella story and familiar to Icelanders from the tales about the youngest sister Helga, also known under the name Kolrassa Krókríðandi [Coal-Bottom Corner-Lurker], and from tales about the farmer's youngest son. However, the coal-biter emerges fully naturalised and individualised in the ancient sagas. (Viðar Hreinsson 1998)

Viðar notes that many coal-biters were endowed with "big" personality traits that drew attention on themselves. They flouted social conventions, had wills of their own and were determined to get their own way. Moreover, the coal-biter motif "can accommodate endless variation, for instance inner conflicts and serious flaws of character" (Viðar Hreinsson 1998). He goes on to analyse the attributes of two of the best-known saga heroes, Egill Skallagrímsson and Grettir Ásmundsson, and points out that in *Grettir's saga* "we see a constant tension and interplay between, on the one hand, pain, loneliness and fear of the dark and, on the other, teasing provocation and tomfoolery".[19] All the features mentioned here are found in many of the autobiographies and show how the authors interpreted themselves and how they intended themselves to be seen by others.

The image of the "great hero" which gained currency with the majority of saga readers early in the 20th century superseded the interest in and identification with the coal-biter. Heroic motifs became more sharply defined and more influential during the time of the independence movement in the second half of the 19th century, and were underscored by constant appeals to the "Golden Age" of ancient Iceland. "At times there is a noticeable tendency to idealise and glorify beyond all restraint," says Viðar Hreinsson in the lecture quoted above. The reflections of the coal-biter motif in autobiographies can be seen as evidence that the sagas had a much deeper resonance to their readers than we find in subsequent periods: to the autobiographers and their peers the sagas were an integral part of their lives, their position unquestioned, offering endless possibilities of approach and analysis. What Viðar calls "the glossy image of the Golden Age"[20] was largely a construct of the middle classes, a weapon to be employed in the service of national independence, and it is this image which has dominated to the present day. But among the rural peasantry, the people who read the sagas constantly and whose lives were fully immersed in them, this idolisation of the sagas did not preclude a continuing creative response to their material. The sagas remained a fixed and reliable reference point in their psychological as well as cultural and spiritual beings, living examples to people in their daily toils, and their leading motifs found their way into the self-image of rural Icelanders when they came to set down their own lives in writing.

One thing is certain: the sagas were a living part of the mental world of many of their popular readers; for this we have the evidence of time and again. To these people the saga world was at times so real and powerful, so "true", that ordinary Icelanders with only the most limited formal education had no hesitation in coming forward to argue the toss with any academic scholar who was so bold as to cast doubt on the veracity of the sagas. Helgi Haraldsson (b. 1891), a farmer from Hrafnkelsstaðir in Hrunamannahreppur in the southern lowlands, achieved national celebrity for the vehemence with which he participated in a number of scholarly disputes in the middle years of the 20th century, for instance over the author of *Njáls saga* (Helgi Haraldsson 1948). And he was not an isolated example. In 1979 Kristín Geirsdóttir (b. 1908) from the remote farm of Hringver in Tjörnes in the north wrote to the prestigious literary journal *Skírnir* expounding her views on the theories of ancient academic saga scholars:

> I have to acknowledge that for all my interest in the ancient writings of Iceland my knowledge of them is not cast in steel. Far from it. I have neither had the stamina nor the facilities to delve into them as I would have wished. But these books have been enormously precious to me from as far back as I remember, and

> if anything is to excuse me for trying to write as I do now it is my heartfelt love for the ancient literature of Iceland. – This may likely be called "sentimentality", and I have noticed that this kind of thing is not in favour among modern literary commentators. But there are also various things in these matters that I have difficulty understanding, because it is hard to reconcile them with my ordinary native common sense. (Kristín Geirsdóttir 1979, 6)

Kristín goes on undeterred to take apart the arguments of academic scholars, using as her weapon her "feeling" for the story world of the sagas as acquired in the setting of her childhood living room. Her 1979 article was followed by two more, in 1990 and 1995, also published in *Skírnir*. Kristín had something to say about the work of just about every critic of the sagas. The youngest object of her disapproval was Guðrún Nordal, now director of the Árni Magnússon Institute for Icelandic Studies, about whose research Kristín writes:

> A recent edition of *Skírnir* (Autumn 1992) contains much of enormous interest. My attention was first drawn to an essay by Dr Guðrún Nordal, "Freyr fífldur" [Freyr cuckolded]. What interested me in this article was, in part, that ever since I was a child Sturla Sighvatsson has left an indelible impression on my mind, both for his complex personality and for his tragic fate. Also lasting in my memory has been the strange story of Hallbjörn of Kiðjaberg and his wife Hallgerður, and his verse "Ölkarma lætr arma",[21] the unforgettable cry of a man at the end of his tether, has affected me more powerfully than just about anything else I know in Norse verse. But never had it occurred to me that there was any connection between the two, the story of Sturla and the one about Hallbjörn and Hallgerður. (Kristín Geirsdóttir 1995, 400–411)

Kristín then goes through the saga against the background of Guðrún Nordal's ideas: "From what I could gather, Guðrún considers that in Sturla's nickname lies an imputation of unmanliness, but this was entirely beyond my comprehension" (Kristín Geirsdóttir 1995, 401). What is notable here is this extraordinary "feeling" for the material that we find in Kristín's presentation of her case, the intuitions of an uneducated working woman from the north of Iceland.

To explain this personal response, we need to look in greater depth at the various motifs we find in the sagas and the power they exerted over ordinary people. Possibly the best way to do this is to analyse precisely how these different motifs are reflected in the autobiographies. Such an analysis increases appreciably our understanding of the independent status of the sagas and serves to identify the particular parameters within which the authors operated, and thus helps us to explain how they understood particular events or relationships, for example with parents and friends. Above all else, this interrelationship between form, motifs such as that of the coal-biter and general individual experience demonstrates clearly that the literary form of the sagas lies at a much deeper level within the psychology of people brought up in 19th-century society and well into the 20th century than we might at first suppose. This striking linkage of form and reality makes the autobiography a particularly significant point of contact between the mental constructs and the experience of people at all levels of Icelandic society.

Modes of Expression

If we attempt to analyse the nature of the significance this influence from the sagas had on society and the writing of autobiographies, two things in particular require consideration: first, how society and the environment influenced people's memories in general, and, second, how the sagas played into people's actual lived experience. Here we must always bear in mind the general truth that in any text form influences content. In this, autobiographies are no exception.[22] Language alone sets parameters and limitations on all experience, and descriptions and accounts of events are not the events themselves but textual recreations of these events. Every text follows certain rules which have nothing to do with the author's actual experience but arise from the structure of the language – the structure of the narrative – which governs a person's options of expression and at times controls it entirely. Accounts of events are thus to a great extent shaped by the form in which they are cast.

A further feature of autobiographies is that they are, in one sense or another, constrained within and marked by the framework set by the life course, which is in turn deeply rooted in the structure of society and receives its strength from the traditions of society – in this case, for example, literature such as the ancient sagas and the religious iconography of the Church.

I have sought to draw attention to significant connections between the ancient Icelandic sagas and the autobiographical writings of ordinary Icelandic working men and women of the 19th and early 20th centuries. These connections were, I believe, positive inasmuch as they deepened and broadened the mental world of people who lived and moved in what was in most ways a simple and unsophisticated society. They provided channels for ordinary people to raise themselves constructively above the daily round of everyday toil. But were there adverse sides to these connections? One of the notable features of the ancient sagas is how seldom the characters give expression to feelings and emotions. This is discussed by the literary critic Torfi H. Tulinius when considering the one-dimensional nature of characterisation in the Icelandic romances:

> In this respect the romances [composed in Iceland] differ from many of the translated courtly romances, in which one finds comparatively lengthy descriptions of feelings and emotions. For some reason the authors and readers of romances in Iceland had no taste for this kind of thing, and it has been suggested that this was because there already existed a rich saga tradition which told first and foremost of people's actions and left readers to speculate for themselves on the emotions that might lie behind them. (Torfi H. Tulinius 1993, 226)

The storytelling tradition that Torfi refers to, and whose origins lie in the narrative technique of the classical sagas, had a profound influence on people's modes of expression in the 19th century. We see this, for instance, in the reticence observable among many of the autobiographers when it came to expressing themselves on matters that touched their emotions. This applies particularly once authors have reached adulthood and left their childhood behind them. Fortunately this reticence is by no means universal, and it seems in many ways as if authors who suffered major hardship and adversity in their youths often succeeded better than others in breaking free of the constraints of the narrative technique. But it cannot be denied that the iron grip that the sagas held over many authors' views of life and reality compromises the candour of many of the autobiographies and lessens their value as sources.

One may, for example, note that few of the autobiographers give much space to domestic life after they achieve the status of heads of households: their attention in these so-called "productive years" was, in most cases, directed to quite different matters, and their spouses, children, family and emotional lives are passed over largely in silence. The turning point – one which the writers often discuss at considerable length – is confirmation. Its impact is often analysed and described in detail in so far as it prefigures the future development of the person involved. This is particularly striking given that, in these same autobiographies, marriage is almost invariably noted merely in passing. The reason appears obvious: men were not supposed to reveal their feelings but to bear their joys and sorrows in silence. In this respect the narrative mode undeniably detracts from the value of the autobiography as a historical source and, what is worse, impedes the individual's personal expression even on day-to-day matters. It is important to be aware of these limitations, since it means that one has to seek other ways of approaching the subject. This may be done, for example, by deconstructing texts produced by people about themselves and reading their accounts in the context of their other experience of everyday life and how they talk about it (Sigurður Gylfi Magnússon 1997a, 45–68).

The ancient Icelandic sagas, we must conclude, exerted a powerful influence on the mental world of the ordinary Icelanders who set about recording their life stories in writing in the 19th century and earlier part of the 20th. This influence comes out, perhaps, as much in their outlook and personalities as in their narrative form. The centrality of the sagas in Icelandic culture leaves its mark on the way in which events are reported in the autobiographies in, for instance, their authors' avoidance of the treatment of emotions – one of the most striking features of saga style. As noted earlier, there is circularity in this process: one part feeds into another, and historians and others who use the autobiographies in their research need to be aware of this reciprocal relationship. The glorification of the sagas remains a potent force, especially on important days and holidays, in the society in which we live and produce our work, and colours our thinking exactly as it did that of the autobiographers.

Notes

1. For the various genres of life writing in Iceland, see Sigurður Gylfi Magnússon 2004 and 2005. English summaries can be found on http://www.akademia.is/sigm/metastories.html and http://www.akademia.is/sigm/dreams.html.
2. These sources have been investigated in depth and used to great and varied effect by members of the Icelandic school of microhistory: see, for example, Sigurður Gylfi Magnússon 1997 and Davíð Ólafsson 2008.
3. There is a useful Dutch database of ego-documents, including large amounts of material related to autobiographies and similar sources, available on http://www.egodocument.net/egodocument/index.html.
4. The importance of the sagas in mental and emotional development of young people in Iceland is treated in greater depth in Sigurður Gylfi Magnússon 1995. See also Sigurður Gylfi Magnússon and Davíð Ólafsson 2002. The sagas of Icelanders are translated in Viðar Hreinsson et al., eds. 1997. This edition also includes the short stories in saga style known as *þættir* ("tales").
5. *Vafalaust er það ekki síst þetta hlutverk sagnanna sem hefur gert þær kærar bændum þeim sem völdu þær til lestrar yfir fólki sínu: þær stöppuðu stálinu í karlmennina og innrættu kvenfólkinu hæfilega virðingu fyrir afrekum þeirra.*
6. Gender roles and categories are discussed in Sigurður Gylfi Magnússon 1997.
7. *Rímur* are rhymed narrative poems, usually on ancient themes, e.g. from the sagas or classical literature. They differ from ballads (*sagnadansar*) in being composed in more highly wrought meters and language and, ostensibly at least, usually reflecting heroic or literary values rather than popular peasant ones. They remained the dominant form of Icelandic verse from the Middle Ages until the 19th century.
8. *Það mætti vel vera, að allur þessi lestur og rímnakveðskapur hafi haft nokkur áhrif á skapgerð mína og viðhorf til líðandi stundar. Þetta var á þeim tímum, þegar fólk var ekki að rengja efni sagnanna, þó að stórkostlegustu ýkjurnar væru ekki af öllum teknar alvarlega. Að minnsta kosti margt af því, sem ég las, var mér blákaldur veruleiki.*
9. *Nógu var úr að velja, ef maður hefði viljað reyna að semja sig að háttum ágætra manna. Að hinu leytinu var ekki heldur skortur eða hörgull á vondum dæmum til að varast (…) Þó að ég minnist ekki þess, að ég reyndi blátt áfram að apa eftir söguhetjunum, þá er hitt víst, að ég dáði þær söguhetjur, sem mestan sýndu manndóm í hvívetna. Að sama skapi hafði ég andúð á hinum, sem mest voru löðurmenni, mönnum sem aldrei mátti treysta og alltaf þurftu eitthvað illt að láta af sér leiða. Siðspeki sagnanna var oftar en hitt afdráttarlaus.*
10. *Sæmilega gekk mér að læra lestur. Var þó heldur latur. Tíu ára fór ég að lesa Íslendingasögur. Og eftir að mér tókst að stauta mig fram úr Egilssögu Skallagrímssonar, vildi ég ekkert frekar lesa en Íslendingasögur. Vígaglúmssögu átti pabbi með gotnesku letri og lærði ég það letur til að geta lesið söguna. Þegar ég hafði náð í og lesið flestar sögurnar, átti ég Grettissögu ólesna. Ég hafði frétt að Ólafur í Melgerði ætti bókina, en það fylgdi sögunni að hann héldi svo mikið upp á Grettlu að hann lánaði hana engum manni. En mig langaði mjög í söguna, því mikið hafði ég heyrt um Gretti talað.*
11. *Ég bar upp erindið með hálfum hug, en Ólafur tók vel beiðni minni og sagði að hann mætti til að lána mér söguna þar sem ég legði svo mikið á mig að fara í hríð til að biðja um hana.*
12. *Þegar búið var að kveikja á kvöldin, var föst venja að lesnar voru sögur allt kvöldið til klukkan hálftólf, að undanskildum þeim tíma, sem gekk til fjósaverka og matar. Kom þessi lestur í hlut stráka í Syðstahvammi. Sögur gengu millum manna að láni og var allt lesið sem í náðist. Oft sömu bækurnar vetur eftir vetur. Íslendingasögur og annað.*
13. *Var lestrinum oftast fylgt með áhuga af eldri og yngri, og er hlé varð á lestrinum ræddu menn um efnið; urðu þá alloft skiptar skoðanir manna og þegar um sögur var að ræða, héldu menn á víxl með söguhetjunum; sumir jafnvel afsökuðu bresti og*

illverk, er unnin voru í sögunni, og reyndu að færa rök fyrir, að svona hlaut að fara, en aðrir mæltu á móti og, urðu um þetta stundum allheitar umræður. Þessar umræður urðu til þess að glæða og skerpa skilning okkar barnanna á lyndiseinkunnum sögupersónanna, og hvernig þær ófu örlagaþráð sinn til frama og upphefðar, láns og gengis, eða til vansa og hrösunar, falls og smánar, til lífs eða dauða. Brann oft hjarta í brjósti mér, og augu mín fylltust oft, ýmist gleði- eða sorgar-tárum.

14 See reference in Jón Karl Helgason 1998, 32. The passage quoted by Jón Karl comes from papers held by the Ethnological Archive of the National Museum of Iceland, specifically from Holger Kjær's research carried out in 1930 into upbringing and education in rural Icelandic society (Holger Kjær I, 5–6). Kjær collected a considerable body of material, concentrating on people born in the middle years of the 19th century. The citations that follow are also taken from Jón Karl's book. This particular quotation was discussed in a lecture given by Viðar Hreinsson at Snorrastofa at Reykholt in Borgarfjörður under the title *Bókmenntir í öskustó: Hugleiðingar um kolbíta fornsagnanna og bókelska almúgamenn* (1998).

15 *Gömul kona sagði mér frá því í æsku, að eitt sinn hefði hún hlýtt á lestur Laxdælu, þar sem hún átti heima. Þegar verið var að lesa um víg Kjartans, kallaði gamall maður hálfgrátandi utan úr baðstofunni:"Æ, hættu að lesa, hættu að lesa. Bölvaður ópokki var hann Bolli, að drepa Kjartan" Sá sem þagnaði og lagði frá sér bókina. En eftir litla stund kom annað hljóð úr sama horni: "Æ, kannski þú haldir ögn áfram að lesa enn" Síðan var lestrinum haldið áfram.*

16 Viðar Hreinsson 1998; Kristín Sigfúsdóttir 1949, 95. The quotation comes from the section of the book titled "Í föðurgarði: Bernskuminningar".

17 For an illuminating analysis of the various courses open to young farmers' sons on entering into life and the consequences these could have for their futures, see Christiansen 1995, 275–294.

18 See for example Viðar Hreinsson 1998. Viðar delivered a lecture on a similar subject in 1997 under the title *Vandræðaunglingar í sveit*.

19 [...] *sjáum við stöðuga togstreitu og leik með sársauka, einsemd og myrkfælni en um leið ertni og prakkaraskap.*

20 *Gullaldarglansmyndin.*

21 The story is found in *The Book of Settlements* (*Landnámabók*), ch. 51. Stanzas in Old Norse skaldic metres are customarily referenced by their first line, as here; the intricacies of skaldic syntax make translation difficult.

22 The ideas put forward here owe much to Hayden White 1973. White's book, one of the core works of historical analysis, ranges across matters such as how the language of any text defines how its matter is presented, establishes systematic parameters for people's thinking and directs it into specific modes of expression.

Kirsti Salmi-Niklander

Monologic, Dialogic, Collective
The Modes of Writing in Hand-Written Newspapers in 19th- and Early 20th-century Finland

Hand-written newspapers belong to what has been termed post-Gutenberg scribal culture, increasingly an object of multidisciplinary research in many countries over the latest two decades. According to Michael Bristol and Arthur Marotti (2000, 13–14), scribal culture

> [...] valued personal intimacy, sociality and participation [...] – all features that generally distinguished it from print transmission. Closer to the world of orality and its sociological assumptions, the manuscript medium could be used to foster familial and kinship ties, group solidarity, local identity, and factional or partisan interests.

In England and France, scribal culture flourished in aristocratic coteries, religious sects and revolutionary movements during the 17th and 18th centuries (Darnton 2000, Ezell 1993, 1999, Gelbart 1987, Love 1993), while in Iceland, scribal culture has played an important role in education, entertainment and emotional support in rural communities until the early 20th century (Davíð Ólafsson & Sigurður Gylfi Magnússon 2002).

In Finland, hand-written newspapers have had an exceptionally rich tradition, providing the possibility for self-taught lower-class people to have their texts read by a larger community; for educated people, they have functioned as an alternative medium to spread ideas during periods of censorship and political oppression.

The focus of the present article is the socio-cultural functions of hand-written newspapers in 19th- and early 20th-century Finland, which was then an autonomous part of the Russian Empire. How did this form of writing practice reflect and serve the social, ideological and emotional needs of those who contributed to and edited them? The interaction of oral and written tradition will be analysed, as well as the individual and social processes of communication in local communities – the production, dissemination and reception of texts.

Based on my research into hand-written newspapers at different times and in different communities I distinguish three modes of writing practiced in the papers. The *monological mode* provides possibilities for mediating ideological messages, the *dialogical mode* for expressing and processing hidden tensions in small groups and communities, and the *collective mode* opens up ways of expressing emotions and experiences. Examples of all these modes can be found in the papers of a single community and in the authorial strategies of individual writers, but their impact varies in different communities and at different historical periods.

From Frustrated Students to Popular Movements

In the 18th and early 19th century, hand-written newspapers were read and produced by the educated people in Finland, especially members of revivalist movements.[1] These hand-written newspapers often resembled circular letters. Theological dialogues by the Lutheran clergyman Abraham Achrenius (1706-1769), *Conventioner af Gamla och Nya Saker*, were distributed by mail among a circle of correspondents in the 1760s. Achrenius argued against the Moravian (Herrnhutian) Brethren, but the model of his journal was adopted from *Gemein-Nachrichten*, a correspondence journal circulated by the Herrnhutians in Germany. Similar journals were produced in Sweden and distributed to Finland (Mäkinen 1997, 126–127, Ruuth 1921, 146–148).

During the first half of the 19th century, hand-written papers became popular in Finnish secondary school students' societies (*konventti*) and in upper and middle-class families (Haavikko 1998, 202–203, Krook 1949, 203–211). Family newspapers were part of the writing culture of upper and middle class people, alongside letters, diaries and occasional poetry (Häggman 1994, Ollila 1998, 30–31, Salmi-Niklander 2005). The most important reason for the revitalisation of hand-written newspapers as a medium of political discussion was the strict censorship during the rule of Czar Nicholas I. The most extreme measure of the Russian government was the Language Statute of 1850, which forbade the publishing of books in Finnish, with the exception of those dealing with economy and religion. Frustrated, university students started to produce hand-written newspapers, an activity that continued long after the statute was repealed in 1860 (Klinge 1967, 11, 135–137, Luukkanen 2005, Ruutu 1939, 65–66).

In the 1870s sewing circles and societies for singing and general enlightenment were established in rural Finland, some of which produced hand-written newspapers. Most members of these societies belonged to the local gentry, but some members of farmer families joined them, too (Liikanen 1995, 190–191, 211–212). The practice of hand-written newspapers was also adopted in popular movements. Artisans started enlightenment societies in Helsinki, Turku and Oulu between the 1840s and the 1860s (Rehumäki 2008). The first temperance and labour societies were established at Helsinki, Oulu and Sortavala in the 1870s and the 1880s, and the nationwide organisation Raittiuden Ystävät ("Friends of Temperance" was founded in 1884. The tradition was taken up by the agrarian youth movement in the beginning of the 1880s (Hästesko 1931, 32–42, Kairamo 1986, 19–20). The papers provided the members with an opportunity, alongside face-to-face meetings, for discussion and even fierce debate on topics such as evolution, temperance, proper behaviour and class relations (Numminen 1961, 459–

471). Unfortunately, most of the earliest papers of the agrarian youth and temperance societies have not been preserved.

The first decades of the 20th century were the heyday for hand-written newspapers in Finland. When the labour movement adopted a socialist ideology and was formally organised, the practice of producing hand-written newspapers spread to new groups and communities in all parts of the country (Ehrnrooth 1992). One reason for their great popularity was the strict censorship printed material was subjected to and the political uprising under Russian oppression 1899–1905, which created strong local activism (Suodenjoki 2010). According to a statistic from 1904, there were 1129 issues of hand-written newspapers edited by 75 temperance societies (Karpio 1938, 450), and more than 200 agrarian youth societies produced their own papers during the first years of the 20th century (Numminen 1961, 160–161).

I will present these modes and practices of writing in three case studies of hand-written newspapers edited by young Finnish adults with limited formal education living in the countryside. The first case deals with a hand-written village journal edited by a young farmer Juho Kaksola (1835–1913) at Hartola, central Finland, from 1862 to 1863. His literary activities were related to the early phase of reading circles, local libraries and enlightenment societies in the Finnish countryside. The second one concerns another village journal, edited between 1882 and 1887 by Kalle Eskola (1865–1938), a crofter's son from Jokioinen, south-western Finland, which was published by one of the first agrarian youth societies in Finland. The third study focuses on the first years of *Virittäjä*, a hand-written newspaper edited by an agrarian youth society in eastern Finland from 1906 until 1957. The beginnings of the paper are related to strong local activism during the period of Russian oppression.

An Oral-Literary Tradition and a Social Practice

A hand-written newspaper is a hybrid form of self-expression, combining oral communication with manuscript and print cultures. In the agrarian youth movement, for example, printed publications and hand-written newspapers were in close interaction: hand-written local papers were cited and commented on in printed publications such as *Pyrkijä*, the journal of the agrarian youth movement, and many societies printed special issues of their otherwise hand-written newspapers on special occasions such as anniversaries. Some papers by student organisations and temperance societies had a partly printed title page, on which the date of the issue could be added by hand.

By *oral-literary local tradition* I mean those expressive genres which involve both oral and written communication.[2] Hand-written newspapers are a case in point: they were mostly produced as a single copy and published by being read out aloud at meetings and get-togethers. Sometimes the papers were circulated from hand to hand or house to house, or were available for readers at a communal reading room or society hall. In most cases, oral delivery was an essential part of the practice, and sometimes contributors would direct their words to their listeners rather than to the readers of the paper.³

My second key term is *conversational community*: a group of people in close interaction, who create, adapt and interpret texts presented in oral and written form.⁴ Hand-written newspapers were produced in communities of the like-minded, and they maintained this relation by creating a common medium for discussion and self-expression. Even those members who never contributed to the paper participated in this process of textual sociability.⁵ The social and collective aspects of writing have been recognised by David Barton, among others, who emphasises writing (and literacy) as a social practice with certain purposes and communicative goals (Barton 1991). Ursula Howard has pointed out that the biased idea of the (male) solitary learner in research on working-class writing leaves out the important social networks and organisations for learning (Howard 1991); Martyn Lyons (2008, 172–173) has similarly stressed that letter-writing can be a collective practice.

Can we talk about "publishing" in the case of hand-written newspapers which were produced as a single copy? I believe we can, because the papers were in many ways treated as publications by their contributors and readers, and by the officials. Both in the student papers and those produced in popular movements, the editorial posts were often highly competitive, and individual articles could elicit lively debates. In 1885 an issue of *Savo-Karjalainen*, the hand-written paper of a student organisation, was confiscated by the press censors. Issues of *Valistaja*, edited 1914–1925 by the working-class youth of Högfors at Karkkila, a small industrial community in southern Finland, were confiscated by the police in 1926, when all socialist organisations in Karkkila were suppressed. So even though these papers were not printed, they were very much part of the public sphere.

Margaret Ezell's concept of *social authorship* is useful here: critiquing the simplified idea of the early-modern manuscript medium, Ezell argues against equating "public" with "published" and "private" with "personal", and outlines the social sphere of writing which resides between private and public spheres. In the social sphere of writing, texts are produced collectively, and they are available for an extensive, albeit select, group of people (Ezell 1999, 22–40). Even when the hand-written newspaper was the work of an individual writer, it was produced to be read by others.

In most cases, hand-written newspapers were put together by groups of people working together. The activity was thus social and dialogic. Even the production of individual pieces was often collective: many people participated in the creation of texts, which were published anonymously or with pen names. *Valistaja*, mentioned above, provides an interesting case of collective writing. A series of travel stories, written by young factory boys from 1922 to 1925, forms a complex net of narratives: the same characters appear in different stories, and the same events are referred to in stories by different writers. The language is replete with dialogue, expressions in local dialect, and there are ironic references to political and religious language as well as citations of popular songs. These stories can be described as a kind of "collective stream of consciousness" of the young factory boys (Salmi-Niklander 2004, 305–363, Salmi-Niklander 2007b).

The language theories of Mikhail Bakhtin provide theoretical tools for the analysis of the multivocal and dialogic features of hand-written newspapers. When people in local communities start to produce oral-literary texts, they take over the language of the press and printed literature, which provides them new ways of discussing space and time, emotions and experiences. This new language, the "speech of the other", the writers relate to their own oral language, creating new, hybrid expressions with ironic and parodic elements (Bakhtin 1984, 184–186, Bakhtin 1994, 278–279). When writers begin to master the literary language, the oral tradition of their own community becomes a "speech of the other" from which they gradually distance themselves.

Village Journals of Juho Kaksola

Two hand-written "village journals", *Leivonen* ("Skylark") and *Kirjelmiä ystäville* ("Letters to friends"), were edited by Juho Kaksola (1835–1913) in 1862 and 1863 at Hartola in central Finland. These journals, 18 issues in all, were given to the Finnish Literature Society in the 1910s together with Kaksola's diary and some speeches by the secondary school teacher Arne Rossander. Kaksola's children later ask for the material to be returned, and typescripts were made of the texts; unfortunately, the original manuscripts have subsequently disappeared.[6]

Juho Kaksola (originally Johan Rolig) was the youngest son of a farmer. His youth was overshadowed by chronic illness. When he began to edit his village journal at the age of 27 he was a serious young man who compensated for his physical disability through the pleasures of reading and writing (Kauranen 2007, 57). The journals provided him with a possibility to mediate his ideas and to earn respect among his peers. Kaksola was a man of progress. For example, he strongly promoted the benefits of the acquisition of writing skills by the common people, fighting against the prejudice that writing would turn common people into "mock-gentlemen".[7] Kaksola was even more radical than many of his more educated peers, also recommending writing skills for women. Apart from his village journal, Kaksola founded a reading society to promote ideas of popular enlightenment. The reading society ordered newspapers and purchased books which were circulated between the members.[8] Half the founding members were women, and there were farmhands, servants and even shepherds among the members, whom Kaksola had recruited in person.

The journals of Juho Kaksola were most probably produced as single copies which then circulated from house to house in his own and the neighbouring villages. It is also possible that the journals were read aloud for groups of listeners at farmhouses, as was customary with printed newspapers. Kaksola's intention was to include texts contributed by other villagers in his journal, but they are mostly filled with his own texts and those he copied from printed publications. Only one lengthy text in *Kirjelmiä ystäville* (May 1863) is written by "a correspondent". It comes close to the moralising observations which Kaksola himself wrote on the excessive use of alcohol at village events.

These comments, targeted at servants and crofters, belong to the temperance discourse of the 1860s (Apo 2001, 207–208). Although the "correspondent" is anonymous, as an editor Kaksola expressed his concern about the possible reactions to this letter, stating that his purpose was not to occasion quarrel, but rather to foster peace and contentment among the villagers.

One can see Juho Kaksola's village papers as his monologue promoting literacy, enlightenment and temperance. The target audience consisted of his fellow villagers. A hidden dialogue with readers can be observed, however. It is apparent that some of Kaksola's writings resulted in debate among the readers, and their reactions provoked him to reveal his personal emotions. In May 1863 Kaksola wrote a lengthy essay, "On the advancement of education and civilisation", in which he related how "all the bewilderment of old times" had given way to civilisation. Refinement in dress and manners are important markers of civilisation, for example, Kaksola wrote. This view aroused opposition: Kaksola was said to defend "luxury". In his reply Kaksola writes with disgust concerning a custom among country women: when spinning, they lifted their skirts and thus revealed a large part of their thighs – the "enlightened new woman" would never behave in such an indecent way. Kaksola had probably been resigned to life as a bachelor, but in 1865, at the age of thirty, he was married to a 17-year-old girl who had had joined his reading society a few years earlier. Kaksola moved to his father-in-law's farm and became its master. He was elected representative of the peasantry at the meeting of the Estates. Kaksola developed the habit of writing a yearly entry in his diary on his wedding anniversary, a practice he kept up until his death in 1913 (Kauranen 2009, 59–87).

Kalle Eskola – a Young Hero of Literacy

Kalle Eskola (formerly Kaarlo Sälli) came from a more modest background than Juho Kaksola. He was born at a crofters' cottage in 1865 at Jokioinen, central Finland. According to the autobiography included in his diary, he was able to complete primary school, so his education was better than that of most of his peers (Kauranen 2009, 136–137, 139). When Eskola was 17 years old he was elected secretary and librarian of the agrarian youth society founded at Jokioinen in 1882 and began editing the society's handwritten newspaper, *Nuorison Ystävä* ("A friend of youth"). He had been an enthusiastic reader of printed newspapers from the age of ten, and had already published in several newspapers and journals.[9] A little later he was elected chair of the youth society, but a local clergyman and the parish clerk managed to have the society suppressed (Kauranen 2009, 140). Eskola's dream of attending a teacher training college was not realised, and he was mocked for his intellectual activities. He continued editing the hand-written newspaper and contributed to a printed newspaper, too, which led to a visit to the local manor house, where the owner threatened to evict the family if the boy continued his writing, and for a while his ink bottle was put under lock and key. In his autobiography, Eskola depicts himself as a hero of literacy, who fights for his right to self-expression.

Only fragments of *Nuorison Ystävä* from the years 1882–1887 have been preserved, altogether 22 pages. They were donated by Kalle Eskola's descendants to the Finnish Literature Society in 2009. They are the oldest remaining documents of this kind, and imitate in many ways printed newspapers with columns, cartoons and vignettes. It is difficult to estimate the number of contributors, because real names were rarely used. Apparently, Eskola used several pen names himself: "Kaarlo", the penname he used in printed papers, is the most common one. "Nukkumatin veikko" ("Sandman's Brother") is another pseudonym. In a poem called *Unelma* ("Dream", 15.7.1882), Sandman is depicted as a "brother" or fantasy friend. During the first year (1882) the initials "D. E." as well as *Kippis* ("Cheers!") and *Lemminkäinen* (a hero from the Kalevala) appear in some of the issues. The styles resemble one another, but the similarity may be explained by the fact that Kalle transcribed and probably revised all the texts he received.[10] At the beginning of 1883, the editor regrets the fact that his writing companions had moved away. After this, the editor probably wrote most of the stories himself. In addition, there were also anecdotes and poems copied from printed publications.

There are some examples of dialogue with other writers. An undated issue from 1884 includes a letter from "Kippis" from Tampere to his "brother" Kaarlo. This indicates that "Kippis" was one of the friends who had moved away. In another issue (1883) Kalle continues an argument between himself and another, pseudonymous writer in printed newspapers (*Keski-Suomi* and *Sanomia Turusta*) regarding the selection of books for the local library. Kalle's papers are dialogic in the Bakhtinian sense, too: the dialogue dealt with literary culture (printed newspapers) and the oral tradition of his own community, creating different fictional literary identities with pseudonyms. Like Juho Kaksola, he had important messages on enlightenment and temperance to deliver – but above all he was a story-teller interested in dramatic stories and comic events.

Stories based on local history constitute the most interesting texts of *Nuorison Ystävä*. "The brass gate of Jaakola" (20.5.1882), for example, is based on a local historical legend set in the distant past. Jaakola, a manor house by the Loimaa river at Jokioinen, had a brass gate which was closed every night. When the Russians attacked the village, the gate was sunk to the bottom of the river together with the church bells, so that the enemy would not get hold of these treasures.

> There on the river bottom the treasures will stay for all eternity; on Christmas morning, when people are riding to church, they hear the bells tolling under the water, and on summer nights one hears the sound of the brass gate, playing its old role in the land of the water spirit Ahti.[11]

The paper died out when Eskola began his military service in 1887. He spent three years in the sharpshooter battalion in Hämeenlinna and trained in Russia, too, the great adventure of his life. After the service Kalle joined his father, who had bought a small farm at Renko. He stayed on, married a local girl and fathered eleven children. Eskola had many confidential posts at Renko, which left little time for his literary activities (Kauranen 136–138, 157–164).

Collective Writing at Hiirola

Virittäjä, the hand-written newspaper of the Hiirola agrarian youth society, differs from the newspapers edited Juho Kaksola and Kalle Eskola as it was a collective effort right from the beginning. Hiirola was a small peaceful village in eastern Finland, and the farms – some wealthy, some more humble – were scattered around the railway station. Besides agriculture, a limestone quarry and some small limestone factories provided employment (Laitinen 1992, 477). The period of Russian oppression at the turn of the 20th century resulted in increased political activity in the village, and the birth of the agrarian youth society was closely connected with this. The members included farmworkers and the offspring of land-owning families and crofters.

One of the active figures was a farmer and lay assessor, Mikko Savander, who opened an informal school in his home for the young people of the village. The study program included reading, writing, arithmetic and religion. In February 1900, this home school was organised into an agrarian youth society.[12] In many youth societies, the formal leaders were middle-aged, established members of the community. For the first three years, the chair of the society was the head of the local poorhouse, but Savander had a strong and long-lasting role in the society. According to an anonymous, unpublished history of the society from 1935, Savander's house became a second home for the young members of the society. His wife Anna served as the matron and his daughter Elin as the librarian. The family provided a pleasant, understanding and memorable place for discussing "serious matters of life". The first members (10 men and 6 women) remained active in the society for more than twenty years. The society organised skiing trips and competitions, social evenings and drama performances.

When *Virittäjä* started at the beginning of 1906, the number of members had begun to increase: in 1906 the society had 34 members, by 1907 the amount had risen to 46 and by 1908 to 55. I have not thoroughly analysed the social background of the members of the Hiirola agrarian youth society, but it is quite probable that many of the new members who joined the society after 1906 were farmhands, crofters and young people from families without land. The sons and daughters of local farmhouses had received primary education at school, in the voluntary home school, and some of them had attended the Otava Folk High School close to Mikkeli. New members brought new ideas and inevitably tensions, too. They were depicted by a woman writing under the pseudonym Tuulikki in *Virittäjä* (No 1, February 1906), in which the members of the youth society were criticised for being "proud and withdrawn". The writer admits that this criticism has a true basis:

> Members of the society, who should fight against storms as brothers and sisters, should not be so inconsiderate as to say: how can I [socialise] with him/her, he/she is only a farmhand or a servant, he/she is not of good reputation.[13] They are yet human beings and bear the hardest heat of the day.

The writer points out that many young men and women avoid the society if they feel that they are despised there – especially those, who had fallen into bad ways, should be helped to rise up, not to be looked down upon.[14]

The hand-written newspaper was produced collectively: all the texts are anonymous or pseudonymous. Each issue was edited by a team of four to six young men and women, but nobody was named an editor-in-chief. Some members of the editorial team were changed in each issue, and their names were in most cases mentioned on the front page. The social, even collective, authorship comes out in the individual texts, too. *Virittäjä* includes *local event narratives*, a genre typical to hand-written newspapers (Salmi-Niklander 2004, 137–138; 2006; 2009). These stories depict small events in the local community, such as social evenings, festivals, excursions and skiing contests. Use of the first person plural is much more common in local event narratives than is use of the first-person singular, and even in those texts where the story is told in the first person singular, the narrator is most often an anonymous observer who does not describe his or her own experiences or feelings.

It is very difficult to trace individual styles or profiles of the contributors, because in many cases several people are likely to have participated in the production of individual texts. It is obvious that the literary competence of the writers varied, however; some could produce crafted, though conventional, stories or essays, using nationalistic discourse with its allegoric observations of nature. The story *Talvi* ("Winter"), for example, by Viiri ("Banner"), included in the first issue (1906), starts with a depiction of a lonely skiing trip in the moonlit forest which arouses the narrator's patriotic feelings:

> When I looked at all this I came to wonder whether I could ever leave my fatherland by moving to a foreign country, how could I stop loving this nation and this country, whose spirit is so rich and poetical. [...] Our forefathers have worked here by the sweat of their brows to leave to their children a more fruitful land. As decent fellows do, they have defended their land and freedom with their blood.[15]

On the other hand, in the third issue (March 1906), edited by five young men, there is a story by a writer with the gender-neutral pseudonym "Punkaharju" (referring to a scenic place in eastern Finland), which depicts the narrator's trip to a fair at Mikkeli. The story is narrated in the first person, but only at the very end it is apparent that the narrator is a man. The end is anti-climatic: the narrator looks forward to the amusements of the fair, he is impressed by the merry-go-round and pretty girls, but does not dare to fulfil his dreams:

> As evening was approaching the pretzels were selling well; the boys bought girls pretzels as large as roots in the swamp, and the girls had their hands full when they left the stalls. I didn't have the courage to say to anyone: will you have a pretzel if I buy you one? I thought that tomorrow I'd be a brave fellow like the others, but when tomorrow came I walked about, nothing came out of it, the day passed in vain like yesterday and that's all.[16]

This story, like many others in *Virittäjä*, was obviously written by a person with little formal education or experience of writing. Is the awkwardness of the writing a parodic element? Is it self-parody or a sign of poor literary skills? The first issues of *Virittäjä* included a few apparently parodic texts, fictional letters from simple country men to their sweethearts, where the parody is created by the contrast of ornate metaphoric language and the simple events of country life.

Virittäjä is an excellent example of dialogic, sometimes even collective, writing, which provided a possibility for expressing hidden tensions in the community, both in open discussion and in fictional narration. By using pseudonyms, individual writers could create different authorial identities and styles. The initiative for the hand-written newspaper in this community coincided with the arrival of new members and new social and political tensions: collective writing provided a medium for processing these tensions. Motives for contributing to a hand-written newspaper in this community were more social than individual. Individual voices can be observed in *Virittäjä*, however, although they are fictionalised with pseudonyms and narrative strategies: stories of fairs and skiing trips are probably based on personal experiences, but these experiences are distanced with metaphors, irony and parody.

Individuals and Communities

There are many differences in the styles and topics dealt with in the hand-written newspapers presented in this article. These differences are related to the historical and cultural changes during the latter half of the 19th century. Juho Kaksola was a "genuine" autodidact, whereas Kalle Eskola and many of the contributors to *Virittäjä* had had some schooling. Both Eskola and Kaksola were enthusiastic and devoted advocates of temperance and popular enlightenment, but they were rather different as writers. Eskola appears to be more humorous and multivocal, preferring fantasy and amusement to serious statements. This is partly due to his personality, partly to the fact that he had read and written more than Kaksola. Both men's literary activities were related to the nation building of the Fennoman movement, but as an active reader, Eskola was more aware of literary trends. The contributors of *Virittäjä* were affected by the political turmoil of the early 20th century, and nationalistic rhetoric and political controversies between the land-owners and the landless population were expressed even in simple stories of skiing trips and visits to local fairs.

As Sami Suodenjoki has recently pointed out, writing was part of popular resistance in late 19th- and early 20th-century Finland (Suodenjoki 2010, 77–85, 129–130, 299–300). The revitalisation of hand-written newspapers as a medium for political discussion was connected to the student radicalism in the 1840s and the 1850s. Writing was a questionable, even a dangerous, activity for self-educated people from the lower classes. Both Juho Kaksola and Kalle Eskola faced mockery from their fellow villagers, and Kalle Eskola even received direct threats from the master of the manor, local church officials and his own father. The founding of the Hiirola agrarian youth society and its hand-written newspaper was related to popular resistance against Russian rule, but one can also see the political tensions between landowners and landless farm-workers in this group of young people.

Ideological discussion and political activism were not the only motivations for producing hand-written newspapers. As social practices of writing, they expressed tensions and created cohesion in individual lives and local communities. Juho Kaksola and Kalle Eskola were strong individuals, ambitious young men frustrated by their limited education and somewhat isolated among their peers, even though both initiated and organised social and cultural activities in their home villages. The hand-written newspaper was one way of gaining respect in their communities. Their literary activities were closely linked with the rise of popular movements such as reading circles, local libraries, agrarian youth societies and temperance societies. Even though these men probably wrote most of the material themselves, the response from their community was very important for them and made the hand-written newspaper a quite different kind of writing compared with private diaries (which both men kept later in their lives).

No single individual writer rises above rest among the young people who edited *Virittäjä* at Hiirola. It is probable that Elin Savander was one of the most active writers on the paper, but her texts cannot be identified. Collective writing was related to the ideals of collective self-education, which formed the ideological background for all popular movements, in spite of their different political ideas: self-education did not only mean new knowledge or new skills, but building up one's character, learning to fulfil one's duty and to benefit the community and the fatherland. These ideals were formulated by Santeri Alkio in the 1890s, and they formed an ideological basis for the labour movement (Numminen 1961).

Monologic, dialogic and collective writing are present in all conversational communities producing social genres of writing, even though these modes of writing gained different meanings and had different emphasis in each community. Delivering ideological messages, processing social tensions and creating new ways of expressing feelings and emotions are important motives for all individual writers and writing communities. Hand-written newspapers and other forms of scribal culture created a social, semi-public sphere in local communities. It provided important training for public life, writing for printed publications and participation in political activities. Many self-educated people learnt to move between private, social and public spheres, getting the best of both worlds; but for many people the semi-public sphere and social writing provided the only medium for presenting their ideas, opinions and dreams to a wider audience.

Notes

1 Mäkinen 1997, 126–127. According to Gunnar Suolahti (1925/1991, 220–221), ministers and judges in central Finland ordered hand-written newspapers.
2 My formulation of the term is related to the ethnographical or ideological ori-

entation in the research of orality and literacy. Researchers with an ethnographic-ideological orientation concentrate on hybrid oral-literate practices ("literacies") challenging the "Great Divide" model of orality and literacy (Street 1993, 1, 8–10; Besnier 1995, 6–12).

3   The oral presentation of both printed and hand-written texts was a wide-spread phenomenon in the 18th and 19th centuries in many countries. Newspapers were read aloud in cafes, pubs, farmhouses and private homes. Letters were shared by family members, neighbours and friends by reading them out (e. g. Lyons 2008, 121–122, 138–150, Sumpter 2008).

4   My definition of the term is somewhat wider than the terms *speech community* and *performance community* discussed by folklorists (Abrahams 1993a, 379–400, 386–387; 1993b, 3–37, 21–22), but more narrow than the interpretative community outlined by Martyn Lyons (2008, 9–11).

5   The term *acts of textual sociability* has been discussed by Margaret Ezell (1999, 39–40) and Kathryn King (1994).

6   The only other example of a village journal edited by a self-taught peasant is a single issue of the journal *Miettiä* ("Thinker") edited by the peasant writer Pietari Päivärinta in 1869 (FLS).

7   These prejudices were described by Antti Manninen (1856/1863) in his pamphlet; see also Mäkinen 2007.

8   Reading societies became popular among the Finnish peasantry during the 1850s (Mäkinen 1997, 138–140, Tommila 1988, 238–239).

9   These included the local newspaper *Aura,* the provincial paper *Keski-Suomi,* childrens' illustrated journal *Lasten kuvalehti* and *Suomen Raittiuden Seuran lehti,* the journal of the Sobriety Society.

10 Ulla Silventoinen has analysed this issue in her paper on Kalle Eskola, written for a course on historical literacy practices at the University of Helsinki in April 2010.

11 *Siellä wirran pohjassa pysyvät ne aarteet ikuisiin päivihin; jouluaamuisin kirkkoon ajettaissa kumahtelevat sieltä jään alta kellojen sävelet ja kesä-öillä kuullaan waskinportin helinätä, siellä näet, Ahtolan linnassa on vaskiportti entisessä virassaan.*

12 The history of the agrarian youth society of Hiirola has been told in two anonymous manuscripts included in the archives of the society, the first written in 1930, the second in 1935.

13 The Finnish third-person pronoun *hän* is gender-neutral.

14 *Sillä seuran jäsenten, joitenka tulisi veljinä ja siskoina taistella myrskyjä vastaan, ei tulisi alentaa itseään niin ajattelemattomaksi että sanoo: kuinka minä voin hänen kanssaan hän kun on vain renki ja palveliatar, eli hän ei ole puhdasmaineinen! Ihmisiähän ne ovat hekin ja kovimman päivän helteen kantavat. Siinä mielessä tulee niin moni nuorukainen sysätyksi pois seuran läheisyydestä, sillä kun hän näin kuulee sanottavan niin varmaa on että hän mieluummin pakenee sinne missä häntä ei ylönkatsota. Näin käy etenkin niille, jotka eivät vaarojen kaltevalla pinnalla pysy horjumatta. Ja näitä juuri tulisi auttaa kohoamaan, eikä hylkiä ja painaa yhä alemmas.*

15 *Näitä kaikkia katsellessani tulin ajatelleeksi, voisinkohan koskaan jättää isänmaatani muuttamalla jonnekin vieraalle maalle, sillä kuinka voisinkaan olla rakastamatta tätä kansaa ja maata, jonka henki on niin rikas ja runollinen. [...] – Otsansa hiessä ovat esi-isät täällä työtä tehneet jättääkseen lapsillensa viljavamman maan. Kelpo poikina ovat he verellänsä puolustaneet maatansa ja omaa vapauttansa.*

16 *Kun ilta alkoi lähemmäksi tulla niin silloin se rinkilän kauppa kävi, kun pojat ostelivat neitosille suuria rinkeliä kun suon juurikkaita jotta tytöillä oli täysi kantamus saattaa kuormien luota pois. Mutta minä en hirvinyt sanoa kellekään, että otatkos rinkilää jos ostan? Ajattelin että kun tulen huomenna, niin olen minäkin reilu poika kun toisetkin, huomeen tulikin tallustelin yhtä turhaan kuin eilinenkin päivä meni ja siinä kaikki.*

Archival Sources

Finnish Literature Society, Literary Archives:
Archive of Juho Kaksola (Rolig), Hand-written newspapers, a diary, other manuscripts and documents.
Archive of Kalle Eskola (Kaarlo Sälli), Hand-written newspapers, an autobiography/ diary, other manuscripts and documents.

Provincial Archives of Mikkeli:
Archive of the Hiirola Agrarian Youth Society, Hand-written newspaper *Virittäjä*, 1906–1957, membership lists, minutes and other material.

Workers' Archives:
Archive of the Högfors Social Democratic Youth Division, Hand-written newspaper *Valistaja*, 1914–1925.

Ann-Catrine Edlund

A Country Maid and her Diary

Methodological Reflections on Historical Literacy Practices

On the morning of Sunday the 9th of January 1938 a 21-year-old woman writes the following passage in her diary: "I have just got out of bed and have had something warm to drink. Everything is so quiet since everyone is asleep. I shall wake Miss Gerda with coffee and bread at 8.30."[1] The writer, Linnéa Johansson (1917–2006), is far away from her home, working as a maid for an inspector in Umeå, where she and the housekeeper Gerda are responsible for a large household. Back at home in Dorotea, in northern Sweden, Linnéa's entries include short mentions of people visiting the farm, her chores and pastimes. Sometimes, like on the 9th of April 1940, the day Germany invaded Norway and Denmark, there are passages revealing something of her emotions: "Syster went to Bodum by bike but the road was bad, I heard that the war has started everything feels hopeless".[2]

Keeping a diary was a fairly common practice in Swedish agrarian society from the mid-19th to the early 20th century. Interest in researching peasant diaries (Swedish *bondedagböcker*) began in the 1970s, and has resulted in a printed national register (Larsson 1992). The Swedish term *bondedagbok* ("peasant diary") has been given a fairly broad definition: the diary keeper must be active in an agrarian environment and make a living in connection with farming, and he or she must also belong to the category of the ordinary or common people (Liljewall 1995, 34). The diary of Linnéa Johansson, who worked as a maid and lived mostly in the countryside, complies with these criteria. Diaries written by peasant women seem to be a comparatively late phenomenon (Liljewall 1995, 334, note 25). The printed register of peasant diaries, which begins before 1900, includes 363 named diary keepers, of whom only 17 are women (Liljewall 1995, 38). Many of these women were, however, co-authors with their husbands, and in some cases continued diary writing after their husbands' deaths.

Most peasant diaries consist of short entries about the weather and the work done at the farm. The texts consist not only of diary entries, but also for example of accounts and annual reports (Larsson 1992, 7). The keeping of diaries began in the modern age, when time and the individual had become salient concepts. The main sources of inspiration were almanacs and the instructions given at agricultural schools (Storå 1985, 83, Larsson 1992, 11).[3] Studies of Swedish peasant diaries have mainly been conducted by ethnologists and historians (e.g. Liljewall 1995, Johansson 1996, Larsson &

Myrdal 1995), but the material has also been analysed from a sociolinguistic perspective (Svenske 1993, cf. Gunnarsson 1995).

Peasant diaries have also been the focus of scholarly attention in other parts of north-western Europe. The network *International Association for the Research on Peasant Diaries* has arranged four conferences on the topic (Ottenjann & Wiegelmann (eds.) 1982, Lorenzen-Schmidt & Poulsen (eds.) 1992, Larsson & Myrdal 1995, Lorenzen-Schmidt & Poulsen (eds.) 2002).[4] It has been difficult to agree on a common term for the diaries, however, since the socio-economic conditions vary to a substantial degree between different places and over time in Europe (Liljewall 1995, 34).

I studied Linnéa Johansson's diary, together with the journal of Julia Englund, who also came from an agrarian environment, in my monograph *Ett rum för dagen* ("Room for the day", Edlund 2007).[5] The comprehensive aim of this study was to analyse the function of diary writing for these two women, living in the northernmost part of Sweden in the 1930s and having little experience of writing. I also focused on the significance of literacy practice for the identity of the diarist: I analysed the ways Linnéa and Julia represented themselves in the narrative which developed throughout their diary writing, and whether their literacy practice involved an increased room for manoeuvre for them, i.e. their chances of acting and expressing their thoughts and feelings.

The aim of the present article is to further the theoretical and methodological discussion concerning historical literacy practices such as the peasant diary. I will here combine my reflections on how to theorise and analyse literacy practices with my observations on the diary of Linnéa Johansson in the period 1934–1942.[6] Linnéa's diaries are preserved from the period 1934–1999, but the focus of my research is on the years when she worked as a maid, often changing employers. My approach draws from the concepts developed in the New Literacy Studies and from actor-network theory.

Diary Writing as a Social Practice

Diary writing is an example of a *literacy practice*, which, along with *literacy event*, are two of the key concepts within New Literacy Studies. Both stress that all use of writing is a social act, and hence emphasise the activity of the participants involved. Literacy events are instances where reading or writing takes place in one way or another, whereas literacy practices are embedded in existing social and cultural practices and always take place within a social context (Barton & Hamilton 1998, Barton 2007, 35–37). According to David Barton and Uta Papen, literacy practices refer to the cultural ways of reading and writing, and literacy events are particular instances of drawing upon one's cultural knowledge (Barton & Papen 2010b, 11). To participate in a literacy practice, it is not sufficient just to have formal reading and writing skills; knowledge of the actual practice is also required. For example, in the early 20th century there were different norms for the writing of letters and the writing of postcards. Postcards did not require the writer to conform to the norms of the written language in the way that letter writing did (Gillen &

Hall 2010, 174–175). The writer of postcards simply had more freedom and greater scope for variation.

Many different scientific disciplines are represented within the field of New Literacy Studies, e.g. anthropology, linguistics and psychology.[7] The unifying factor is a new approach to reading and writing where the concept of literacy is put forward as a social practice and not just as a cognitive skill. Literacy varies across time, cultures and contexts, and several different literacies must therefore be considered. Within a given culture, different literacies are associated with particular aspects of cultural life. It is, for instance, possible to distinguish between *work-place literacy* and *academic literacy*.[8]

To regard diary writing as a social practice may, at first sight, seem problematic, since a social practice is normally understood as interplay between individuals or groups of individuals, which is ostensibly not the case when a person makes private notes in a diary. The literacy event of diary writing is nevertheless here perceived as part of a social practice, based on the premise that diary writing is part of a process of identity construction – a process where the writer is in dialogue with him- or herself, using writing as a technique, and pen and paper as tools. In this daily literacy event, individual activities and experiences are made visible at the same time as the writer positions him- or herself in relation to the social contexts that he or she, as an individual, is a part of.

By using the diary text as a basis it is possible to investigate how subjective identity, also called *the self*, is formed. The continuous narrative in people's lives is here regarded as a fundamental condition for the formation of the self. Linnéa Johansson's diary is not a narrative in the usual sense, but it develops from day to day, and forms a narrative of a kind. Certain episodes are chosen to be written about, some moments are described. With a free interpretation of the psychologist Mark Freeman's words we can say that we live episodes, but we do not know the plot of the narrative of which these episodes are a part (Freeman 1993, 29).

The theoretical inspiration of the forming of the self has mainly been derived from the work done by the philosopher Seyla Benhabib and the historian Joan Scott (Benhabib 1995 & 1997, Scott 1992 & 1999). Both emphasise the individual's own participation in the processes of identity construction, where each separate individual is assumed to be a co-creator in the narrative about his or her life. Separate individuals thus possess a certain room for manoeuvre and it is therefore possible for them to influence their situation, in one way or another. I regard Linnéa Johansson as a co-creator in the narrative of her life, in the story or stories that construct her self. One of these narratives is the written text that develops throughout her diary writing. Naturally, she is not the sole participant in the forming of her life story and in the construction of her self. There are several cultural and social conditions related to the construction of identity which are specific for the time and the place where she lived and worked. In Seyla Benhabib's terminology, she has many established stories to relate to (1997, 138), while Joan Scott states that individuals are "subjects whose agency is created through situations and statuses conferred on them" (1992, 34). The diary material makes it possible to study **one** process of identity construction where the subjective identity, the self, is both created and recreated.

Vernacular and Dominant Literacies

Diary writing is an example of vernacular literacy – writing for everyday purposes. Other examples of vernacular literacy practices from early 20th-century Sweden are letters, postcards and song books. Today's vernacular literacies include emerging digital literacy practices such as Facebook, text messages and blogs. The concept *vernacular literacy* is used in New Literacy Studies and stands in contrast to dominant literacy.[9] The distinction between vernacular and dominant literacies illustrates the fact that certain literacies become more visible and influential than others. Dominant literacies are connected to organisations and institutions such as education, law, religion and the work-place. They are characterised by their formalisation and standardisation and are also highly valued in the culture. Dominant literacies are also clearly defined by the needs and objectives of the institution/organisation, and access to knowledge is controlled by experts and teachers (Barton & Hamilton 1998, 252, Barton 2010, 110f.). An example of a dominant literacy is academic literacy, as expressed in literacy practices connected with the doctoral dissertation. The form of the dissertation is regulated and standardised and highly valued in our culture. The university as an institution has set up clear demands and goals for the work. Other university teachers mediate knowledge about this specific literacy practice and they are also the ones who assess it. Vernacular literacies, on the contrary, are rooted in everyday experiences and serve everyday purposes: they are "essentially ones which are not regulated by the formal rules and procedures of dominant social institutions and which have their origins in everyday life" (Barton & Hamilton 1998, 247).

How do vernacular literacies then differ from the dominant literacies in society? Firstly, these literacy practices are less valued, by society as well as by the participants themselves. Secondly, vernacular literacies are learnt informally, and learning and use often take place simultaneously. The activities are usually initiated by the writers themselves. Those of us who have logged onto Facebook in recent years have all learnt what and how to write while participating in this very practice. No one has informed us how to behave on Facebook, apart from the rudimentary instructions on the web. Vernacular literacies may also differ from more formal genres as regards spelling and grammar because of the nature of the communication and the social interaction in the actual context (Barton & Papen 2010b, 10). With regard to formal standards these differences do not necessarily mean that the participants lack competence. It is important to emphasise that the relation between dominant and vernacular literacies vary over time and within different social contexts.

As for Linnéa Johansson's diary writing, it emerged voluntarily and on her own initiative. Before keeping a diary, Linnéa had already participated in another vernacular literacy practice, the reproduction of songs. She regularly copied song lyrics and other texts in her two song books, and added a date and her signature after the text she had written down. There are also sporadic diary notes directly connected with the lyrics she copied. It seems that the noting down of the date has functioned as a kind of an invitation to write something about what had happened during that day, what the weather was like or who visited the farm. Linnéa's notes in the song books are both extensive and regular during this three-year period, between 1931 and 1934, a total of 164 copied texts on 288 notebook pages (Edlund 2003 & 2007). This recurrent literacy event laid the ground for her future diary writing. At about the same time as she stopped copying texts in her song books she began keeping a diary, which she continued to do until 1999, toward the end of her life.

From the Writer's Point of View

Studies on vernacular literacy, work-place literacy and academic literacy have mainly concerned contemporary literacy practices. In this research, the methodology of ethnography has been employed, where the basic unit for analysis is the literacy event. Observations, in-depth interviews and textual analysis have been ways to attempt to understand literacy events and their significance for the participants (Barton & Hamilton 1998, Karlsson 2006). David Barton and Uta Papen emphasise the importance of applied methods in the study of literacy practices: "In order to understand writing as social and cultural practice, we need research tools allowing us to explore the activity and contexts of writing and the meaning their users, readers and writers, bring to these" (Barton & Papen 2010b, 9).[10]

The ethnographic research tradition, as described in Barton & Hamilton 1998, focuses on four aspects: the study of real-world settings, a holistic approach, multi-method research and interpretative analysis that aims to represent the perspectives of the participants (1998, 57f.).[11] The researcher of historical literacy practices cannot draw on an identical methodology, however, although it is still possible to employ an ethnographic approach. The study of a historical literacy event presents some difficulties, since the researcher has to rely on the testimonies given by literacy artefacts and other historical documentation that can shed light upon the social contexts where the texts have been written and read.

I have employed an ethnographic approach in the study of Linnéa Johansson's diary in order to examine the functions of her literacy practice and the writer's representation of herself in her diary. I will start my methodological reflections by presenting the ways I have contextualised Linnéa's literacy practice, after which I present four components which are part of her literacy practice: *the literacy event, the artefacts, the text* and *the language*. The participant is an additional component in literacy practices, which will not be further discussed here, since Linnéa is the sole participant in her diary writing practice.[12]

The first methodological step in the analysis of diary writing as a literacy practice is to situate this practice in a cultural and social context – to place the diary keeper, the literacy event, the text and the artefact in a specific historical time and space. I have relied on the method used in cultural anthropology and ethnography, where an *emic* perspective, "the native's point of view", is the basis for interpretation and reconstruction. My method is to a great extent inspired by the cultural anthropologist Clifford Geertz (Geertz 1991 & 1993). I have tried to get as close to the diarist's living conditions as possible. I strive to see places, people and events from Linnéa's perspective by building up interpretative contexts in which I can place her diary practice. It would have been considerably more difficult to construct the historical context in which Linnéa lived had I not had the unique opportunity to interview her and take part in her oral narrative in 2001–2002. I have come to know her, not just through her writing as a young girl, but I have also met a woman who looks back on her long life.

I have also attempted to reconstruct Linnéa Johansson's physical environments with the intention of investigating the relation between the lived space of the writer and the written space of the diary. This investigation has taken place in cooperation with the artist Maria Sundström.[13] Together we visited some of the places where Linnéa had lived in order to deepen our understanding of the conditions of her life. We followed the young Linnéa to her home village, Stavsjö, which is now desolate and where house foundations as well as arable land has been reclaimed by nature. We also visited Svanabyn in Dorotea, where Linnéa worked as a maid for several periods of time.[14] We gathered contemporary illustrations, mainly private photographs. Historical archive material is of course also an important source for contextualisation – in the study of Linnéa Johansson's diary practice this was not used to any great extent, only in the reconstruction of her living environment when she worked in the town of Umeå in a middle-class environment, where we have traced maps, pictures and building plans.

The Literacy Event of Diary Writing

It is obvious that Linnéa Johansson wrote regularly in her diary, as can be seen from the dating of the notes. But where and when did she write? Did she have a strict writing routine or did the moment for her writing vary? Did she write in her diary when other people were present, or was her writing a more private, perhaps even secret, occupation? There are a number of clues in Linnéa's diary entries which actually afford a glimpse of her literacy events of diary writing. Linnéa's frequent stating of the day's date is one clue. Notes from one and the same day often repeat the date, as each noted event is accompanied by the day's date.

> Elna and Viola came from Sund then went to Stavsjö 19 March 1934. I wash clothes 19-3-34. Artur came here and went home 19 March 1934. Linnéa J. We made the cheese 19 March 1934 (Edlund 2007, 192).[15]

Why did Linnéa choose to date each separate entry? One explanation may be that she wrote several times a day: each entry was dated, because she did not know if the last entry also was the last for that day. This would mean that Linnéa had taken out her notebook and written in it on four separate occasions on this one day in March 1934. If we assume that the number of datings is the same as the number of writing occasions, we can estimate that Linnéa wrote on average two to three times a day (Edlund 2007, 193). Another clue to Linnéa's literacy events is what I have chosen to call *on-the-spot accounts*. Linnéa usually writes about events that have occurred, using past tense, but sometimes she describes what is happening at that very moment: "At the serving table at the Berglund family in Östermalm Friday Oct 29 1937. Linnéa Johansson" (Edlund 2007, 196).[16] Through these on-the-spot accounts one can sometimes determine at what time of the day she is writing her entry and sometimes also where she was at that moment. With the help of the dating of the entries as well as of the on-the-spot accounts we can conclude that Linnéa did indeed write in her diary several times a day, probably whenever she had a free moment from her chores.

The Artefacts

The literacy artefacts of diary keeping – both the look of the notebook and the choice of the pen or pencil – can also provide a clue to the writing event. Durability and permanence in literacy artefacts are emphasised by the literacy researchers David Barton and Mary Hamilton in their article "Literacy, Reification and the Dynamics of Social Interaction" (2005). They use *actor-network theory*, developed by the sociologist Bruno Latour (2005), which highlights the complexity of the relationship between social structure and agency, and also pays attention to the roles of the artefacts in the organisation of society (Barton & Hamilton 2005, Brandt & Clinton 2002). Actor-network theory suggests that agency also resides in artefacts, since aspects of human agency can be delegated to these objects. Literacy artefacts play a particularly important role in linking local and global practices since they serve to build and sustain networks across time and space, given their ability to endure, travel and integrate (Brandt & Clinton 2002). Artefacts ought to be regarded as social participants since they also contribute to the stabilisation of social relations (Latour 1998, 274).

Actor-network theory thus emphasises the social function of the diary itself. The diary participates in a literacy practice where personal experience is reified in a written form that is permanent. The diary can thus be said to participate in an identity-forming process where the subjective identity, the ego, is both created and recreated in the narrative which develops day by day. The diary's sustainability is made up of the permanence of the texts. The diary is a permanent object as long as it is not destroyed – the written texts are also permanent, provided that the writing isn't erased or written over or that the pages are torn out. The diary is also mobile and easy to move, in time as well as in space. It is thereby possible to maintain long-lasting connections and networks across time and space – creating conditions for making this artefact into a particularly efficient and capable social actor (Edlund 2008, 67).

The notebooks where Linnéa writes her diary entries are small and dainty and therefore easy to move and store. Linnéa herself has said that she stored her diary by her sleeping place or in a hiding-place, where the book was concealed from the curious eyes of the other members of the household. In her writing, Linnéa uses ink, pencil and indelible pencil. Writing with ink required a permanent writing place. But the most common writing tool for Linnéa was the pencil. The small notebook and the pencil could accompany her in her apron pocket, which made it possible for her to write wherever she was.

The Texts

The texts have not been analysed to any great extent in the New Literacy Studies: the focus of analysis has usually been on the production processes and the use of texts, not on their content and form. The research carried out in *Cultural Practices of Literacy* is one instance where the analysis of texts and the genres they belong to is included in the study of literacy practices, however, here within the field of literacy education (Purcell-Gates 2007a).[17]

In my "Room for the Day" (Edlund 2007) the diary text was first of all studied in order to contextualise the diary practice. The text is in itself an important source of information on the living conditions of the diary writer. Naturally, the picture that can be drawn from the text is never complete – and never can be. What is written down only constitutes segments of everyday life. Secondly, I concentrated on the functions of the diary practice and the issues concerning the writer's identity – how the writer represents herself in the text. My textual analysis of the diary has been inspired by Critical Discourse Analysis, where texts are seen as parts of social events (Fairclough 2003, 21). Norman Fairclough presents three major types of text meaning: action, representation and identification. "Or to put it differently: the relationship of the text to the event, to the wider physical and social world, and to the persons involved in the event" (Fairclough 2003, 27). Applying this notion, I regard the diary texts as an expression of identity forming. In her diary notes, Linnéa relates herself to the surrounding world and presents her perspective on the events that are described.[18]

The focus in the textual analysis depends naturally on the issues of the individual study.[19] My analysis focused on the themes of the texts and the perspective through which they are described. Which activities and events does Linnéa write down in her diary? Which attitudes and values are present in the text? The analysis, conducted from the perspective of the text, indicates the writer's point of view. It might be expected that the diary notes would be written entirely from the writer's own perspective, but the young Linnéa writes from the farm's perspective and primarily describes the activities of the men in the household, rather than her own chores as a maid. As for the attitudes and values appearing in the diary text, the entries are undoubtedly more documentary than self-reflective, but there are some evaluating comments as well as descriptions of the writer's state of mind. Finally, I used textual analysis in order to find out whether the diary practice offered an increased room for manoeuvre for Linnéa Johansson. Is it possible for her, via her diary writing, to engage in activities which would have been difficult to perform in other ways at that moment in history in her social position? Such as challenging activities or exploring activities?

The Language

The language, or language varieties, that are involved in literacy practices also represent an important component of these practices (Purcell-Gates 2007b, 11). Linnéa Johansson's first language was the dialect spoken in her home area. In school she was introduced to written Standard Swedish, her second language, where lexicon and syntax differed substantially from the local dialect. Today this written standard has a spoken variety that is very similar and is mainly spoken on radio and television, but during the early 1900s the first encounter with this standard language was normally in the school.[20] Linnéa's opportunity to attend school was limited, because her mother died when she was 11, and her total schooling only amounted to about two years.

Although Linnéa spent such a short time at school it is obvious from her writing that she had learnt the spelling norms for Standard Swedish. There are, however, some features in her writing that are closer to the spoken language. When she uses dialect words she often marks this graphically by using double inverted commas. When the potato harvest is finished, for example, she uses the dialect word *pären* for potatoes, placing it in between quotation marks, instead of the standard form *potatisar*. This use of graphic notation for many of the dialect features indicates that Linnéa is very much aware of the standardised written language and has the ambition to comply with these norms in her diary writing (Edlund 2007, 201).[21]

The Written Narrative of a Young Country Maid

Linnéa's written narrative develops in the five notebooks she filled with diary entries between 1934 and 1942. During these nine years she mainly worked as a maid for a total of 18 different employers, both in agrarian as well as middle-class environments. Every day Linnéa writes down her notes in her diaries wherever she is, and she probably also sits down to write several times during the day. The fact that she uses a pencil simplifies her writing since she doesn't need a permanent place for writing. Linnéa is a comparatively conscious writer with the ambition to follow the norms of the written language. She is also anxious to maintain the chronological structure of the diary and therefore uses brackets to mark notes that break the chronology.

I regard the diary artefact as a participant in a social practice where ideas about subjective identity are created and recreated. My study shows how the diary can engender an increased room of manoeuvre for the diarist. The character of Linnéa Johansson's literacy practice changes during the period under investigation. In her first diaries, when she lives in an agrarian environment, the farm is in focus, and Linnéa herself seems to be barely present in the written space. The master on the farm is the main character, and apart from him there is a great gallery of characters, consisting of all the visitors who came to the farm. But when Linnéa's literacy practice takes place in the unfamiliar middle-class environment, she directs her attention to herself and not the household. In this written room Linnéa is the protagonist. It is Linnéa's chores which are made visible, and it is Linnéa's free time and her joys and sorrows, which take up space. The room which the literacy practice creates in the middle-class environment is built for Linnéa's own needs. In this strange environment she needs someone to talk to, and that is how she uses her diary. Thus, in Umeå, Linnéa initiates a literacy practice where she is a more obvious subject – in an environment where she is alone and vulnerable. She also brings parts of the literacy practice which she establishes in the middle-class environment to her continued writing in the agrarian environment.

The literacy practice can be said to have given Linnéa Johansson a somewhat more increased room for manoeuvre in relation to the private employers that she worked for as a maid. Through her diary she gets a chance to confirm the work that she has done and at the same time complain about the hardships connected to her work. Her literacy practice also makes a challenging activity possible, viz. a careful questioning of her employer's social position (Edlund 2007, 229). Thanks to the literacy practice she also gets a chance to explore a new identity. During the period 1939 to 1940 Linnéa sometimes writes her last name as *Robertsson* rather than *Johansson*.[22] She had wanted to change her name, but to do so was unthinkable, and the diary gave her a chance to explore how it would feel to bear the name of Robertsson, to explore and try out an alternative identity – only in the written room can she be *Linnéa Robertsson*.

An Ethnographic Approach to Historical Literacy Practices

In this article I have discussed methodological problems and possibilities in the study of historical literacy practices, especially vernacular literacies. As defined by the New Literacy Studies, all uses of literacy are regarded as acts which are part of different social practices. The use of literacy is thus a social act which not only requires cognitive skills but also knowledge of the social and cultural contexts of the literacy practices in question.

In applying ethnographic methods on historical material, it is important to contextualise the literacy practices as much as possible. One should strive to re-create the interpretative contexts in which these literacy practices can be placed in order to attain "the writer's point of view". Naturally, no thorough understanding is possible: one can only aim for a comprehensive interpretation. As Barton and Papen write, "We do not presume that we know the kind of writing practices that are used in the communities we study" (Barton & Papen 2010b, 10). My description of a diary writing practice and its historical context can never reach the reality which it describes, but must be regarded as a scholarly attempt to interpret, understand and describe the conditions of a diary keeper and her diary in her historical and social environment.

Out of the five components in the study of the historical literacy practices presented in this article (the participants, the artefacts, the literacy events, the texts and the language or language varieties), the sole "real" participant in a specific literacy practice is the writer herself. However, the second component, the literacy artefacts, holds a special position among these components. It is mainly due to them that we can approach historical literacy practices: the artefacts function as re-creators of the social contexts which the literacy events are a part of. Thanks to their permanence, they have the ability to maintain long-lasting connections through time and space.

The third component, the literacy event, provides the most difficult task for its re-creation and analysis. In my study, the diaries and the content of the entries could provide clues to the specific writing activity. On the other hand, the fourth and fifth components of the literacy practices (the text and the language/language varieties) can always be analysed. The type of textual analysis and its thoroughness naturally depends on the issues of each individual study. It is the question of the aim and scope of the study that sets the boundaries for the depth of the analysis.

Notes

1. *Jag har nu nyss stigit opp och fått nånting varmt i mej. Allt är så tyst för alla andra sover, jag skall väcka tant Gerda med kaffe å bröd kl. 8:30* (Edlund 2007, 195).
2. *Syster var till Bodum hon cyklar men dåligt väglag, fick veta att kriget börjar allt känns så meningslöst* (Edlund 2007, 129).
3. A great source of inspiration for diary writing was the printed almanac published by the Royal Swedish Academy of Sciences. The almanac had a wide circulation in Sweden and is one of the most widely-read books in older times, alongside the Bible, the Catechism and the Hymn Book. By the end of the 18th century the circulation figures were as high as 300,000 (Melander 1999).
4. For bibliographies of peasant diaries, see Lorenzen-Schmidt & Poulsen (eds.) 1992 & 2002.
5. The other diary analysed in the monograph belongs to Julia Englund, Nederluleå, Norrbotten (1882–1951). Englund's diaries are preserved from 1932 to 1948, in total 679 pages.
6. The years 1934–1942 in Linnéa Johansson's diary make up a total of 497 pages. In all, her diaries are preserved from the period 1934–1999.
7. A new concept, the *anthropology of writing,* has recently been introduced for the study of writing as a social and cultural practice by David Barton and Uta Papen (2010b, 9). See also Barton & Papen 2010a.
8. For an outline of the growth of Literacy Studies/New Literacy Studies, see Barton 2007, 22f., Barton & Papen 2010b, 11ff. See also Baynham & Prinsloo 2009 where both the state of the art and the future of literacy research are discussed.
9. Jennifer Sinor uses the term *ordinary writing* for everyday writing in her study of a woman's diary from the late 19th century. She contrasts ordinary writing with literary writing (Sinor 2002, 5f.).
10. Methodological issues for future literacy research are discussed in Baynham & Prinsloo 2009.
11. For a detailed presentation of ethnographic methods of literacy studies, see Barton

2000 and Heath; Street 2008.
12 Barton & Hall (2000, 6) distinguish four components while studying letter writing as a social practice: the texts, the participants, the activities and the artefacts.
13 Our joint project resulted in an exhibition *Mobila tidsrum* (*Mobile Time Rooms*) which is presented in greater detail in both text and pictures at www.mariasundstrom.se/mobila%20tidsrum.html
14 For a more detailed presentation of our cooperation, see A.-C. Edlund 2005, Edlund & Sundström 2007.
15 *Elna å Viola kom från Sund for sedan till Stavsjö den 19 mars 1934. Jag tvättar kläder den 19-3-34. Artur kom hit och far hem den 19 mars 1934. Linnéa J. Vi gjorde osten den 19 mars 1934.*
16 *Vid serveringsbordet hos Berglunds på Östermalm fredagen den 29 okt. 1937. Linnea Johansson.*
17 The focus on texts is here theoretically framed by North American genre theory, where genres are considered as socially constructed language practices. The concept of *sociocultural domain* is used to capture the genre as well as the social domain. Memory/record keeping, personal care and bureaucracy are examples of these sociocultural domains (Purcell-Gates 2007c, 200). A Swedish contemporary example of a literacy study where texts have been analysed is Karlsson 2006, in which literacy practices in work places are investigated.
18 I discuss *the functions of the texts*, while Fairclough chooses to discuss *text meaning*: "I prefer to talk about three major types of meaning, rather than functions" (Fairclough 2003, 27).
19 The analysis can either focus on selected features of a text or many features simultaneously (Fairclough 2003, 6). Examples of text analysis issues could be genres, intertextuality, styles.
20 In school the children were taught how to write according to the standard norms, but they were also introduced to a reading pronunciation (Teleman 2003, 406). For an outline of the growth of a standardised Swedish written language, see further Teleman 2003.
21 Different studies show that ordinary people seem to strive to comply with the written norms in their writing (L.-E. Edlund 2005, 331).
22 The use of different signatures is also being discussed in a study of a young boys writing in the late 19th century (L.-E. Edlund 2005, 329).

Anna Kuismin

From Family Inscriptions to Autobiographical Novels
Motives for Writing in Grassroots Life Stories in 19th-Century Finland

Life Stories of Petter and Kustaa

> Then I started sailing on them russian boats and sailed on baltic seas until the war began then I bought a horse and went around Finland driving cargo then came to turku and it was a jubileum there in Turku then I arrived at Peterhof on peter's day then the sitka boats came to krontat I lied to the Russian that my brother is on them boats so I was given a passport and then I went to rontat and started working weekly wages five roubles a week and went around the world three times [...].[1]

The original of the above extract, presented here in a translation which attempts to capture the orthography used by the writer, is from *Petter Wenäläinsen muistij Kirja koko Elämän* ("Petter Wenäläinen's notebook of [his] whole life"), preserved at the Literary Archives of the Finnish Literature Society. According to his narrative, Petter Wenäläinen (b. 1833) grew up in Virolahti near the Russian border in south-eastern Finland, started herding sheep at the age of four and lost his father when he was five years old. He worked as a farmhand, delivered post in Viipuri, drove cargo, smuggled liquor and sailed on the Russian-American Company's steamboats, before starting a stonecutting business and hauling building material to St. Petersburg. He was married four times.

Wenäläinen began writing his life story in 1885 and continued adding short passages up to 1909. It is apparent from his text that he had not written much in his lifetime. The incentive for recording his exploits must have come from Captain Lars Krogius Jr. (1860–1935), whose father Wenäläinen had served as a sailor; Lars was born during a sea voyage to Sitka. There are passages in the little notebook which reveal their friendship. When Wenäläinen was in trouble, the Captain lent him money, and in 1907 Krogius, then director of Finland Steamship Company, and his sons visited Wenäläinen on their cycling tour. The fact that it was Krogius's son Birger who donated the notebook to the Finnish Literature Society also points to the patron friend as being behind Wenäläinen's effort to set his life on paper. It is likely that Wenäläinen's life story would have remained unwritten without this incentive.

The oral tone of Wenäläinen's narrative is very different from that of the autobiography of Kustaa Roslöf (1830–1898), a self-taught itinerant schoolmaster from south-western Finland. Unlike Wenäläinen, who hardly used commas and full stops, Roslöf could write "properly", in a style reminiscent of stories read at Sunday Schools:

> I was a dearly loved son to my parents. They taught me to know God in my earliest childhood. Especially my mother often spoke about God and Jesus, Heaven and salvation. She said that only good children – those who avoid evil, confess their crimes, repent, rely on Jesus and pray to Him, can enter Heaven. My father, who worked as a blacksmith, took good care of me; he wanted me to be an obedient and humble child. My parents were very dear to me, and my father's father, who shared our bread, was as dear to me as my father. Reading God's words and singing hymns were a daily practice in our home.[2]

Kustaa Roslöf mentions in his preface that he had occasionally thought about writing something about his life, but it would have ended there that had not a "Christian brother" encouraged him to do so. Also the title of the little book Roslöf had printed in 1892, *Muuan heikon ja paljon puuttuvaisen kristiveljen omakirjoittama elämänkertomus* ("Life story of a weak and greatly lacking Christian Brother, written by himself"), points to the community of the like-minded to whom the writer is addressing his words. Roslöf's apologetic justification for writing about his own life is common in autobiographies; this convention conveys the attitude that one should not flaunt one's accomplishments or draw attention to oneself (cf. Liljewall 2002, 225–226). Roslöf does not, however, hide the fact that he had taught himself Swedish so that he was able to translate a book into Finnish. He also taught himself some Russian and read books about world history.

Until recently, it has been thought that the unschooled people in 19th-century Finland did not leave many self-written documents behind. Yet the material now being unearthed from various sources shows that this assumption does not hold true: common people did produce various kinds of texts – contracts and petitions, hymns and secular verse, religious or philosophical musings, hand-written newspapers and ethnographic data, as well as plays and fictional stories.[3] For every surviving text, dozens of others must have been lost or destroyed. One of the surprising discoveries is the fair number of autobiographical texts unearthed from public archives, private homes and forgotten printed sources. Petter Wenäläinen and Kustaa Roslöf are but two examples of autobiographical writers discovered in this way.

Wenäläinen was writing for his friend and patron, Roslöf for fellow Christians. The reasons for taking up the pen were many, as were the messages embedded in the life stories. My aim in this article is to explore the explicit and implicit motives behind the texts written by self-educated, Finnish-speaking, 19th-century non-elite people about their lives.[4] In doing so, one has to take into account the contexts in which the texts were produced and, in some cases, disseminated or published. For whom was the life story written, what was the nature and scope of the intended audience? How does this material compare with the texts analysed by Britt Liljewall (2002) and Martyn Lyons (2008)?

Literacy and Common Writers

Fully literate people – those who possessed both functional reading and writing skills – comprised only a small minority of the population in 19th-century Finland, especially during the first six or seven decades of the century. In the mid 1830s, C. Ch. Böcker, secretary of the Finnish Economic Society, gathered information about the numbers of people who could write, among other things. According to a rough estimate based on his findings, which do not cover the whole country, about 5 % of Finnish men were fully literate; there were no inquiries made into women's literacy. Regional differences were striking: the highest percentages were acquired from the Swedish-speaking Åland Islands. By 1880, about 13 % of Finns over the age of ten knew how to write, and at the turn of the century, 40 % of those who had reached the age of 15 possessed the skill (Leino-Kaukiainen 2007, 426–430). On the whole, the statistics of literacy are not very reliable.

The literacy instruction provided by the Finnish Evangelical Lutheran Church concentrated on instilling reading skill for everyone. It was executed by various means such as home instruction, circulating schools held in bigger farmhouses and yearly examinations held in villages. The ability to write was not considered necessary, and the idea that too much study would wean children from manual labour was often shared both by the clergy and the common people themselves (Mäkinen 2007). In practice, reading was often a mechanical skill, and the required religious texts were learnt by oral repetition rather than by studying them. If common people wanted to take up the pen, they had to find the ways and means themselves, often in the face of prejudice and practical difficulties such as procuring paper and writing instruments, which required money and shops to purchase them from. Writing could be practiced on sand, snow, birch bark and shingles by using sticks, poles and pieces of coal or self-made ink and quills. Tuition was sought from peers, older villagers, local pastors and their sons – or just from the model alphabet.

The descriptions found in grassroots life stories of the struggles in learning the writing skill as well as maintaining it exemplify Jan Blommaert's notion of the importance of material infrastructure for effective literacy (Blommaert 2008, 40). In reading manuscripts produced by unschooled non-elite people, one has to pay attention to the materiality of the texts and the mechanics of writing: for a grown-up ploughman starting to write, even holding a pen was an obstacle to overcome. And the attempt to acquire the skill of writing was not always applauded or even met with approval in their local communities.[5]

One of the earliest incentives for learning to write came from revivalist movements; hymns to be sung at meetings were written down, for example, and letters were exchanged among believers. Some writing practices were rooted in trade and administration. Writing was also enhanced by increased mobility brought about by freedom of trade and immigration as well as new occupations in post offices and on the railways. Increasing nationalism engendered channels of publication for writers from lower ranks, too, and the gradual improvement of the status of the Finnish language as well as the Municipal Administration Reform of 1865 provided opportunities for non-elite people in managing local affairs in their mother tongue. Associations such as the temperance societies established in the 1880s and 1890s were yet another indicator of an evolving civil society, creating ways of using one's ability to write – since the 1860s, the "enlightened" common people and the Fennoman intelligentsia had found a common ground in promoting the ideals of temperance (Salmi-Niklander 2007a, 173). Last but not least, the growing numbers of books published in Finnish from the 1870s onward contributed to the formation of the Finnish-language literary institution.

In spite of its somewhat negative connotation, the term *common people* is used here to signify the non-elite people who mainly earned their living by doing physical work and had little or no formal schooling. One could talk of "ordinary people", but writers were exceptional in their communities. As Finland was predominantly rural, most of the grassroots writing took place in the countryside. There were often great social differences between well-to-do farmers owning their land and their crofters, cottagers, farm-hands and so on, but many distinctions separated the common folk from the nobility, the clergy and higher civil servants who commanded Swedish, among other things (Laurila 1956, 31). Itinerant schoolmasters often came from the lower ranks of society and were self-taught. There were also soldiers, rural craftsmen and shop assistants who acquired the skill of writing. Women took to the pen later than men – writing, long associated with power, belonged to the male sphere.

In order to gain a better understanding of the writing of common people I began gathering data on their years of birth and death, birth- or dwelling places, occupations and the types of texts they produced. I chose to disregard writers born after 1880 because I wanted to have texts from individuals who had reached adulthood before the era of mass education. To date I have compiled a list of 409 individuals, out of which 39 are women. The writers can be divided into the following categories:

1) Activists of revivalist movements and other religious writers, who composed hymns, wrote epistles and prophesies, described their religious development or chronicled the revivalist movement in which they were involved; this group includes the first female non-elite writers.

2) Ideologues and enthusiasts, who advanced, above all, popular education and nation-building by collecting folklore or producing ethnographic narratives, writing poems or editing hand-written newspapers.

3) Pillars of local communities, who took care of ecclesiastical and honorary offices; some ended up as representatives of the Peasant Estate in the Diet. These writers often contributed to local and national newspapers and worked towards establishing elementary schools and libraries in their own localities.

4) Philosophers, who tended to be isolated in their own communities, but found an audience by sending their diverse writings to the Finnish Literature Society.

5) Marginal figures, including eccentrics, social outcasts and prisoners, some of whom lived by composing mocking songs, peddling broadside ballads and by begging.

6) Aspiring authors, who took advantage of the opportunities created by the Finnish-language newspapers and publishing houses during the last decades of the 19th-century to get their writings printed.

This grouping is in some ways problematic. All categories contain writers whose world view was coloured by religion and/or nation-building and popular education, and most groups include people who gathered oral tradition and produced ethnographic data for the Finnish Literature Society or the National Board of Antiquities. The purpose is simply to present the range of contexts of common people's texts. There were people who wrote about their lives in all categories presented here.

Life Story Corpus

The corpus of grassroots texts I have put together consists of 65 writings, 55 of them produced by men and 5 by women. This truly heterogeneous material comprises autobiographies, memoirs, autobiographical novels and poems, fragmentary or unfinished texts as well as narratives covering only one or two aspects of the writer's life. For want of a better term I will speak about *life stories*. Fifteen texts in my corpus were published within the writers' lifetime, seven of them through what can be termed vanity publishing. The original manuscripts of these printed texts have not survived, which means that the extent of the role played by editor cannot be determined. The shortest texts fill one or two pages, the longest about 300.

Most of the material comes from archival sources such as the Literary Archives of the Finnish Literature Society, National and Regional Archives, the National Library of Finland and the Prison Museum. Some of these texts have been donated to the archives by scholars or the writers' descendants. Autobiographical material was also solicited. Some of the "Peasant Poets" who were asked to provide personal information for a biographical dictionary sent the Finnish Literature Society their life stories, for example. The Society also received unsolicited material including poems and life stories from common people. In the 20th century it became customary to invite lay collectors of folklore to write about their lives for the archives of the Society. I have also found texts in recent publications put together by families or local historical associations, as well as on the Internet.

The oldest writer in my corpus was born in 1751, the youngest in 1880. The age at which life stories were written down varies a good deal, but the average age is about fifty. Writers came from many parts of the country, although south-western Finland, the oldest inhabited part of the country with relatively high literacy rates, has many hits on the map, as does the province of Savo, where there was a lively tradition of poetry in the Kalevala metre. Not every writer was unschooled in the strictest sense of the word: some attended primary school, though mostly for a limited period; some had a chance to spend a semester or two at a folk high school (*kansanopisto*) or at a teacher's training college. In addition to having learnt to write, there were individuals who had taught themselves Swedish, arithmetic and bookkeeping, among other things.

Most of the writers born in late 18th and early 19th century were farmers, while those born during the latter half of the 19th century represented a wide range of occupations. There were individuals who kept looking for new sources of livelihood throughout their lives. Aleksanteri Lindqvist (1858–1917), for example, worked in a bakery, in the police force and for the railways, tried stonecutting and bricklaying, went to sea, toiled as a shoemaker in St Petersburg and ended up as a pedlar of books. One of the items he must have sold was his own life story, *Huwittava kertomus eli Kokemusten koulu* ("An entertaining story, or the school of experiences"), printed in 1891. Some of the writers rose from rags to riches or gained important confidential posts, but there were also cases of "downward mobility" (cf. Kauranen 2007). One of them was Johan Ihalainen (1799–1856) from Rautalampi: he started as a tailor, but due to a crippling illness became a pauper, living on poor relief. Around 1850 Ihalainen sent his patron Wolmar Schildt (1810–1893), a medical doctor from Jyväskylä, an autobiographical poem in which he asks for writing instruments and paper. Another version of this poem had been published by Elias Lönnrot, compiler of *The Kalevala*, in his magazine *Mehiläinen* ("The Bee") in 1837.

Most life stories are narrated in the first person singular, but there are some cases in which the third person singular is used, which does not necessarily mean that the stories would have been more embellished or fictionalised than those written in the first person. Nearly a quarter of the texts are in verse, mostly in the Kalevala metre (alternate rhyme, four-line stanzas, seven or eight syllables). For people living in a society still strongly marked by oral tradition, verse was a natural way in which to express oneself. Besides, the old epic and lyric poetry in the Kalevala metre was collected and published as a part of the nation-building efforts. Some of the stories are in prosimetrum, where prose narration breaks into verse form or vice versa. The longest narrative poem, comprising 5410 lines, was produced by Johan Léman (1800–1869), son of a sailor who started as a coachman, became a warden of the Oulu town hall and ended up as a bailiff. The carefully constructed title page and the corrections in the neatly crafted manuscript indicate the writer's wish to have his text printed. Pekka Huuskonen (1880–1975), a gardener from Ruovesi, wrote down his life story in verse for the first time in the 1930s and had an updated version (3600 lines) printed in 1963.

Teaching, Repentance and Revenge

One of the motives for writing one's life story originates in the desire to pass on information of one's background and the course of one's life to family members or other limited circles of readers. Pietari Västi (1751–1826), a farmer from Ilmajoki, left behind a short text entitled *Muisto vasta tulevaisille* ("To be remembered by those who come after [me]"). It is organised as a chronological list of years starting from the year of Västi's birth; the second entry mentions the year when Västi's father died. As if anticipating a question from a reader, the third entry is justified in this way:

> Because there is no other way one can learn to know life and understand the habits of other people, in 1763 I went to work at Penttilä, serving there for 2 years, 1 year at Rahkola, 1 year at Ruskala in Kyrö.[6]

Perhaps Västi had no need to work outside his home; hence the explanation for his employment. He also explains that he enlisted in the army in 1769 because he wanted to learn more about life. The rest of the events recorded, such as getting married and receiving positions of trust in local administration, include no explanations. Breaking off in the middle of a sentence, the document is either unfinished or a fragment of a longer text.

It is perhaps an exaggeration to call Västi's catalogue of events a life story. However, it is something more than the practice of writing called *family inscriptions* (Fet 2003, 390), which refers to a register of births, deaths and marriages marked on the inside cover of the Bible or the Hymnal; Västi does not merely record the events of his life but also gives the motivation for some of his actions. His text resembles the oldest texts in Britt Liljewall's corpus of Swedish life stories written by non-elite people. The life story of Jesper Jacobsson (born 1714), for example, a farmer from the island of Gotland, consists of a list of personal details. As Liljewall states, however,

> [...] the contours of a life formed by the individual himself stand out, in spite of the limited contents of the text. It can be seen as a life story, even if the different entries are isolated from each other and are not linked in a coherent or continuous story or narration (Liljewall 2002, 216).

Chronological lists of memorable events also figure in Finnish common people's early diaries (Kauranen 2009).

Israel Hemberg (1797–1877), a factory worker's son from Turku who started as a trader of furs and ended up owning several farms, left behind a document which can be seen as an *exemplary narrative* or a *pedagogical text* (Lejeune 1989, 170). In this untitled text, preserved in the family and written around 1860 in a language reminiscent of old Biblical Finnish, Hemberg compactly narrates his achievements in life. At the end of the story the writer presents himself as an ideal citizen, obviously a good example for his offspring:

> According to my own judgement, I have been a model for many people to follow, due to my diligence and avoidance of drunkenness and lawsuits. Thank God my health has been good so that I have been able to look after my own affairs as well other people's causes. I have rebuilt my burnt-out home village, looked after my old relatives and tried to bring my children up as good workers and civil people. I have been married for 39 years with a good and hard-working spouse, and even though I started as a beggar boy, I have always striven to get ahead.[7]

According to Philippe Lejeune, parents have always imparted their experience to their children: "But perhaps they do so in a more emphatic way when they have the feeling that they are the founders of a dynasty, and they are transmitting, along with their experience, their business" (Lejeune 1989, 170). Hemberg does not, however, write much about the accumulation of his property. Instead, he lays emphasis on the new methods of farming and his positions of trust. Interestingly, the short document includes a passage in which the writer regrets the fact that he had neglected the use of his writing skill, until he woke up from "the sleep of slowness" and started practising it.

Apart from producing an exemplary story with an educational purpose, a common motive for autobiographical writing was to justify and defend one's actions. Matti Saxberg Kolho (1826–1908), a farmer from Keuruu, left his family a text that can be seen an *apology*, a genre with deep roots in Western culture. When he was young, the writer explains, there was a strong revivalist spirit which moved people, and he too heard its call. At the time of writing (1872) he felt again that he was encircled by sin. A series of misfortunes had taken place in Saxberg Kolho's life, starting with a boating accident in 1845 in which 26 people were drowned, including his mother and sister, while he himself was saved. His uncle had been murdered in 1861. Saxberg Kolho's financial troubles had begun in 1862 when he had to start supporting another uncle's large family. On top of this, he was forced to pay his brother-in-law's debts. If the writer could be sure that everything had happened out of God's will, he would not grieve for his misfortunes, "but because I think it has been my own fault, I have filled myself with too much food and drink and worry of livelihood".[8]

In addition to financial problems, Saxberg Kolho reveals trouble of a more personal nature, causing him a great deal of anxiety:

> In the evening of my life my wife does not believe my words even though I have sworn by my soul and life and heaven and earth, even if I wrote the truth with golden words on every wall she would not believe me.[9]

Wailing like Job of the Old Testament, the writer continues his text with a prayer. The document ends with a forceful warning: "The person who deliberately destroys this piece of writing will destroy him- or herself". The text is private in nature, yet its title, *Muistoks jälkeenjääneille elämästäni* ("Remembrance about my life for those who will come after [me]"), points to future readers. Another autobiographical document lists more or less the same events but also covers the years from 1872 to 1902. It bears the following wish: "Let this piece of writing remain to the times to eternity so that I would not be thought as a liar."[10] Neither of the texts reveals the nature of the accusations made by Saxberg Kolho's wife.

Even though Saxberg Kolho was plagued by worries about his posthumous reputation (cf. Liljewall 2002, 220), his text cannot be seen as an act of revenge like *Elias Sutelan elämäkerta eli onnettomuuksien ajama* ("Biography of Elias Sutela, or driven by misfortunes"), published in Oulu by the writer himself in 1899. In his preface Sutela (born c. 1827) declares that he is going to relate all the twists and turns of his life so that the reader can decide if the author's life has been a dance on roses or on thorns. The reader will learn from his story, Sutela promises. The lofty purpose is hardly realised because the writer concentrates on listing his grievances: time and again he has been robbed or deceived. "Life is not child's play for an honest person who tries to strive forward but is met with misfortunes, one after another, and has to suffer because of people who have no conscience", Sutela claims. The last sentence holds a verdict: "But God Almighty will pay them according to their deserts."[11] By having his text printed Sutela obviously wanted to avenge himself on the people who had wronged him. The writer had his story published as an eight-page chapbook, but it is not known how it was sold or who might have purchased it.

Apology and Confession

Kustaa Kallio (1846–1901), a farmhand and later smallholder from Vanaja, begins his life story by remarking that only a few people in the "immense numbers of mankind" had written their life stories – understandably, the unschooled writer did not know much about the long autobiographical tradition in Western culture. Kallio explains that he writes for his kin; he sets out to do this even though he knows that his life is hardly worth remembering. The word used here (*jälkimuisto*) refers to obituaries of remarkable people read at church services or published in newspapers. After this apology the writer offers a justification for wanting to leave behind his autobiography: perhaps his children will not mind if he leaves them some lines describing "the most important moments in my life, because they will keep on narrating, with the familiar father's voice, long after I am lying six feet under".[12] Kallio was aware of the fact that writing would be a better way to preserve the message he wanted to convey than the reflections his children might or might not remember. Interestingly, the image of the written text preserving oral utterances points to the transition from oral or semi-literary culture into one in which the written word had an increasingly significant role both in the lives of individuals and society in general.

The life story of Kustaa Kallio has the generic traits of the *confession*. As a young man Kallio had tried to separate the weeds from the good and useful plants, but once he had carelessly touched "a burning plant". From then on, his life had been an almost constant struggle, both internal and external. The cause and nature of this struggle is not revealed; Kallio's children undoubtedly knew it well. At the end of his text the writer returns to the justification of his life story: he is no proper author nor does he want to become one, but his children know his weaknesses and will forgive him. The text dates from 1897; perhaps Kallio knew that he had not many years to live and wanted to settle his accounts with the people closest to him. Going over his memories of childhood, the death of his mother, the injustices his parents encountered and the changes in society he had witnessed over his lifetime suggest that writing must have been highly therapeutic for Kallio.

The autobiography of Zefanias Suutarla (1834–1908), brought out in 1898 by Werner Söderström, the major Finnish-language publisher at the time, presents a case where there are several motives for writing, some of which seem even to conflict with one another. The title of the book, *Suomalaisen Talonpojan elämänvaiheet. Kertonut tosielämän pohjalla Suomalainen Talonpoika* ("Life of a Finnish farmer. A true story told by a Finnish farmer"), points to the intended representativeness of the text. The protagonist is called by a shortened version of the writer's first name Zefanias (Vani), and the story is written in the third person. Vani started as a farmhand but after having married a widow became a master of a fairly big farm, thus climbing the social ladder. He became engaged in local activities such as founding a dairy and a flour mill, received positions of trust and was elected representative for the Parliament as a member of the Peasant Estate. Not all of his ventures were successful, however: he lost money in shipbuilding, for example, failed in the education of his own son and was taken to court by his ungrateful stepchildren, who wanted more than their share of the estate. In exploring the reasons for these misfortunes Suutarla finds fault both in his own and his wife's conduct. But society is to be blamed as well: for example, if his son had been able to have further education in his own language instead of having to go to a Swedish-speaking school in town, he might have fared better. "Life of a Finnish farmer" includes a fair amount of self-analysis, and it relates Suutarla's bitter memories of his own upbringing as well as the development of his religious views. It is one of the few stories in my corpus where sexuality is touched upon.

Besides its apologetic and confessional features, Suutarla's autobiography bears traits of an exemplary narrative with a political end. It presents an individual who seeks learning, progress and the common good. The text shows how a man born in humble circumstances transcends his origins but encounters obstacles in a society in which the language of the majority is regarded as inferior. Suutarla stresses his decisive role in founding a local primary school and a library, in addition to other efforts in advancing the position of Finnish language and culture in general. In this way the book continues the tradition started by Pietari Päivärinta's *Elämäni* ("My life") which was published by the Society for Popular Education in 1877. Päivärinta (1827–1913) was a self-taught cantor (parish clerk) and farmer, who subsequently became a prolific and popular author. Päivärinta's *Elämäni* is not strictly autobiographical. When compared to a memoir Päivärinta wrote later in his life, one can see how some details are twisted to make *Elämäni* into a more representative and dramatic story.[13]

Stories of Awakenings

Religion was part and parcel of most life stories, as a self-evident basis in one's world view: the Bible is quoted as a source of wisdom, and God directs one's path in life. At times some writers seem to be following the model of a sermon. The number of pure *conversion narratives* or stories of *spiritual awakening* is rather small, however. It is also interesting to note that there are writers who describe their thorny path to God's mercy through temptations and revelations; yet this development is not always in the foreground of the text. Johan Poikonen (1794–1867), for example, took up the role of chronicler or a participant observer in his 14-page manuscript entitled *Muistelmia yhellelle renkimiehelle elämän waiheista* ("Memoirs of a farm hand on the course of his life"). The writer refers to himself as "that man", "he" and "Johan Poikonen, a farm hand", who witnessed, among other things, the schisms between the followers of Paavo Ruotsalainen (1777–1852), the lay leader of a revivalist movement called *körttiläisyys*.[14] According to Britt Liljewall, writing one's life story was legitimised within the revivalist movements by the fact that it was performed in honour of God and as a testimony of his mercy, and was therefore not evidence of preoccupation with oneself (Liljewall 2002, 227).

It seems that Poikonen wanted to provide material for future historians of the revivalist movement, but he also had his own reputation at stake: Lauri Juhana Niskanen, another influential lay figure in the movement, had slandered him for years. At the end of his story Poikonen sums up his spiritual development in this manner:

> In this short and simple way the outer events in the life of the above mentioned farm hand have been told, as far as the inner things are concerned there have been many misgivings and lapses due to the inherited faults of his but nevertheless he has received the doctrine of justification that neither the devil nor the hypocrites have managed to overthrow perhaps the terrible waves of unbelief have roared during the times of anguish but the secret hand of the almighty has always kept in him the fine belief and longing for christ who from sheer grace forgives the sinners and in this belief he is going to stay until the last breath of his life.[15]

Matti Haapoja (1845–1895), a farmer's son from Isokyrö, was convicted of several murders. He experienced a religious awakening after having become acquainted with Mathilda Wrede (1864–1928), a noblewoman who visited prisons. According to Haapoja, his story, entitled *Yhren onnettoman nuorukaisen elämänvaiheet* ("Life of an unfortunate young man"), could act as a warning because it shows what happens to people who "forsake God and overlook the mercy of the Saviour."[16] This conflicts with the impression that the prisoner does not really seem to repent his crimes, however. Haapoja also mentions that his text might become useful for someone wanting to write a book about his life. A subject of newspaper articles and broadside songs, Haapoja was aware of the attention he had attracted and was likely to attract in the future. The wish to be remembered by the general public probably motivated the writer more than the explanation given in the manuscript.

Incidentally, Haapoja's conversion did not last long, and he ended his life by his own hand after having killed two prison guards.

> 'Bless the LORD, O my soul: and all that is within me, bless his holy name. Bless the LORD, O my soul, and forget not all his benefits.' When I look back on my life I cannot but say out loud these words of thanks of David when I think how great his mercy on me has been.[17]

Maria Österberg (1866–1936), daughter of an impoverished farmer from Lohja, begins her Lapsuuden muistelmia ("Memoirs of childhood") with this passage from the Psalms.[18] Österberg sent her story to the Finnish Literature Society in the 1890s. She writes about the unhappy marriage of her parents, her father's violence and alcoholism, which drove the family into extreme poverty. Regardless of the harsh life to which she was subjected, Maria pursued her ardent desire to read and write. Receiving the Bible from the local pastor as an acknowledgement for her achievements in the confirmation classes was a high point in her first fifteen years. At the end of the text she presents herself as a quiet woman who has not had a youth like other people. However, she claims to be content with her life: she earns her living as a seamstress, teaches at the local Sunday School, collects folklore and writes ethnographic narratives for the Finnish Literature Society.

Maria Österberg was not involved in revivalist movements; her religious quest was conducted in solitude. She sought spiritual enlightenment from devotional texts such as the Finnish translation of *Paradiesgartlein aller christlichen Tugenden* (1612) by the German Pietist Johann Arndt (1555–1621). This book had urged her to pray and communicate closely with God. She also mentions "conversion stories"; they had helped her understand that one had to undergo a real change of mind in order to receive God's grace. These literary references show the importance of models both in terms of living one's life and shaping it into a story. Interestingly, Österberg did not include her real name in her text but used the pseudonym "Phoebe", which probably refers to a servant of the Church mentioned in St Paul's letter to the Romans (16:1).

It is not known whether Maria was aware of the fact that her elder sister had also written her life story for the Finnish Literature Society. Matilda Österberg (1863–1903, later Grönqvist) had started to collect folklore in 1887, and the following year she sent the Society a text with the remark "a true story" along with the folk tales she had noted down. *Pieni Mökki Haavistossa* ("A little cottage in an aspen grove") is written in the third person; the protagonist is called Sofia (Matilda's second name), while her siblings bear their real first names. Many of the incidents Matilda tells about the childhood of Sofia and her siblings resemble those depicted in her sister's story. The few books available were treasures children cherished:

> The New Testament gave them topics to talk about and things to be amazed at. There were lots of stories of Jesus, how He was born poor and low and how He had done a lot of good for people and finally suffered a bitter death, only for the sake of people – all this was more than they could understand. They would follow

Jesus, from the stable in Bethlehem to the Mount of Olives, marvelling at His great love for mankind. They decided to offer their lives for Him who had done so much for their sake.[19]

Besides religion, Matilda Österberg's story lays great emphasis on temperance. "A little cottage in an aspen grove" ends with a scene in which the grown-up children and their mother are gathered in their garden. A passerby asks why they have joined the temperance society. The answer given reproduces the discourse used in books and magazines advocating temperance, popular education and the true faith in God.

Neither of the Österberg sisters had specifically expressed a wish that the Finnish Literature Society should help them to publish their stories, but it is apparent from Maria's use of the pseudonym and the feigned style of Matilda's story that the desire is there. Perhaps the sisters felt that women should not make themselves too visible in public. It seems that the Finnish Literature Society provided Maria and Mathilda Österberg – and many other self-educated people who kept sending their texts to the Society – a niche for practising different types of writing. Even though their life stories were not commented on by the Secretary of the Society they must nevertheless have felt that they had an audience in him. They received books and small remunerations for the tales, proverbs and ethnographic data they sent to the archives in Helsinki. Maria and Matilda were probably aware that their texts would be stored, and that one day they would find more readers.

Kustaa Roslöf, mentioned at the beginning of this article, was a religious man throughout his life. He became acquainted with the revivalist movement called *rukoilevaisuus* (Beseecherism or Prayerism) but did not uncritically adopt their mores. Instead, he was active in local efforts such as founding a primary school. Roslöf's story promotes Christian values but reminds his peers about the importance of education and general knowledge: one should not pay attention only to spiritual matters. His impact can be seen in the fact Isak Ojala (1839–1911), another self-taught schoolmaster, started his life story by copying Roslöf's words almost verbatim, although without acknowledging the source. Ojala's text dates from around 1907–1909. He relates two sets of awakenings in his *Kertomus elämäni taisteluista* ("Story about the struggles of my life"). The first one is spiritual; even as a child Ojala had been part of the same revivalist movement as Johan Poikonen. Obviously, the road was not straight, and one occasionally strayed from the path of virtue.

Besides a narrative of his spiritual development, Isak Ojala relates an awakening to the ideas of nation-building which he learnt from some educated Fennoman gentlemen – sons of the local pastor and their visitors – and through the texts published in the *New Suometar*, the organ of the Finnish national movement since 1869. Ojala became so taken with the Finnish cause that he would gladly have given his life for it. He organised a joint meeting in which emotions were running high: Ojala took one of the visiting gentlemen from Helsinki in his arms, feeling that class distinctions had disappeared. They all were just sisters and brothers of their fatherland, united in the desire to build a Finnish nation.

The national awakening led Ojala into giving patriotic lectures, urging people to subscribe to the *New Suometar* and join the Popular Education Society. His patriotic ardour started to paralyse his spiritual life, however. He sought advice from Lauri Kivekäs (1852–1893), the student leader of the Fennoman movement. According to Kivekäs, it was a Christian's duty to support the Finnish cause: patriotic spirit originates in the Christian love of one's neighbour and working towards the common good. Eventually the religious side took the upper hand, thanks to the influence of a new pastor who did not take part in the nationalist zeal. Ojala turned his attention to improving the singing of hymns at the church and campaigning for a local primary school. Both Isak Ojala and Kustaa Roslöf ended up in similar positions in their mature years: religious pursuits were combined with efforts to promote education, both in terms of establishing schools and advancing popular education in general.

Conclusions and Reflections

As I have shown, the motives of 19th-century Finnish common people for writing about their lives were manifold and often intertwined with one another. One of the most common reasons stemmed from the need to pass on information and values to one's descendants or peers – something that has motivated people from time immemorial. However, it is interesting to note that with the newly acquired skill of writing came the realisation that the written document was more permanent than oral transmission in fulfilling this task. There were local and individual differences in the nature and scope of generic traditions, depending on the availability of reading material, among other things.

While some writers were driven by a desire for self-justification, there were others who wanted to avenge the wrongdoings to which they felt they had been subjected, or to provide a testimony about a revivalist movement in which they had been involved. The desire to promote temperance, national sentiment, diligence and love of God appear in many texts, a clear indication of the success of nation-building and popular education projects among the common people. Although several different kinds of awakenings are depicted, the awakening to socialism does not figure in my material. The reason for this probably stems from the fact that a great part of the material is taken from the collections of the Finnish Literature Society, one of the major forces in nation-building. The autobiographical material stored in the Finnish Labour Archives, for example, may have a different story to tell, but falls outside the time limit I have set for the texts in my corpus.

On the whole, many of those who took up the pen to write about themselves wanted to improve their lot in life, but those who succeeded in life, in one way or another, were not the only ones to produce such narratives. This, among other things, distinguishes the Finnish corpus from the English and French working-class autobiographies analysed by Martyn Lyons, who has noted that the "fate of those who tried the road to self-improvement, but failed, defeated by poverty or other pressures, can only be imagined" (Lyons

2008, 2). In the case of Finnish common people's life stories one does not have to resort to imagination: there are texts written by both winners and losers. One of the reasons for this difference might be that Lyons analysed only published texts.

According to Britt Liljewall, writing for "traditional culture's sake" – in the interest of preserving traditional culture – was one of the motives in Swedish common people's life stories (Liljewall 2002, 228–230). This motive does not really appear in the Finnish material. The difference between the corpora could be explained by the fact that some of Finnish writers sent non-autobiographical ethnographic descriptions focusing on traditional life to the Finnish Literature Society, which left them free to concentrate on other aspects in their life stories. In addition, many writers were driven by the ideals of progress, so that superstitions, old-fashioned methods of farming and attitudes concerning upbringing of children are criticised and set in juxtaposition with rational new ways.

There also seems to be a difference concerning the role of introspection in life stories. According to Liljewall, explicit analyses of inner motives are very rare in the Swedish material (Liljewall 2002, 231), and Martyn Lyons similarly claims that English and French working-class autobiographies tended to avoid introspection and personal revelations (Lyons 2008, 8). While it is true that especially the oldest Finnish life stories and some of the texts solicited by the Finnish Literature Society lack introspection, there are definitely also writers who bare their souls. Even Petter Wenäläinen reveals something of his feelings in his straight-forward narrative stream – after the death of his second wife he felt as if he were in some kind of a penitentiary, and on one occasion he relates a dream in which he finds himself in a humiliating situation.

The life story of Heikki Kauppinen (1862–1920) provides a case in which the inner motive for writing is explicitly stated. Born out of wedlock and orphaned at the age of fifteen, Kauppinen worked as a farm hand at the vicarage of Vieremä in the province of Savo. The pastor's sons, Pekka and Johannes Brofeldt, encouraged Kauppinen to improve his literacy skills; eventually he was qualified to teach at a circulating school. They had also helped Kauppinen to have his first story published in a literary magazine. In 1885 the young schoolmaster produced a prose narrative in which he analysed his desire to write about his life in the following manner:

> If someone walks through a deep forest trying to get somewhere, even if he has no clear knowledge about his goal, because he cannot see any goal, only the things around him, and he only vaguely remembers the journeys he has undertaken, so there comes a point at which he stops to think about the distances he has covered. So will I do, too, and even if my life is no joy, at least in parts, so why shouldn't I write about it, to remember it, for myself only.[20]

Even though Kauppinen stated that he was writing only for himself, he showed his text to Johannes Brofeldt, who had already published several works of fiction under the name of Juhani Aho. In his letter to his protégé, Brofeldt commented on the story and gave advice on how it could be worked into a short story, in case he wanted to do so (Makkonen 2002b, 269). It is apparent that Kauppinen was motivated both by self-therapy and the desire to improve his writing in the literary sense of the word. Subsequently, he became a published author under the name of Kauppis-Heikki; his life story, however, was not brought out until 1912. Kauppinen was one of several writers from the lower strata of society to enter the Finnish-language literary circle with the help of a middle-class mentor. For example, Heikki Meriläinen – originally a country blacksmith who had learnt to write at the age of 23 – was encouraged to write by Lydia Stenbäck, editor of a literary journal. In 1888, Meriläinen published an autobiographical novel, an achievement worthy of attention.

The earliest Finnish life stories had taken over generic traits from family inscriptions, devotional books and oral poetry. And while there were significant differences between the processes and practices of common people's writing and earlier writing, there were also continuities: autobiographical poems in the vein of the Peasant Poets continued to be written well into the 20th century. Like Johan Ihalainen, the impoverished tailor, Juho Tanholin (1863–1928) earned his living by begging and writing mock-songs. However, his circles were much wider than those of the earlier poet. Tanholin, poet and a collector of folklore, corresponded with various scholars and writers, asking for financial help. When F. A. Hästesko, a folklore scholar and a lecturer, met Tanholin in 1913, the poet began to narrate the story of his life before he was asked to do so:

> So, let's begin from the beginning. I was born on 20 October 1863. My mother was a so-called fallen woman, Kaisa Tanholin. They say that my father was a student who had spent his holiday here at Viitasaari. I was born at Viitasaari, in this "land of poems". I am a child of downstairs, left without education; the same desire to study and the same pain in my stomach have followed me as long as I've lived.[21]

It seems that Juho Tanholin had made his life story into a commodity, to be performed both orally and in written form. It was part of the public persona he used for soliciting rewards from the Finnish-minded *literati*.

Notes

1   *Sitten läksin ryssän laivoin seilaman ja seilasin sitten itämerilä siksi kuin sota aiko siten ostin heposen ja ajelin rahti ympäri Suomen mata sitten kuin sota lopui, nin läksin tas ryssän laivoiin ja mänin Oulun mata myöten siten tultin turkun ja se oli jupelin jula silon Turussa sitä tultin pietar hovin pietarin päivänä siten tulit sitkan laivat krontatin nin minä valehtelin ryssälen että minun veljen on nisä laivoisa että sain passin pois ja sitten mänin rontat ja rupesin viko palkalen, visi rula viiko ja sitten otin hyrin nikolai pervaisin jossa olin kolme sitkan reisuva ja käin kolme kerta manpallon ympär [...].*

2   *Olin hellästi rakastettu poika wanhemmilleni, jotka myös johdattiwat minua Jumalan tuntoon jo warhaisessa lapsuudessa. Äitini warsinkin puhui usein minulle Jumalasta ja Jeesuksesta, taiwaasta ja autuudesta ja sanoi että waan hywät lapset,*

jotka wääryyttä wälttäwät, rikoksensa tunnustawat ja katuwat sekä Jeesukseen turwaawat ja Häntä rukoilewat, pääsewät taiwaaseen. Isäni, joka takoi pajassa, piti tarkkaa huolta minusta, että olisin ollut tottelewainen ja nöyrä lapsi. Wanhempani oliwatkin minulle erittäin rakkaat ja isäni isä, joka wanhuksena asui samassa kodissa ja sowinnollisesti samassa työssä ja ruoassa wanhempaini kanssa, oli yhtä rakas kun isänikin. (Roslöf 1892, 5)

3   For example, the catalogues compiled by Kaisa Kauranen (2005) include information on the texts of some 200 self-taught 19th-century writers in the collections of the Finnish Literature Society.
4   See also Stark 2008 and Kuismin 2010.
5   Stark 2008. See also Kaisa Kauranen's article in this volume.
6   [...] *niin kuin ei opi ihminen tuntemahan tämän elämän vaiellusta niin että tulla tuntemahan muiden ihmisten tapoja niin 1763 anooin itteni palveluxen 2 vuotta pentilän talos 2 vuotta rahkolas 1 vuoden Kyröös ruskalan talos* [...].
7   *Olen omasta mielestäni ollut monelle esimerkkinä, ahkeruuteni takia samoin kuin sen vuoksi, että olen välttänyt juoppoutta ja käräjöintiä. Jumalan kiitos terveyteni on ollut hyvä, niin että olen taitanut toimittaa omat ja muidenkin asiat. Olen palanutta syntymäkylääniikin rakentanut uudelleen, hoitanut vanhat sukulaiseni hautaan sekä myös omat lapseni koettanut kasvattaa ahkeriksi työntekijöiksi ja siveellisiksi ihmisiksi. Olen ollut naimisissa 39 vuotta hyvän ja toimeliaan puolison kanssa ja vaikka aloitin kerjäämällä, olen aina pyrkinyt eteenpäin.* (Makkonen 2002, 24)
8   *Jos tietäisin että se on Jumalan tahto en huoliskaan surta, mutta kun luulen omaks vijakseni ja syykseni, niin olen täyttänyt itten ylön syömisellä ja juomisella ja elatuksen murheella.*
9   *Ja vielä päälliseks tällä elämäni ehtoolla ei usko vaimmoni minun sanojani vaikka olen vannonut sieluni ja henkeni taivaan ja maan kautta, ja vaikka kultaisilla kirjaimilla joka seinään totuuden sanosin ei hän taitais minua uskoa sittenkään.*
10 *Ja säilyköön tämä kirjoitus ijäisiin aikoin asti etten tulis valehtelijaks.*
11 *Niin – ei elämä ole leikkiä sille, joka rehellisyydellä koettaa eteenpäin päästä ja kuitenkin joutuu onnettomuudesta toiseen ja tunnottomain ihmisten tähden saa kärsiä. Mutta Kaikkiwaltias maksaa heille kyllä ansioidensa mukaan.* (Sutela 1899, 8)
12 [...] *vaan kuin lapseni ovat minulle rakkaita hee ehkä eivät ota pahaksi jos heitille jätän nämät rivit kertomaan elämäni tärkeimpiä hetkiä sillä nee kertoovat silloinkin vielä samalla tutulla Isän äänellä kuin jo itse olen aikaa maannu turpeen alla."* (Makkonen 2002, 137)
13 See also Kuismin 2011.
14 See Petri Lauerma's article in this volume.
15 *Näin on lyhyesti ja yksinkertaisesti annettu tietää sen eillä mainitun renkimiehen tilaisuus ulkonaisten waiheien puolesta, mitä sisälliseen tulee niin siinä on ollunna paljo puutteita ja hairauksija perintö wijan tähe, waan kuitenni wanhurskauttamisen oppija on saanunna saatana eikä ulkokullatut peräti kukistaa ehkä hirmuset epäuskon aallot on ahistusten aikana kowin pauhanneet, waan kaikkiwaltijaan salainen käsi on aina ylös pitännä sen hienon uskon ikäwän kristuksen puoleen joka sulasta armosta armahtaa syntisiä ja tässä uskossa aikoo hän wiimmeiseen hengenvetoon asti.*
16 *Sillä tarkotuksella alotan tämän Kirjoitukseni, jos olis jollekin jälkein tulevaielen vaika vähänkin ohjen nuorana kun tästä saavat nährä kuinka sellaisen ihmisen käypi jo täälä maanlisesti, joka hylkää jumalan, ja ylön kattoo vapahtajan armon* [...].
17 *Kiitä Herraa minun sieluni ja kaikki mitä minussa on Hänen pyhää nimeänsä. Kiitä Herraa minun sieluni ja älä unhota mitä hyvää Hän sinulle tehnyt on." Katsoessani taaksepäin mennyttä elämääni en voi muuta kuin lausua nämä Davidin kiitokset herralle muistaessani kuinka suuri Hänen armonsa minua kohtaan on ollut.* (Makkonen 2002, 291)
18 Psalms 103: 1–2, King James's version.

19 [...] *siitä [Uudesta testamentista] löysivät he kaikki puheenaineensa, sitä eivät voineet kylliin ihmetellä. Siinä on niin paljon kertomuksia Jesuksesta, kuinka Hän syntynyt, köyhänä ja halpana, tehnyt paljon hyvää ihmisiille, ja vihdoin kärsinyt katkeran kuoleman, ja kaikki vaan ihmisteen edestä, tämä oli enemmän kuin voivat käsittää. He seuraisivat Jesusta, Bethlehemin tallista aina Öljymäelle asti, ihmetellen Hänen suurta rakkauttansa ihmisiä kohtaan. He päättivät uhrata koko elämänsä Hänelle, joka niin paljon on tehnyt heidän edestänsä.* (Makkonen 2002, 281)

20 *Jos joku kulkee synkkää metsää pyrkiäksensä johonkin, vaikkei hänellä ole varmaa tietoa siitä, mihin hän pyrkii, syystä ettei hän voi nähdä mitään päämäärää, ei muuta kuin mitä hänen ympärillään on, ja vain hämärästi muistaa mitä matkoja hän on kulkenut, niin hän jolloinkin pysähtyy ajattelemaan, minkälaiset ne matkat olivat, joita hän kulki. Samoin teen minäkin, ja vaikka ei elämäni olekaan ilahduttava, ainakaan paikoitellen, niin miksi en sitä kirjoittaisi itselleni muistoon: ainoastaan itselleni.* (Makkonen 2002, 257)

21 *Siis alkakaamme alusta. Syntynyt olen lokakuun 20 p. 1863 niin sanotusta langenneesta naisesta Kaisa Tanholinista. Isäni, niin kertovat, on ollut joku ylioppilas, joka Viitasaarella on lomaansa viettänyt. Viitasaarella olen syntynyt, näillä 'rannoilla runollisilla'. Alakerran lapsia olen, ilman sivistystä jäänyt, sama opiskelun halu ja sama sairastelu vatsassa ja hartioissa on koko ijän seurannut.* (Möttönen 2005, 7)

Life Stories referred to in the article

Haapoja, Matti: Yhren onnettoman nuorukaisen elämänvaiheet. National Library of Finland.

Hemberg, Israel: [Untitled]. Published in Makkonen 2002a, 22–23.

Huuskonen, Pekka: *Runo – eräs elämäntarina – 900 värssyä.* 1963. [Published by the author].

Kallio, Kustaa, Muistoja elämästäni & sukuni alkuperästä. FLS LA. Published in Makkonen 2002a, 136–159.

Koskelainen, Aatu (1918): *Leivän ja seikkailun haussa. Hämäläisen mökinpojan tarina.* Werner Söderström, Porvoo.

Léman, Johan: *Oulun Raadi Huoneen Wahtim Johan Lemannin Lyhykäinen Elämäkerta. Itseltänsä näin Runon Muowoin kokoonpantu. Oulusa 1839. 1nen Osa.* Finnish Literature Society, Literary Archives.

Leppänen, Alfred: Lapsuuden & nuoruuden matkamuistelmia. Published in Makkonen 2002a, 202–236.

Lindqvist, Aleksanteri (1891): *Huvittava kertomus eli kokemusten koulu. I osa.* [Published by the author].

Ojala, Isak, Kertomus elämäni taisteluista. Finnish Literature Society, Literary Archives.

Poikonen, Johan: Muistelmia yhellelle renkimiehelle elämän waiheista. Archive of the Church Historical Society, Finnish National Archives.

Päivärinta, Pietari 2002 [1877]: *Elämäni. Perhe-elämällinen kertomus.* Helsinki: SKS.

Roslöf, Kustaa 1892: *Muuan heikon & paljon puuttuvaisen kristiveljen omakirjoittama elämänkertomus.* [Published by the author]

Saxberg-Kolho, Matti, "Muistoks jälkeenjääneille elämästäni". In Maija-Stiina Roine 1998, *Kolhon kylän tarina.* Published by the author.

Sutela, Elias 1899: *Elias Sutelan elämäkerta eli onnettomuuksien ajama. Kertonut itse.* Published by the author.

[Suutarla, Zefanias 1898], *Suomalaisen Talonpojan elämänvaiheet. Kertonut tosielämän pohjalla Suomalainen Talonpoika.* Porvoo: Werner Söderström.

Västi, Pietari: [Untitled]. *Kotiseutu* 13 (2), 54–55.

Wenäläinen, Petter: Petter Wenäläinsen muistij Kirja koko Elämän. Finnish Literature Society, Literary Archives.
Österberg, Maria: Lapsuuden muistelmia. Published in Makkonen 2002a, 290–322.
Österberg (later Grönqvist), Matilda: Pieni Mökki Haavistossa. Published in Makkonen 2002a, 272–287.

Kaisa Kauranen

Odd Man Out?
The Self-Educated Philosopher and his Social Analyses of 19th-Century Finland

Kustaa Brask[1] (1829–1906), despite having attended no more than a few weeks of the local itinerant school and living a modest life as an unmarried crofter in Joroinen, a municipality situated in the province of Savo in eastern Finland, was the author of an extensive body of writings which he sent to the Finnish Literature Society. Brask's manuscripts add up to about 5700 pages of texts about religious, philosophical and societal matters, agriculture, popular education and history. His manuscripts also contain poems and drafts of school textbooks as well as collections of folklore and ethnographic material. Brask's texts are difficult to classify. The "speeches", as he often calls his writings, usually run to a few dozen pages; the longest piece is 294 pages. Besides endeavouring to articulate his contemplations on the relationship between man and nature, Brask reflected on emotions, intelligence, memory and the soul, among other things. He wrote about the life around him, revealing tensions in the local community during the last decades of the 19th century. Brask produced most of his writing at a relatively advanced age; in fact, his most active period began in the 1880s and continued almost right up to his death. His archived writings open up interesting perspectives into rural Finland – class relations, customs, ways of thinking, prevailing mentalities. They also enable the researcher to gain new insights into the spread of written culture among the rural lower classes.

Brask was writing at a time when fully literate people were more of an exception than a rule. Itinerant school teachers in Brask's childhood rarely taught children to write, as only reading was considered necessary – according to an estimate made in 1880, only about 13 % of Finns knew how to write at the time, while by the turn of the century, ca. 40 % of the population over the age of 15 possessed that skill. Regional differences were striking, and in the eastern rural areas where Brask lived the percentage of the fully literate population was lower than the rates mentioned here (Leino-Kaukiainen 2007, 430–434).[2] Written culture spread through Finland later than it did in the other Nordic countries. There are historical reasons for this: the language of governance and the elite was Swedish, whereas the language of the majority of the population was Finnish. Book publishing in Finnish was meagre until the last decades of the 19th century. Improving the status of Finnish and creating a standard language was a lengthy project, and it was espoused by a number of common people, too. In Brask's case, not only did he turn to studying and committing his thoughts to writing, he also wanted to spread the fruits of literacy skills and the public enlightenment among his own social class.

An important question in the study of early self-educated writers is the interaction between the writer and the community. What sort of relationship did Kustaa Brask have to his peers and to those above him? How did Brask's activities as a writer affect his standing in the community? What kind of perception of society emerges in Brask's texts and what was the status of written culture in it? How did his keen interest in reading and writing shape his views about the hierarchies in his own community and in society at large? The present article deals with these topics through an examination of a range of texts by Brask, including historical and societal writings, with an emphasis on those concerned with literacy and popular education.[3]

It is obvious that Kustaa Brask was no ordinary crofter, even though his penchant for the written word did not make him entirely unique either. There were others among his class who had expressed themselves through writing, as can be seen from many of the articles in this volume. Studies from a number of countries have shown that more ordinary people than has previously been thought not only possessed writing skills but also actively used them,[4] and at the end of this article I will attempt to situate Brask as a writer within a broader context – both within Finland and internationally.

Kustaa Brask's Life Story

Although Brask wrote only sparingly about his own life, the brief autobiographical texts that have been left to us are useful for outlining the story of his life. His father was a crofter at Joroinen and his mother the daughter of a farmer from the same locality. Brask spent his entire life on the same croft, never marrying, living first with his parents and then with one of his brothers and his family. The croft was part of the Frugård Manor, which was owned by a noble family named Grotenfelt.[5] Already as a child, Kustaa Brask had been exposed to religious literature. At the age of eleven he had been given a Bible, which he managed to read in its entirety in the course of two years. Brask makes no mention of how he learnt to write, but states that his father "was not against learning". Brask's texts reveal that his excessive interest in books and writing was considered strange by the people in his village; three of his younger brothers displayed a similar passion for learning, however.

In 1850 the young Brask was afflicted with a severe illness which lasted for many months. The symptoms were the feeling of *polte* ("burning") all over the body, visions, delirium and restlessness, all of which Brask described vividly decades later. The people around him associated his illness with his prodigious reading, especially of religious texts. At the hospital Brask was diagnosed with "mania", which, in those days, often signified a state of delirium brought on by infectious diseases accompanied by fever. This indeed may have occurred in Brask's case. After two months in hospital Brask was sent home; the records indicate that he was healed (*förbättrad*).[6] Brask wrote that he felt branded and mocked after his illness, but there is no evidence of him being regarded as a "village idiot" later in his life. Instead, he looked after the modest local library and was known to have acted as an agent for book sellers. According to family history, he prepared documents for people unable to write and provided "home-schooling" for his brother's children, teaching them to read, write and do sums (Brask, N. 2001, 10).[7] Naturally, Brask also took part in the work done at his and his brother's croft, which was one of the biggest at the Grotenfelt manor, and the family got along fairly well, according to the standards of the times (Brask, N. 2001, 6, Åström 1981, 69).[8] Although Brask referred to his writings as "speeches", there is no documentation as to whether he had ever actually presented them orally to an audience. In company Brask tended to be withdrawn and self-effacing, and the fact that he was hard of hearing no doubt also made him less keen to speak in public. Family history recalls his decision to reject a position as Sunday school teacher even though the job was specifically offered to him (Brask, N. 2001, 9). In some of his accompanying letters to the Finnish Literature Society he remarked that his writings were "available for some people to read", though he did not specify whom he meant.

Prior to making contact with the Finnish Literature Society, Brask was an active contributor of reader's letters to at least two newspapers for twenty years (1858–1877).[9] The topics he discussed were typically the yearly agricultural cycle and matters dealing with municipal administration, such as the care of the poor and the advancement of popular education at Joroinen. Brask's published pieces were presumably heavily edited. According to the editor's comment, Brask's contributions began to expand to such a degree that they could not be published as they stood (*Tapio*, 27 Feb. 1869). When the newspaper's cramped columns could no longer accommodate Brask's sprawling pieces, he began to seek out new outlets by offering at least one of his textbook manuscripts to a commercial publisher. The text was rejected, however, and Brask sent it further to the Finnish Literature Society in 1876. Brask delivered part of his texts to the Society through members of the Grotenfelt family. G. O. Grotenfelt, owner of the Frugård Manor and Vice President of the Court of Appeal in Viipuri, was a member of the Society, as were his nephew and his nephew's two sons. The Grotenfelts were conscious of Brask's literary pursuits, but it is not known if they actively encouraged him.

What possessed Brask to write such extensive essays and have them sent to a learnt society in Helsinki? On the one hand, he wanted to inform the elite in Helsinki about the living conditions of the poor and the social ills in the countryside; on the other hand, he wanted to address the common people on topics relevant to them or about which they – at least in his opinion – needed additional information. These included, for example, methods of farming, practical work skills, children's upbringing, Christian teachings and "the science of the soul" as psychology was called in Finnish at the time. Because of his knowledge of the conditions in which the rural common people lived, Brask considered himself to be better equipped than members of the educated classes to write booklets to advance the cause of public enlightenment. In his letters to the Society Brask repeatedly expressed his keen wish to see his writings in print.[10] Brask's ruminations were never published, however, as such texts hardly had any place in the publishing agenda of the Finnish Literature Society, which focused more and more on academic publication. Nor did the Society send his texts to any other publishing house, as had been Brask's wish. Although his orthography was nearly flawless, Brask's texts were cumbersome and abstruse and would have needed extensive revision to make them readable for the wider public. Brask might have continued writing and sending his text to the Society because he was aware of the fact that the officials of the Society had important positions; maybe he kept hoping that his writings would have an impact on societal matters through them, even without publication. Besides, now and then the Society sent him payments in the form of either books or small sums of money. Brask did not want to have his writings returned to him, perhaps harbouring the hope that, housed in the archives, his work would at least be preserved – and thus available to be read by future generations.

It is difficult to know what books Brask had at his disposal as no documents describing the contents of the modest lending library at Joroinen have been preserved, When offered books as compensation for his collections of folklore, he chose works on history and folklore, a book on law and official terminology, a textbook on botany and Sakari Topelius's *Luonnon kirja* ("Book of nature") as well as the *Kalevala* and the *Kanteletar*, both published by the Finnish Literature Society.[11] The Bible was essential to Brask, and he was also a keen reader of the newspapers, although he could not afford to pay any subscription. He seems to have had little time or appreciation for novels and fictional stories

Popular Education and Class Differences in Rural Finland

Brask sought to provide background for his essays with summaries of historical events and processes. In a way, he used history to situate himself within hierarchical society. In his examination of Finnish popular education, for instance, Brask looked back to the arrival of Christianity in Finland. Informed by his faith, he regarded the conversion of the Finns as a huge leap forward for a people who had previously lived as pagans, since the new religion brought not only God's word but also written culture and law and order. The arrival of organised religion and the societal changes it wrought came slowly but surely to alter the lives of the people; rural people eventually began to learn the literary skills, observed Brask, and he himself certainly was among those to seize this opportunity. He considered his own writing as a part of the Christian written tradition. In Brask's endeavours to work towards the enlightenment of the rural population, Christianity and secular education went hand in hand. As he saw it, the general acceptance of Christian beliefs was only superficial – the great majority of Finns were "baptised pagans", Brask wrote in 1901. Memorising the Catechism could not be equated with understanding and adopting its message. More than anything, it was the fear of punishment – not genuine conversion – that had compelled the common people to abandon their old ways of life, Brask stated.[12]

Brask also had something to say about revivalist movements. He saw one of the four main Pietistic revival movements in Finland, known as *körttiläisyys,* as responsible for the spread of writing, book culture and voluntary reading in his own region. Yet their doctrine diverged significantly from Brask's own religious outlook, thus leaving him spiritually indifferent. It appears that Brask found no spiritual home in any religious circle. He recounts his youthful disagreements with the local Lutheran clergyman and the schoolmaster, two authoritative figures who had ridiculed Brask's religious views. This experience indubitably left him suspicious or at least cautious in his dealings with the clergy and he defended the right of the "poor working class" to study and interpret the Bible independently.[13]

Even though Brask often reiterated his opinions on the general reluctance of the Finns to accept Christian teachings and book learning, another common theme in his writings offers an alternative vantage point on the matter. What kinds of opportunities existed for a poor Finnish person to enter the world of proper education and thus benefit from its civilising effects? The fates of the crofters and the landless were dire. The offspring of the poor were condemned to roam the villages begging, whilst their parents were weighed down by "cold, exhaustion, hunger and deprivation". Ceaseless work or worry about their very survival left little room in the imagination for notions such as "citizenship" and "literature". When a person's primary goal in life was avoiding hunger, he or she was in no position "to hanker after schools, learning, knowledge, skills, customs".[14] The lives of the landless were always haunted by uncertainty about the future. Lodgers had no home of their own, they just stayed temporarily in the dwellings of other people, and crofters lived in constant fear of eviction. According to Brask, the landless were strangers in their own land, always ready to take their leave, never feeling at home anywhere.[15]

The internal hierarchy of the rural population – that is, its division into independent farmers (*talolliset,* in Swedish *bönder*), crofters, craftsmen, farm hands, farm maids and lodgers – recurs repeatedly in Brask's writings. Even though each group had its own particular task, Brask underscored the fact that they were all united by their participation in cultivating the land: all of them were, in Brask's words, "bread-labourers". Nevertheless, the landowning farmers and the landless were separated by an ever-widening gap – a social and economic divide which Brask regarded as extremely unjust. He severely criticised farmers who attempted to distinguish themselves from their fellows by trying to raise themselves to the status of gentlemen, the class of people who did not earn a living by doing physical labour. Brask observed, for example, how some farmers no longer sat down to eat with their paid labourers and served them food of poorer quality than what they ate themselves.[16] For Brask, it was this kind of man, one who stood in the fields observing his subordinates, who emerged as the ultimate symbol of injustice.[17]

The changes in class relations at Joroinen were undeniably real. At their root, among other things, was the increased prosperity enjoyed by the farmers who made money by selling lumber; this additional capital enabled them to buy farmland from the gentlefolk who were relocating to urban centres. Some major purchases were also made with borrowed money, although the new owners did not always manage to pay off their debts. This led to rapid changes in ownership of some properties, causing unstable conditions for the crofters.[18] The indebted farmers sought to remedy their own situation by imposing greater financial demands on the crofters – a phenomenon which was widespread throughout the country at the end of the 19th century – which put great strain on the relations between the two classes (Peltonen, M. 1992, 285). In his view, an established upper-class landowner was a more reliable landlord than an ambitious farmer. Brask paid considerable attention to the selling of land and the changes it brought about. One reason for Brask's preoccupation with this question might have been his anxiety about the possibility of the Frugård manor being sold – an event which would have placed Brask and his kin at the mercy of the "social climbers" he so despised.

The writings in which Brask discussed conditions in rural Finland are highly charged and even contradictory or inconsistent. Some of his pieces are forceful accounts of instances of injustice and dire poverty. At his most extreme, he sums up the lot of the landless as slavery glossed over with an agreement.[19] He condemned the land-owning farmers and criticised them acrimoniously, identifying strongly with those who found themselves in difficulties. Despite these expressions of discontent, Brask often retreated from such bold assertions, thus opening and closing his "speeches" with Biblical references justifying the natural order of things: every society is made of rich and poor, and each person must accept his destiny. Although Brask himself, as an opinionated writer, had certainly shaken free of the traditionally subservient role offered to him by society, the hierarchical structure of the society in which he lived persisted in informing his thought.[20]

While Brask sympathised with the plight of the poor and wrote a great deal about improving the conditions of the crofters, he did not mince his words when pointing out the failings of the landless population either. According to him, they neglected to save for the future but simply squandered what little extra money they had. As Brask saw it, they possessed no higher goal in life than a quest for pleasure – drinking, playing cards and lazing about were their favourite past-times. Moreover, if anyone in their ranks ever tried to improve himself or his methods of working, it only resulted in envy and bad blood. Brask often depicted the strained relations between people in his own community; according to him, disputes, sarcasm, mockery and contempt aggravated day-to-day existence. Brask sought to ameliorate this by promoting the civilising effects of education and Christian teachings. In his view, the most important task was to provide guidance to children, who had yet to pick up their parents' vices. Brask formulated a "gentle" philosophy of education, which was based on encouraging a child's innate curiosity and eagerness to learn. He opposed corporal punishment and coercive measures in children's education. The task of bringing enlightenment to adults was a far more challenging enterprise, however, and Brask's belief in the possibilities of this project kept changing, almost from text to text.[21]

In his essay on human happiness from 1888 Brask vigorously defended every individual's right to learn as well as to enjoy the benefits and pleasures to be gained from learning. The intellect was a gift from God, and every human being was entitled to have the time and freedom to use this gift. Reasoning skills enabled each worker to carry out his tasks with greater effectiveness; indeed, working methods would no doubt be developed and improved through brainwork and by obtaining new knowledge. In Brask's view, this principle was equally valid for physical as well as intellectual work. The ability to think and reason enabled a person to choose his own thoughts – to nourish the good and to discard the bad. In the final analysis, the intellect was the path to God: reason was a quality of the soul, and the word of God was meant to enlighten the soul, thus ensuring its path to "justice, truth, purity and beauty".[22]

In his writings Brask observed that books had gradually found their way into households where they had previously had no place. Especially among the farmers there were people who subscribed to newspapers and kept themselves informed of important events.[23] The gap between those in possession of land and those without had apparently become so wide, though, that Brask could not find kindred spirits among the socially active farmers. Brask never mentioned friends or acquaintances with whom he would have shared his interests of the topics he so avidly read and wrote about. Documentary evidence reveals Brask's intellectual isolation in his community. Yet the injustices and disadvantages he witnessed compelled him over and over again to sit down at his table and write.

Looking up to the Gentry

For historical reasons, there were a fairly large number of upper-class people in Joroinen during Brask's time. In the 19th century, the local gentry consisted of the owners of the manors and local civil servants, whose roles often overlapped. For Brask, society was essentially divided into two groups, gentlefolk and "bread labourers". He barely noted the distinctions and hierarchies internal to the upper classes. Writing about days gone by, Brask commented on local officials who had not cared if the common people failed to learn to read, not to mention learning to write. These people, Brask pointed out, equated the common man with a workhorse – and believed that such men should be happy with their lot in life.[24] The campaign for popular education nevertheless influenced not only Brask but also those belonging to the local upper strata. At Joroinen, members of the gentry were instrumental in the establishing of schools and libraries. Brask observed that the efforts of the educated "Fennomans" were bearing fruit: knowledge had gradually become accessible in Finnish also to the working classes.[25]

Brask noted that his peers usually thought that civil servants were not engaged in any real work, but pointed out that an orderly society could not function without them. His favourable attitude to civil servants presumably derives in part from the fact that he saw them as disseminating new enlightening ideas. In Brask's eyes, the typical land-owning farmer regarded his crofter primarily as a beast of burden (as did some former officials), but a proper gentleman was involved in the cause of popular education.[26]

Brask occasionally dealt with the question of social mobility, considering the possibilities an individual had for crossing the divide separating the gentry from the bread-labourers. In an essay written in 1888, Brask approved of those who sought to rise in station by working toward an occupation of higher status – as long as the individuals in question had demonstrated natural ability for the work and had acquired the necessary training. He was convinced that the inclination for learning could be found in all levels of society. Brask also made note of individuals entering the civil service only through birth and a desire to take advantage of the benefits. If their inherent talents were insufficient for carrying out the work, the common people suffered due to the ineptitude of those more powerful than themselves. Brask's writings also reveal the belief in human equality: obligations and rights should be equally shared, and no one should be excluded from the "ownership and enjoyment" granted to another.[27] Interestingly, many of Brask's writings contain statements invalidating his previous position, thus returning to a stance upholding the ideology of the old hierarchical society.

The recurrently inconsistent nature of Brask's writings can at least partly be explained by his position as a crofter of a manor house of family Grotenfelt. As mentioned earlier, some members of the large Grotenfelt family, and even the owner of the Frugård manor, were members of the Finnish Literature Society.[28] Brask's caution regarding his depictions of the gentlefolk is understandable as both he and his brother Konstantin with his family were wholly reliant on their noble landowners. The crofter and the landlord were never on an equal footing, as Brask himself wrote.[29] According to the typical agreement, the landowner had the right to dismiss any crofter who failed to treat his master with the appropriate deference (Rasila 1961, 58–59, 67). According to the agreement signed by Kustaa's father, Adam Brask, in 1836, the crofter would face eviction in case of arrogance (*sturskhet*) or disobedience (Åström 1981, 115 & 1989, 174). Even if we consider the matter solely from the perspective of prudent self-defence, few crofters would have risked the future of their holdings by writing critically about the owner class of their croft, or even having an open dispute with it. In practice, the crofter's freedom of expression was limited. Where the limits exactly went was surely unclear for anyone at that time of hidden unrest, not to mention Brask himself, in his contradictory and repressed position. The concepts *hidden transcript* and *public transcript* used by anthropologist James C. Scott (1990) in analysing authoritarian societies reflect the conditions of Brask and his fellow crofters in 19th-century Finland. The *public transcript* describes the open, public interactions between dominators and oppressed, while the *hidden transcript* refers to the critique which those in power do not see or hear (Scott 1990, 2–5). It seems that Brask did not dare openly to criticise the land-owning class he depended on, but there are cracks in his argumentation, as I have shown above. In addition, his folklore material includes more open criticism of people in power.

Although Brask shared an interest in written culture with members of the educated elite, he could never have been their social equal in a society defined by class hierarchies. Anna-Maria Åström's studies of manor life in Savo reveal the vast and irreconcilable gap separating the common people from the gentry. The common people were wholly excluded from upper-class culture; in fact, local legends recorded in the area bear witness to the cultural and social divide between the tellers of tales and the gentlefolk. As far as the ordinary country people were concerned, the gentlefolk hailed from another world altogether (Åström 1993, e. g. 286–299, 323). According to Åström, most of the narratives construct an atmosphere rank with "gloom", with the gentlefolk cast in a distinctly disagreeable light. Of all the supernatural beings populating the folk imagination, the devil was the figure most frequently associated with members of the upper strata of society. Compared to the active role of the wicked member of the upper class, the narrative roles ascribed to the common people generally tended to be passive (Åström 1995, 212–222, 232). Breaking from the legend tradition, Brask primarily wrote about the gentry with approval; yet in his proverb-like aphorisms, his view towards the "rich" is much more severe. It seems that the "anonymous" folklore genre gave also for Brask a safer channel for expressing his critical opinions of the ruling classes.

Brask seemed to inhabit two entirely different worlds. On the one hand, he was a member of a family of crofters working the land, but on the other, he was an intensely committed enthusiast for the written word. To be sure, the books and newspapers in which he immersed himself were largely authored by members of the educated elite. Furthermore, the world of ideas and knowledge to which the common people gained entrance through reading was deeply imbued with written culture; in other words, this world represented part of the "Great Tradition" to which the common people could not achieve full membership, despite the complex interplay between the great and little traditions (Burke 2007, 25–26, Redfield 1967, 40–59). Further, Brask's extensive knowledge of the Bible and resolute religious commitment made him rather exceptional among his peers as well. The more Brask delved into the products of written culture, also putting his own thoughts into writing, the more he distanced himself from the mostly oral culture of his local milieu. A chasm had thus opened up between the rustic writer and his neighbours. Evidence of his sense of estrangement emerges in his texts, wherein he articulates his disapproval of the conduct and habits of landless people and the crofters – as though he could not even have been counted among them.

In many ways Brask's status as both a crofter and a writer was inextricably bound to his relationship to the upper classes. Brask's critical scrutiny of the precariousness of the crofter's position – in addition to the unclear legislation – was essentially directed at the land-owning farmers. Yet censure of the legislation was nevertheless indirectly also criticism of the upper classes, for they were primarily responsible for the legislative process. Out of these contradictory and competing ideological positions emerged Brask's own philosophical approach to life, where the ideology of the "old" hierarchical class society was competing with the "new" ideas about egalitarianism, enlightenment and popular education.

A Writer and his Community

Martyn Lyons, who has studied autobiographies written by French working-class people, states that working-class writers inevitably imitated patterns picked up from their study of the written culture. Yet however much these self-taught writers attempted to emulate canonical works of literature, their efforts were rarely applauded by members of the intellectual or literary elite, the people to whom they offered their writings. Without the advantages of formal education, the working-class writer found himself on foreign ground. What is more, the worker who had the audacity to step into the domain of written culture and to embrace its modes of thinking may have created social tensions among his peers, who most probably found his behaviour unsettling and peculiar (Lyons 2008, 111–112, 127–128,135–138).

Lyons's analysis can also be applied to the case of Kustaa Brask. From an early age, Brask's devotion to reading and writing set him apart from the others in his community. In his essays, he dealt with demanding and complex issues and failed to meet the conventional standards set by the educated class. Brask was aware of the possibility that his landlord or landlord's relatives would have an access to his texts, which had an impact on the way he presented his views. Unlike his Central European counterparts, Brask lacked the support of a reference group in a nascent labour movement or any other mass organisation which would have served to bring people of similar status together. The rise of organisations and political movements in Finnish rural areas coincided with the last few years of Brask's life and the period after his death. Brask's zeal for reading and his endeavours to produce his own works of writing drew him intellectually closer to the upper classes than to "his own people".

In a Nordic context, Davíð Ólafsson's analysis of the Icelander Sighvatur Grímsson (1840–1930) also provides a comparative perspective on the life and works of Kustaa Brask. Sighvatur Grímsson was a fisherman and a farmer who, in addition to carrying out his daily work, worked as a writer and scribe in his community. It must be noted, however, that he did not write in isolation but operated within a broad network of people, including other lay writers as well as readers of texts. According to Davíð Ólafsson, the last category included just about any Icelander, because hand-written copies and printed narratives were read aloud during evening gatherings, when people did handicrafts and passed the time in company. The old written culture of Iceland, combined with the non-existent printing houses, gave rise to a vibrant tradition of copying, in which Grímsson was an exceptionally active participant, an "extreme case" (Davíð Ólafsson 2009; also the present volume).

Brask could also be described as an extreme representative of early "common" writers in Finland. Studies conducted in Finland have brought to light a number of writers who have been viewed with suspicion and wonder in their own original reference groups (see, e.g. Stark 2006b) and have had some kind of connection to the gentry or to the intelligentsia.[30] The connections were many; some had learnt to write with the private assistance of a local member of the gentry, others had borrowed newspapers and books from them or had been given writing supplies. Many of the autodidacts were writing to newspapers and had established contacts with editors. While some writers had received words of encouragement from upper class friends, others had even been granted financial assistance. For Brask and many of the others the connection to the Finnish Literature Society was crucial.

In their own local settings these writers often felt like misfits – as they doubtless were, for the possession of literacy skills combined with active involvement in the task of writing was truly unusual. Still, these writers often had an impact on their communities, for example in local government, and not all of them ended up living in isolation. Some went on to attend farming schools or similar educational institutions, while others became men of business and thus moved at least partially into another social class. These earlier writers from among the ordinary people shared many common characteristics. Almost all were eager to study books and newspapers, and the causes of public good and popular education were close to their heart. Indeed, in their intellectual pursuits they formed a group – a community of sorts – even though many of them were not personally acquainted. An important connection nonetheless was established, for example, when they read each other's writings in newspapers – often hidden behind pseudonyms – and perhaps even composed their own responses. So far, only little is known of the communication between these early writers. Correspondence between them, if it existed, must in most cases have disappeared. In Brask's case, too, there remains uncertainty as to whether he had some sort of contact with like-minded individuals at least at some point of his life.

The rise of 19th-century popular movements – the temperance movement, the agrarian youth associations, the women's movement and political parties – constituted a powerful force for social change in Finland. Those with the desire to be politically and socially active were therefore compelled to master the new medium of expression. The ability to write was essential for recording minutes of meetings, producing handwritten newspapers and corresponding with fellow ideologues from other localities. Furthermore, the nature of writing changed profoundly as it became a means of communication among those working towards a common goal. Writing as a social practice began to flourish (Salmi-Niklander 2009, Suodenjoki 2009). Although too old to join any of the popular movements, when an agrarian youth association was established in 1896 at Joroinen, Brask followed their activities with interest. His ambivalence toward these popular movements was in keeping with his character. He feared that the association's activities would distract its members from religion and practical work. At the same time, he was tentatively pleased to see young people getting involved in educational pursuits. Despite occasional bouts of pessimism, Brask saw that various social classes were beginning to have access to the civilising benefits of education, and that humanity as a whole was only at the beginning of the road of progress.

NOTES

1 Brask signed his manuscripts and letters "G. F. Brask", for "Gustaf Fredrik". I use the Finnish form of Brask's first name, Kustaa, because it most probably was the name by which he was usually addressed. I have, however, retained the name G. F. Brask in the notes and list of sources simply because it is the name under which his writings have been archived.
2 The areas of southwestern and western Finland (southern Ostrobothnia) were more advanced in the development of literacy than the country's more easterly regions. Even as early as the 18th century, the revivalist movements spawned networks of writers in western Finland. Composing hymns and circulating of devotional texts meant the establishment of a local copying and manuscript tradition, which can be seen to be analogous to the phenomenon described in Iceland. In central and eastern Finland, however, literacy and the ownership of literary works were less common. Brask's testimonies to the shortage of books in his home region correspond with the information to be found in estate inventory deeds.
3 The present article is based on my forthcoming doctoral dissertation, which deals with Kustaa Brask's world view and his position as an early writer of the working class (Academy of Finland Research Project *Itseoppineet kirjoittajat ja kirjallistumisen prosessit 1800-luvun Suomessa; Self-taught writers and literacy processes in 19th-century Finland*; project number 1121270). I am grateful to Maria Virtanen for her collaboration upon which the present article is partially based (Kauranen & Virtanen 2010).
4 For *ego-documents*, see the European Science Foundation's project www.firstpersonwritings.eu/index.htm. In Great Britain a three-volume bibliography of autobiographies of working-class people was compiled in the 1980s (Burnett, Vincent & Mayall 1984–1989). For studies on the autobiographical writings by French workers, see Lyons 2008 and Traugott 1993. On the writings by self-taught Nordic people, see Lorenzen-Schmidt & Poulsen (eds.) 2002. For Finnish research, see e.g. Makkonen 2002; Kauranen 2006, 2007 and 2009; Laitinen & Nordlund 2008 and Nordlund 2007.
5 Many parishes in southern Savo were settled by upper-class families. They controlled manor estates which also had crofters' holdings. Manor houses began to spring up in the 17th century, due to the area's close proximity to the Russian border; the owners were often in the service of the Swedish army. During the Russian rule in the 19th century the noble owners of the estates were often employed in the public service; see Åström 1993, 33–37. For a history of the Grotenfelt family, see Grotenfelt, N., Grotenfelt, E. & Grotenfelt, K. (eds.) 1917.
6 Hospital records 1847–1859, Act:1, Series A Records. Provincial Archives of Mikkeli.
7 Information about Kustaa Brask preserved in the family has been obtained from Niilo Brask's notes (2001) as well as from an interview with him. KIAÄ 2006:234, SKS KIA. Niilo Brask is Kustaa's brother's grandson (b. 1920).
8 According to church registers Kustaa was the master of the croft at least until he was 60 years. Between 1890 and 1900 his three year younger brother Konstantin became the master, after which Kustaa's title was "master's brother".
9 The Finnish-language newspapers *Suomen Julkisia Sanomia*, from 1866 *Suomalainen Wirallinen Lehti* as well as *Tapio*. Brask's contributions to these newspapers can be read in http://digi.lib.helsinki.fi/sanomalehti/secure/main.html (see also http://fi.wikisource.org/wiki/Gustaf_Fredrik_Brask).
10 E.g. G. F. Brask in his letters to the Finnish Literature Society 11 Dec. 1886, 16 July 1887, 16 Oct. 1891, 20 Dec. 1897.
11 The *Kalevala*, first published in 1835, is the Finnish national epic, and the *Kantel-*

etar (1840) is its "sister work", a collection of poetry primarily sung by women.
12 Brask, G. F. 1890, B175:35; Brask, G. F. 1897b, B175:107; Brask, G. F. 1901, B175:47, SKS KIA.
13 Brask, G. F. 1899, B175:52; Brask, G. F. 1903, B175:54; Brask, G. F. 1904, B175:53, SKS KIA.
14 Brask, G. F. 1892b, B175: 55; Brask, G. F. 1894, B175:41; Brask, G. F. 1899, B175:52, SKS KIA.
15 Brask, G. F. 1890, 12–13, B175:35; Brask, 1892a 12–13 B175:38, SKS KIA.
16 It was a distinction that was both symbolically and concretely important. For more about the eating practices of landowners and paid labourers in light of oral historical materials collected in the 1930s, see Mikkola 2009, 277–280.
17 Brask, G. F. 1898, B175:31; Brask, G. F. 1892a, B175:38, SKS KIA. Brask sometimes pondered the possibility that crofters would be able to cultivate their independently-owned farmland, but the complex issue of landownership rights and Brask's perception of it must be left outside of this article.
18 N. Karl Grotenfelt (1931) deals with the history of the estates in Joroinen one by one, thus making it possible to track the changes of ownership. For more on the subject, see Kauranen & Virtanen 2010, 74, note 68.
19 Brask, G. F. 1892a, 12, B175:38, SKS KIA.
20 Brask, G. F. 1890, B175:35, SKS KIA.
21 Brask, G. F. 1887, B175:120; Brask, G. F. 1890, B 175:35; Brask, G. F. 1892a, B175:38; Brask, G. F. 1894, B175:41; Brask, G. F. 1899, B175:52, SKS KIA.
22 Brask, G. F. 1888, B175:21, SKS KIA.
23 Brask, G. F. 1897a, 21, B175:68, SKS KIA.
24 Brask G. F. 1899, B175:52; Brask, G. F. 1897b, B175:107, SKS KIA.
25 G. F. B. in his newspaper artcles in e.g. *Suomalainen Wirallinen Lehti* 2.12.1870 and 13.1.1877. Brask, G. F. 1897b, 17–24, B175:107, SKS KIA.
26 Brask, G. F. 1887, B175:120; Brask, G. F. 1901, B 175:47; SKS KIA.
27 Brask, G. F. 1887, B175:120; Brask, G. F. 1888, B175:21, SKS KIA.
28 Kustavi Grotenfelt, the grandson of G. O. Grotenfelt's brother, was even one of the leading figures in the Finnish Literature Society.
29 Brask, G. F. 1904, 4, B175:53, SKS KIA.
30 My view is based on Laura Stark's article and the autobiographies and diaries published by Makkonen 2002 and Kauranen 2009, research conducted within the network *Kansanihmiset ja kirjallistuminen* ("Common people and the processes and practices of literacy") as well as manuscripts stored at the Literary Archives of the Finnish Literature Society.

Archival Sources

Provincial Archives of Mikkeli
Mikkeli County Hospital Archive, Hospital records (Sairaspäiväkirjat) 1847–1859.

Finnish Literature Society, Sound Recordings Archive
Niilo Brask's interview 19 July 2006, interviewers Kaisa Kauranen and Maria Virtanen. KIAÄ 2006:234.

Finnish Literature Society, Literary Archives (SKS KIA)

The Archive of the Finnish Literature Society. Received letters 1876–1905.

Brask, Niilo 2001: Torppari, kansanrunouden kerääjä Gustav Fredrik Brask ja hänen kirjoituksensa SKSn arkistossa (first version 1989).

Brask, G. F (1887): *Puheita: Ihmisen olennosta* ("Speeches: on human beings"). B 175:120.

Brask, G. F (1888): *Puheita Ihmis elämästä, ja Ihmisen onnellisuudesta, ruumiillisesta ja hengellisestä* ("Speeches concerning human life, and about human happiness, in body and spirit") B 175:21.

Brask, G. F (1890): *Puheita Työwäestä, ja leipä työn tekijäin tilaisuudesta* ("Speeches concerning the working class, and the circumstances of the bread-labourers"). B 175:35.

Brask, G. F (1892a): *Puheita: Ihmiskunnan wähijen osuuksijen, Perhekuntina eläwijen, olosta, ja talouden pidosta* ("Speeches: on humanity's underprivileged, conditions of families and the managing of households"). B 175:38.

Brask, G. F (1892b): *Puheita Maa Torpista, eli Mökkilöistä Sawossa, ja Joroisissa* ("Speeches on Crofts, that is Cottagers in Savo and Joroinen"). B 175:55.

Brask, G. F (1894): *Puheita: köyhyyden syistä, Suomessa. Ja muutamija sanoja köyhyyden syiden poistamisesta* ("Speeches: concerning the causes of poverty, in Finland. And a few words about getting rid of the causes of poverty"). B 175:41.

Brask, G. F (1897a): *Puheita: Joroisissa tietoon tulleista, ja opettawaisista, Asijoista, ja tapauksista* ("Speeches: Concerning Joroinen's learned and things instructive, matters and cases"). B 175:68.

Brask, G. F (1897b): *Puheita: Jumalan hywyydestä, Suomalaisille* ("Speeches: About God's Goodness, for Finns") B 175:107.

Brask, G. F (1898): *Puheita: Hywästi eläwäisyydestä* ("Speeches: on good living"). B 175:31.

Brask, G. F (1899): *Puheita Suomalaisista, ja nykyisen ajan tunnoista, suomessa* ("Speeches about Finns, and sentiments of this day and age"). B 175:52.

Brask G. F (1901): *Puheita: Leipää kaswattawista työn Tekijöistä, Suomessa Sawossa ja Joroisissa* (Speeches: bread-labourers in Finland, Savo and Joroinen"). B: 175:47.

Brask G. F (1902): *Puheita Työtä tekewän kansan tilaisuuden korjauksesta* ("Speeches concerning the improvement of the situation of the working class"). B 175:50.

Brask, G. F (1903): *Puheita Suomalaiselle, maalla asuwalle, Työ wäelle* (Speeches to the Finnish rural working-class"). B 175:54.

Brask, G. F (1904): *Puheita, Mökkilöissä asumisesta, Suomen maan, Sawossa* (Speeches, concerning living in cottages, in Finland, in Savo"). B 175:53.

Guðný Hallgrímsdóttir

Material without Value?
The Recollections of Guðrún Ketilsdóttir

One of the ways in which women have been marginalised in Icelandic cultural history can be seen in the way women's manuscripts have been catalogued. At present, roughly 15000 items are preserved in the manuscript department of the National and University Library of Iceland. Most of these are from the 19th and 20th centuries, but there is also a good deal of material from the 17th and 18th centuries. The collection is mainly the work of 19th-century amateur collectors. In all parts of Iceland there were people who borrowed, copied and collected these old, mouldy manuscripts, their goal primarily being to provide themselves and the members of their households with interesting reading matter such as sagas, poetry, autobiographies, chronicles and so on. These amateur collectors and copyists, who often knew one another, played an important role in the dissemination and preservation of Icelandic culture at a time when the production of printed books was limited (Helgi Magnússon 1990, 186–187).

Book publication, starting from the time printing was first introduced in Iceland around 1530, showed little variety in subject matter, the vast majority of books published being of a religious nature. The bishops in Iceland controlled what was printed, a situation which did not change significantly until the 1830s (Helgi Magnússon 1990, 187). Starting in the mid-19th century, the National Library of Iceland began to purchase manuscript collections from private owners. The goal was loftier than that of the collectors of earlier times. A booklet published by the National Library of Iceland on factors leading to the foundation of a national library in Iceland states, among other things:

> During the time of the independence movement in Iceland, it was important for the nation to have a history and culture which in some way made it a nation, and for it to have a building or institution which would preserve books and manuscripts in order to support this image. (Örn Hrafnkelsson 1997)[1]

In 1913 Páll Eggert Ólason (1883–1949), a lawyer, was hired to classify and catalogue the manuscripts in the Library's collection. He was meant primarily to attend to a card catalogue of all the printed books, however, and he thus worked with the manuscripts in between other things. The catalogues, the first volume of which appeared in 1918, eventually became five in number and encompass over 8000 items. In his introduction, Páll Eggert states the following:

> The National Library contains far too many useless manuscripts; this undoubtedly stems from the fact that catalogues were not made immediately, apart from acquisition catalogues, and thus more has been admitted to the collection than was needed, because the librarians did not know what was already there. (Páll Eggert Ólason 1935–37, vii)[2]

It can be inferred from this statement that he would not himself have chosen to preserve all the manuscripts that had found their way into the library and perhaps explains why so many manuscripts in his catalogues are described simply as miscellanies (*Margvísleg brot*). Organising the great quantity of manuscripts no doubt required a tremendous effort, and Páll Eggert must have made some assessment of the cultural value of the manuscripts as he catalogued them. He appears not to have had a very high regard for women's manuscripts, certainly, as they are often catalogued under the names of their husbands, fathers or brothers, suggesting that women's manuscripts were primarily registered and listed in order to preserve and maintain the history of the "worthy men" they had links to during their lifetime. One result of this is that Icelandic women, especially women of the lower classes, are largely invisible in the cultural history of previous centuries. There exist, however, thousands of manuscripts written by and for women in the vaults of the manuscript department, manuscripts containing letters, poetry and all kinds of personal accounts – catalogued and accessible to a varying degree.

In the present article I will focus on one such account, *Æfisaga Guðrúnar Kétilsdóttur*, the autobiography of Guðrún Ketilsdóttir (1759–1842), a female servant from northern Iceland. The original manuscript of her story is now lost but probably dates from around 1840, making this one of the oldest sources concerning a specific Icelandic woman. In the folklore collection *Gríma*, where the story was eventually published, it is stated that when Guðrún was a guest at Syðra-Laugaland, the home of Sigfús Jónsson, the district administrative officer, she was asked to tell the story of her life (*Gríma* 1929, 71). There are three manuscripts in the library preserving texts of her story, all of them bearing the same title, *Æfisaga Guðrúnar Kétilsdóttur*. According to the catalogue, these manuscripts date from 1850 to 1870. In one of them, written by Þorsteinn Þorsteinsson, it is stated that the account is told by Guðrún Ketilsdóttir herself and written down verbatim (NULI ÍB 841 8vo). The second manuscript is written by Geir Vigfússon and dates from around 1870 (NULI ÍB 438 4to). The scribe of the third manuscript is unknown but the text is more detailed than the other two and appears to come closest to reflecting Guðrún's own spoken language (NULI ÍB 883 8vo).

What is the value of a single text like this preserved from earlier times? How well does it mirror the past? Can such limited material tell us something about the person behind the story? These questions are especially important in historical studies of women, because there the sources are often more scarce and haphazard than those concerning men. My intention is to show how rich a text such as Guðrún's life story can be for research, despite having been thought worthless. In the manuscript catalogue, Guðrún's autobiography is classified as a humorous story (*kímisaga*), a classification which is at best misleading and not a little patronising. I have sought all available sources in order to learn more about her life and the society in which she lived. Local and regional magistrates' archives as well as historical sources related to the parishes have proved invaluable in providing information on people who were directly or indirectly related to Guðrún. Parish registers and visitation books, for example, contain information about the members of each household: their names, age and status, their knowledge of the Christian faith, reading skills and behaviour. As my article will show, together with Guðrún's life story, this material opens up a window on the life of a common woman in 18th- and 19th-century Iceland.

Childhood and Youth

Guðrún Ketilsdóttir was born at Samsstaðir in Eyjafjörður in 1759 and worked her entire life as a servant in the vicinity of Akureyri. In the pastors' records of home visitations, Guðrún is always presented positively and if the text of the life story is examined it becomes evident that Guðrún was, despite her lower-class standing, an extremely proud woman who enjoyed the respect of those around her. Hers is the story of a working-class woman who, through diligence and determination, managed to live a decent life during one of the most difficult periods in Iceland's history. Guðrún's story was recorded directly from her own telling of it. The order of events is not chronological and the narrative moves back and forth in time according to whatever comes to Guðrún's mind at any given point. Because of this, the narrative becomes somewhat confusing in places, but it is convincing and gives the impression of sincerity.

Guðrún begins by saying where she was born and where she lived as an infant, but remains remarkably silent about her family, making no attempt to connect herself to the society of which she is a part. In fact, she is presented to the reader as an individual without family. There is, however, evidence that she must have been in regular contact with her family throughout her life. She had five siblings who survived to adulthood, and both her parents lived to an advanced age. All these people lived in the same districts as she did; some were hired labourers throughout their lives, while others ran prosperous farms. Most of Guðrún's siblings had children who were baptised and confirmed in close proximity to her; some of them also died young. It can thus be regarded as highly unusual that such an individual should recall her life without saying anything about her parents and siblings.

On the other hand, the concept of family was perhaps much broader in earlier times and encompassed a larger group of people than is the case today. The legal obligation for those who did not own their own land to be tied as labourers to a specific farm for a year at a time and the power which officials had over workers' conditions, along with the legal obligation to support relatives, deprived families of a certain degree of autonomy over their destiny. Many workers were forced to adjust to new masters and to different conditions every year. Constant movement between farms with the attendant upheaval in the workers' immediate environment, even affecting with whom they shared a bed at any given time, made all family ties much looser. In her story, for instance, Guðrún has a lot to say about the people with whom she lived in each place. She speaks warmly of the county administrative officers and pastors who may have been the persons who had the greatest influence in shaping her fate. The county magistrates provided her with good or bad positions, while the pastors ministered to her at various times, so they may perhaps have been Guðrún's real family.

Guðrún herself had a childhood no different from that of most other children in the agrarian society of 18th-century Iceland. She quickly learnt to take responsibility for herself and was required to work hard all the time. When she was only eleven years old she was sent away to work at the farm Gröf:

> My life at Gröf, everybody knew – it was horrible. From there I went to Páll at Þórustaðir, he was mean and his will was the same, he stole from me my grey sheep and was the trickiest of them all, I would rather walk on my head than stay there. (NULI ÍB 883 8vo)[3]

Like most people in her position, Guðrún realised that it could be beneficial to win the favour of the people she worked for. An obedient, hard-working and loyal maidservant was desirable for any good home. To be regarded as valuable and placed with good people was very important for hired labourers. Guðrún had a strong desire to survive in this society; the visitation records of the pastors contain the following testimony about her: "Makes a good impression, is well-behaved and helpful, hard-working, pious, conscientious and true" (NAI: Hrafnagil BC/2, BC/3, Munkaþverársókn BC/1).[4]

At around the age of twenty, she was registered as a labourer assigned to the farm Kaupangur with the farmer and county administrative officer Guðmundur Guðmundsson. She says that she was treated very well and that everyone loved her because she always presented herself well and did what she was told (NULI ÍB 883 8vo).[5] Ten years later, she had become a maidservant at the home of the district magistrate himself, Jón Jakobsson at the farm Stórhóll. According to her narrative, Guðrún enjoyed "tremendous respect".[6] The county magistrate's household was large, with 18 registered members there the year she started her service. One can hardly imagine a higher status for a servant than to get to work for the county magistrate, and this was a position Guðrún Ketilsdóttir had attained through her own merit.

Guðrún was an extremely industrious worker. When she was employed at Stórhóll, she went along with other workers to gather highland moss (lichen) at lake Mývatn. Such trips could last as long as two weeks if the harvest was good; on this trip, Guðrún managed to fill nine barrels, which was more than two horses could carry. In contemporary sources it is stated that a woman could be expected to gather four barrels of moss per week (Jónas Jónasson 1975, 37). When Guðrún was employed at the farm Grýta she had mown three acres of outfields per day, she reports. It can be seen from various sources that an able-bodied woman could at most be expected to mow two acres per day (Jónas Jónasson 1975, 81). However, it was not enough to be hard-working and loyal in order to maintain a good position. Female labourers like Guðrún also had to take care not to get pregnant, for doing so could cost them dearly. She often had to contend with men, married as well as single, who were determined to sleep with her:

> Þorsteinn tried to get me into his bed but I managed to fight him off. Guðmundur in Hamrakot also tried it on with me but I am more moral than to lie with just anyone who wanted to. When he saw me naked he wanted to have me to lie with but I defended myself vigorously and didn't let him have it. (NULI ÍB 883 8vo)[7]

It can be seen from Guðrún's statements that sex outside marriage was a very serious issue for women in the 18th century. It was not only their honour that was at stake; these women feared, perhaps most of all, the terrible fate that awaited their unborn children. Pregnant female labourers faced having their children taken from them and placed in foster care, as labourers' wages were not sufficient to bring up children, even the wages of healthy and hard-working women like Guðrún. It may not be strange that she was forced to fight men off, as, according to her own account, she was rather beautiful: "I had white lines along my nose, red disks in my cheeks, blue-eyed, small-eyed and with high eyebrows" (NULI ÍB 883 8vo).[8] Her clothing was no less impressive, for she says that she wore a handsome headdress and a red silk kerchief on her head and a ribboned cape over her shoulders (NULI ÍB 883 8vo).[9]

For almost her entire life Guðrún worked as a servant in other people's homes and thus never had a fixed address. This must have been hard, as the new masters often had different rules and customs which the servants had to learn to adhere to. According to the Discipline-decree of 1746 servants were almost totally at the mercy of their masters; this decree, which contains stipulations as to the legal status and behaviour of servants (farm-hands and maids) was in force in Iceland down to the beginning of the 20th century. But even if the freedom of the servants was limited, Guðrún seems to have been relatively independent: she owned some sheep, a horse and five chests which contained more than "empty darkness" as she put it. In one of the chests she had raisins, which she could give to those she liked. She also mentions that she owned a pickling barrel with lots of things in it. The chests were important to Guðrún because she could lock them and store her most precious things, clothing, utensils, wool for knitting and the food she was given as part of her keep. It was usual at the bigger farms to weigh out in one go the food the farmhands were to live off for a long period. So Guðrún may have had bread, lard and dried fish in addition to some luxury goods such as alcohol and liquorice.

Guðrún used the contents of her chests not only to feed herself but also to barter with and obtain the goodwill of others. In one place she says that she had given the Reverend Hallgrímur many drops of liquor (NULI ÍB 883 8vo).[10] Alcohol was a luxury in the 18th century and it was unusual for female servants to have such delicacies to offer. She mentions also that she bought a good piece of meat, with lots of fat on it and a little later, while in Siglufjörður, she bought a lock costing one *riksdalir*, which at this time might have been as much as six months wages for a good servant. Despite the harsh provisions of the Discipline-decree Guðrún did not seem to have felt totally at the mercy of her masters. As a matter of fact she seems to have had several methods of survival as a single maidservant and be able to make at least some decisions regarding her own wellbeing. Through hard work and efficiency she was a sought-after worker and could choose her masters. With the contents of her chests she could buy favours or barter when she was in need of something. With her sheep she could provide products which her masters found attractive and through her splendid dress she earned the respect of her contemporaries.

Guðrún and Illugi

It was during her stay at the farm of Sigluvík that Guðrún met a young man named Illugi who was later to play a major role in her life. Before long their acquaintance reached a more serious level and Guðrún's attempts at resistance were for nought. When she had got to know him better, she described Illugi as follows:

> When I had got there, there were sailors, among whom was one from Hrafnagil, that accursed fox whose name was Illugi, a handsome man but there are many wolves in sheep's clothing; so it was with him. He offered me all his service but an unknown product separates many from their wealth. He had fair hair and wore a blue jersey, a green shirt, a hat and good shoes. (NULI ÍB 883 8vo)[11]

Illugi was from the farm Kotá in Hrafnagilshreppur. In the pastors' visitation books from his childhood years it was stated that Illugi's parents were simple-minded and ignorant, with five small children to support. At the age of only ten he became a pauper (*hreppslimur*) and was placed on the farm Hrafnagil where the parish priest, Erlendur Jónsson, lived. At 18 he was registered as unruly (*óstýrilátur*), at 19 as a lay-about (*flysjungur*) and in his 20th year he was not even listed with the rest of the members of the household but only said to be a pauper placed there by the parish. At 21 he was said to be stubborn (*stífsinna*) and lazy (*latur*), then finally he was registered as a farm hand (*vinnumaður*) at Hrafnagil (NAI: Hrafnagil BC/2, BC/3). In other words, Guðrún was right: this was a wolf in sheep's clothing. Such a lad would hardly have been considered an appropriate match for a sensible and diligent maidservant. But Guðrún was in love:

> Then a courtship began between me and Illugi. I had five chests, there was more in them than empty darkness; there were raisins in one which I sneaked to him because I thought he was a man and not a devil. (NULI ÍB 883 8vo)[12]

Guðrún moved to Kristnes to live with Illugi in the autumn of 1793. According to the visitation book from 1794, Guðrún was registered as a domestic servant:

Kristnes in Hrafnagilshreppur, Eyjafjörður, January 1794

Jón Guðmundsson	farm owner	37 years
Björg Guðmundsdóttir	his wife	43 years
Steinunn	their daughter	1 year
Jón Jónsson	foster child	2 years
Guðrún Arnfinnsdóttir	maidservant	26 years
Illugi Jónsson	labourer	27 years
Guðrún Ketilsdóttir	domestic servant	34 years (NAI: Hrafnagil BC/3)

Domestic servants were slightly better off than ordinary maidservants. They were some kind of in-between group between the farm owners and the labourers. They did not live in their own buildings, but in the owners' houses, but were in other respects "left to themselves"; they themselves were responsible for their maintenance and determined their tasks (Gísli Gunnarsson 1987, 31). According to the same visitation book, Illugi, Guðrún's fiancé, was a simple labourer. Guðrún says that she had a barrel of sour whey in the fall when they move to Kristnes and many things in it, but that Björg, the lady of the house, had stolen it all. This Björg did not let it suffice to sneak into Guðrún's whey barrel either, for she seems also to have had some relations with the fiancé, for they were very secretive, says Guðrún of the relationship between Illugi and Björg, the lady of the house. It was not easy for Guðrún to accuse the lady of the house of stealing from her whey-barrel or for allegedly having an affair with her fiancé. Although Illugi's womanising had clearly hurt her deeply, the young couple became engaged in the summer and on July 19 in the same year they were married in the Grund parish, where they were said to reside (NAI: Grundarþing/ Laugaland BA/2).

Many historians have confirmed that economic conditions were more important than love in determining the choice of marriage partners in the 18th and 19th centuries. As far as Illugi was concerned, it can certainly be argued that economic reasons were important in his choice of Guðrún as his wife, as she was clearly quite a catch. In Guðrún's case, however, love appears to have been the deciding factor in her choice of partners; at any rate, nothing appears to have happened which would have forced her into this marriage. She was, for instance, not pregnant by Illugi at this time. She herself was reasonably well-off economically, which could not exactly be said of her fiancé, for Illugi was an impoverished labourer who was not likely to do great things. And she married him despite his unfaithfulness. Guðrún must therefore have been in love. Bitter, she continues her account of Illugi's behaviour; now his flings had become violations of marriage vows. Regarding Illugi's behaviour, Guðrún says: "Then he took up fornication and went from girl to girl, while I was forced to suffer it and and be silent and everyone grows cowardly when he grows old." (NULI ÍB 883 8vo)[13]

In 1796, when they had become labourers at the farm Stokkahlíð, Guðrún, then 37, gave birth to their first and only child, Jón. The couple's marriage did not improve as a result. At this point in the story, Guðrún says that Illugi's behaviour became even worse, "for he was a scoundrel and a rascal except to the sluts that he slept with" (NULI ÍB 883 8vo).[14] In 1799 the family moved to the farm Hof in the Möðruvallaklaustur parish. Illugi is registered there as the owner of the farm. Their son Jón is 4 years old; Guðrún says that he resembles her in diligence and uprightness. The marriage of Illugi and Guðrún at Hof was not working out and in 1803 they decided to part and moved away from the farm. Guðrún says of their time at Hof and the reason for their divorce:

> Then we moved to Hof where we had 14 yearling sheep and a heifer; he took it to market for his accursed debts and then I declared myself free from him. Then he took my clothes away; he was fifty dollars in debt; they seized 20 dollars [interest] and then he had 16 left. He had them for Kristín, for he lay on her like his breeches. (NULI ÍB 883 8vo)[15]

Probably Illugi was revelling in town at that time while his wife was trying to run the farm alone with the child. After they lost the farm, Guðrún was left behind downcast and poor. Illugi had even sold her clothes, including the ribboned cape and her red silk kerchief. She had sacrificed everything for love. The same year that Guðrún and Jón dissolved their household she was registered as a maidservant in Skagafjörður, 44 years old. Guðrún seems to have suffered hardship and not had anywhere to stay after she left Hof. She describes this journey thus:

> [...] then I went to the farm Barð in Fljót, where I stayed the night and Þorsteinn tried to get me into his bed but I managed to fight him off. Guðmundur in Hamrakot also tried it on with me but I am more moral than to lie with just anyone who wanted to. So I lay outside in the field during the spring night in sunshine and southern winds, more dead than alive – Guðbjörg gave me some rye bread so that I could regain some strength. Then I returned to Eyjaförður. (NULI ÍB 883 8vo)[16]

The autobiography does not say why Guðrún chose to leave Eyjafjörður with her son, but perhaps this was to keep the boy from being taken and put into care. When she left Illugi she had lost everything and the authorities would probably have taken Jón and placed him as a pauper in Hrafnagilshreppur, the parish where his father had been born, as according to law the parish was obliged to provide for paupers born there. By leaving Eyjafjörður she could at least delay this happening for a while until the boy was older.

A few years later Guðrún is again registered in Eyjafjörður, but according to the parish register of Hrafnagil she does not seem to live in the vicinity of her son, who has been placed as a worker on a farm in Hrafnagil parish, 14 years old; he is later confirmed there, in 1811. Guðrún was present at her son's confirmation, however, for she mentions with resentment how meagre the refreshments were and that he did not receive any confirmation gifts (NULI ÍB 883 8vo).[17] Illugi was found rambling here and there around the country; in 1823 he got a young female servant pregnant, but the child died within the year. Jón was employed as a servant in various places in Eyjafjörður but then settled down in Svarfaðardalur, where he married. And then, only 28 years old, he drowned on a trip to Siglufjörður, leaving a wife with two young children to support and a third on the way. According to genealogical records, Jón was regarded as a promising father, upright, as his mother had said, and quite competent (Stefán Aðalsteinsson 1978, 297).

One can deduce from Guðrún's life story that it was not easy growing old as a maidservant, not least for a person with neither family nor fixed abode. In her later years she does not seem to get on so well with her masters, she is bitter and complains about their betrayal and lack of respect. "Now they all say, there goes that damned witch, Guðrún Ketilsdóttir – but I'm regarded well by good people, for no one does this except the damned joksters who care nothing for either God nor men" (NULI ÍB 883 8vo).[18] It is possible to follow Guðrún's later years in the pastors' house visitation books from Öngulsstaðahreppur, where she had been granted permanent residence by law. Each year she is found in new homes within the district with names which she doubtless felt provided little dignity, i.e., as a ward of the district (*hreppsómagi*). Guðrún died in the Munkaþverá parish on 9 December 1842, in her eighties (NAI: Munkaþverá BA/2).

A Tale of Foolishness?

As can be seen from the above, Guðrún Ketilsdóttir's autobiography is a remarkable source of information on the life of an ordinary Icelandic working-class woman from earlier times. Guðrún's story was written down word for word as she told it, so her character emerges quite palpably from the text; one can clearly feel Guðrún's presence in it. The narrative is singularly entertaining. Guðrún uses short sentences and relates things directly without mincing her words.

In Páll Eggert Ólason's manuscript catalogue one version of Guðrún's life story (NULI ÍB 438 4to) is classified as "a humorous composition" (*kímilegr samsetningr*), and the word for life story is placed in parentheses. The entry reads simply "*Guðrún suða Ketilsdóttir (ævisaga)*", "*suða*" meaning "buzz" (Páll Eggert Ólason 1927–32, 828). This classification is significant in many ways. First of all, Páll Eggert says that he has followed the rule that he uses the headings in the manuscripts themselves when listing them in his catalogue. In this instance, however, he appears to have departed from this practice.[19] The table of contents for all five volumes of the manuscript catalogues contains a tremendous number of biographies of both women and men. Although the word indicating a life story is clearly present in the title in all three manuscripts, Páll Eggert chooses nonetheless to place it in the category of "folk belief and folk wisdom". In this category one finds tales of elves and ghosts, things related to witchcraft, monsters and superstition. Thus the story is clearly defined as a humorous tale of a foolish person and every effort is made to cover up the fact that this really is an autobiography.

At around the same time as the indices to Páll Eggert's manuscript catalogues were published, Guðrún's story appeared in print in the periodical

Gríma, a collection of folk wisdom edited by Þorsteinn M. Jónsson. Jónas Rafnar, a respected scholar from Eyjafjörður, also worked on the publication; he appears to have prepared the manuscript for publication and written a preface. It appears that Þorsteinn and Jónas, like Páll Eggert, found Guðrún funny, for in the table of contents for *Gríma* Guðrún's story is listed under the category of humorous tales (*Kímnisögur*). They chose to name Guðrún's story as an example of "foolishness" (*Flónska*). Jónas Rafnar emphasis Guðrún's talkativeness and peculiarity:

> Guðrún Ketilsdóttir, who was commonly called Gunna buzz, died in December of 1842 at the age of 83. During her last years she wandered itinerantly around Öngulsstaðahreppur. Gunna was constantly chattering, wherever she was; when she was walking alone between farms, she spoke to herself, so that the buzz was heard far off. In her determination to speak she threw everything together into a mishmash, so that it was difficult to follow the subject; the life story reflects this. (*Gríma* 1929, 71)

Jónas Rafnar's patronising attitude is revealed in his naming of Guðrún as *Gunna suða* (Gunna the buzz). It was not uncommon in earlier times for paupers and destitute people to be mocked and made fun of by those in power. In church records and parish censuses, there is no mention of the nickname "buzz" for Guðrún, even though it would have been quite natural for her to have one, since she had a sister who was one year older who was also named Guðrún (it was common in times of high infant mortality for siblings to be given the same name, in order to ensure that a name which was traditional to the family would survive). Both sisters lived in the same district and thus could easily have been distinguished in pastors' records with nicknames. This was, however, not the case: they both were always listed by their full names until their deaths. Furthermore, in the journal kept by Ólafur Eyjólfsson, secretary of the district magistrate at Grund, Guðrún appears often to have stayed at Grund during her travels in the area. Whenever she is referred to in Ólafur's journal, she is listed by her full name, Guðrún Ketilsdóttir. Most people in Ólafur's list are, however, only listed by their first names or identified with the farm that they came from. When Guðrún died, Ólafur mentioned her death on 11 December 1842 in this way: "News arrives of the death of the old woman Guðrún Ketilsdóttir" (NULI Lbs. 1343–1347).[20] Jónas Rafnar's preface clearly reveals his attitude toward Guðrún and her life story. In addition, he makes interesting comments on Guðrún's plain-spoken narrative style; for he says that the narrative is presented unaltered except that a few instances of obscene language are modified, though without changing the meaning. The editors thus present the text as a humorous story of a foul-mouthed, foolish old woman.

The attitude apparent in the writings of Jónas Rafnar and Páll Eggert seems to be related to a certain division between rural and urban culture on the one hand and between learned and lay scholars on the other, a division which developed toward the end of the 19th century. The so-called lay scholars were greatly interested in all manner of stories, poetry and learned tales which they collected and copied with great enthusiasm. Most of them came from rural areas and their main aim was to get their hands on interesting reading matter for the entertainment and enlightenment of themselves and the members of their households. Around the turn of the 20th century Icelandic society underwent great changes as new modes of production resulted in increased urbanisation and the creation of an urban middle-class. At the same time the publication of historical material was mostly taken care of by university educated historians. During the time of the fight for independence these men had the main responsibility for forming the self-image fitting for the new Icelander. There was increased emphasis on the so-called Commonwealth period (930–1262), when Icelanders were free and independent, and on the few important men who were considered to have made a deeper impression than others in the history of the nation.

The way in which women's manuscripts have been presented in manuscript catalogues must have had a significant effect on scholars' selection of sources about women. The relative paucity of women's manuscripts in the manuscript catalogues did not come about because women did not write, but must rather be attributed primarily to the viewpoints of the men who assembled the manuscript catalogues. Undoubtedly the many boxes and tattered handwritten books which can be found in the storage facilities of the manuscript department conceal interesting manuscripts preserving women's self-expression. Following a thorough investigation of the catalogues, I am convinced that there is a lot of material that has never found its way into the catalogues, but rather wound up in manuscripts attributed to others (most often men), been overlooked due to a perceived lack of cultural importance or fallen prey to collection pruning, cast off as so much dross.

Notes

1 *Á tímum sjálfstæðisbaráttu Íslendinga skipti það máli að þjóðin ætti sér sögu og menningu sem á einhvern hátt geri hana að þjóð og hafi hús eða stofnun er geymi bækur og handrit til að styðja þessa ímynd.* (Örn Hrafnkelsson 1997)
2 *Í Landsbókasafninu er að finna allt of mikið af ónýtum handritum; stafar það vafalaust af því, að skrár hafa ekki verið gerðar jafnóðum aðrar en aðfangaskrár, og hefir því verið tekið meira inn í safnið en þörf var á, með því að bókaverðir vissu ekki, hvað fyrir var.*
3 *[...] æfina mjna j gröf allir vissu hún var bölbúð – þaðann fór jeg til Páls á Þórustöðum hann átti bágt og viljinn var eins hann hafdi af mer gráu gimbrina mína og var manna víðsjálastur firr vildi jeg gánga á höfðinu enn vera þar.*
4 *Kemur vel fyrir, er skikkanleg og gagnleg, iðjusöm, fróm, hirðusöm og trú.*
5 *[...] fór því til Guðmundar í Kaupángi hann var mér besti maður og var jeg þar í mesta gengi og allir elskuðu mijg því jeg kom allstaðar fram tíl góðs og betur gengdi.*
6 *[...] fór jeg þá í Eyafjörð gekk mer vel fór jeg að Stórhóli í vist var þar í mesta jfirlæti [...] þá var jeg þéruð af öllum þá sögðu þeir sælar veri þér og komið þér sælar.*
7 *[...] Þorsteinn vildi fá mjg til fílgilags enn jeg beit af mer Guðmundur í Hamarkoti vildi það eirninn enn jeg var ráðvandari enn svo að jeg lægi undir hvurjum sem hafa vildi. [...] þegar hann sá mig bera vildi hann fá mjg til fílgilags en jeg varðist brinju búin og ljet hann ekki fá það.*
8 *[...] þá var jeg falleg þá var jeg með kvíta tauma ofan með nefinu rauða diska í*

kinnum bláeigð smáeigð hafinn brínd.
9 [...] brúkaði vænann fald og rauðann silkiklút um höfuðið og borða lagða hempu jfirum þverar herðarnar.
10 [...] gaf jeg séra Hallgrími margann brennivíns dropa.
11 [...] þegar jeg var þángað komin þá vóru þar sjómenn meðal hverra eirn var frá hrafnagili sá bölvaður refur og het Íllhugi álitlegur maður enn margur hilur úlfin undir sauðar gærunii svo var um hann bauð han mér alla þenustu enn ókunnugur varningur firrir margann fje hann var með bjart hár í blarri peisu grænum bol hatt og góða skó.
12 [...] þá kom tilhugalífið með okkur Íllhuga jeg átti 5 Kistur þar var meira í þeim enn mirkrið tómt í eirni vóru rúsjnur og laumaði jeg i hann af þeim þvj jeg hugsaði að þetta væri maður enn ekki djöfull.
13 [...] þá fór hann í sitt hóru rí og fór stelpu af stelpu enn jeg mátti slama og þeija og ergist hver með aldrinum.
14 Vestnaði nú Illhugi þvj hann var þræll og fantur nema við hórur sínar sem hann lá í.
15 [...] fórum við þá að hofi og áttum 14 gimbrar og kvígu han fór með það í sínar bölvaðar skuldir og sagði eg þá laust við hann tók han þá af mér fötin hann var í 50 rd. skuld í kaupstað, þaug hlupu 20 rd. og hafði han þá til góða 16 rd. og hafði hann þá handa Kristínu því hann lá í henni eins ogbrókinni sinni.
16 [...] þá fór jeg að Barði í Fljótum var þar um nóttina þorsteirn vildi fá mjg til fílgilags enn jeg beit af mer Guðmundur í Hamarkoti vildi það eirinn enn jeg var ráðvandari enn svo að jeg lægi undir hvurjum sem hafa vildi lá jeg þá úti á klaufabrekkum vorlánga nóttina í sólskini og sunnanvindi að komin dauða Guðbjörg gaf mier svartabrauð að endurnæringu fór jeg þá í Eyafjörð.
17 [...] dáindis að var Jón minn konfermeraður enn lapþunnir vóru grautarnir þar og aungvann bita fiekk hann firir utan mat sinn.
18 [...] enn nú sega þeir allir þarna fer kelíngar skrattin hún Guðrún Ketilsdóttir vel er eg metinn af góðum mönnum því ekki gjöra þetta nema bölvaðir gárúngarnir sem ekki skeita um guð nje menn.
19 The title of Geir Vigfússonar manuscripts is Æfisaga Guðrúnar Ketilsdóttur auknefnd Suða. Af henni sjálfri sögð og af ýmsum samansett í eitt ("The life story of Guðrún Ketilsdóttir nicknamed Buzz. Told by herself and composed by various people").
20 Diaries of Ólafur Eyjólfsson from Laugaland.

Archival Sources

National and University Library of Iceland (NULI):

NULI ÍB 438 4to: Various fragments with Geir Vigfússon's hand.
NULI ÍB 841 8vo: Miscellany, assembled by Þorsteinn Þorsteinsson from Upsir.
NULI ÍB 883 8vo: Manuscript from Jón Borgfirðing.
NULI Lbs 1343–1347: Diaries of Ólafur Eyjólfsson from Laugaland.

The National Archives of Iceland (NAI):

NAI Grundarþing/Laugaland BA/2: Visitation book.
NAI Hrafnagil BC/2, BC/3: Parish register.
NAI Munkaþverársókn BA/2: Visitation book.
NAI Munkaþverársókn BC/1: Parish register.

Kati Mikkola

Self-Taught Collectors of Folklore and their Challenge to Archival Authority

The year 1809 – when Finland was ceded from Sweden to Russia and became an autonomous grand duchy – represents a decisive moment in Finnish history. The new status served to spark a social desire for the creation of a Finnish national identity – an aspiration that had already begun to take shape in the late 18th century in the minds of intellectuals at the Academy of Turku. This Finnish cultural nationalism primarily centred on the question of language. J. V. Snellman (1806–1881), a Hegelian philosopher and politician, emphasised the importance of Finnish language and literature in fostering a national consciousness. One of the first measures of the Finnish Literature Society, founded in 1831 to promote the creation of Finnish literary culture, was to support the excursions made by its first secretary, Elias Lönnrot (1802–1884), to note down oral poetry in the easternmost parts of Finland and in eastern Karelia, where the tradition was still alive. The *Kalevala*, an epic poem compiled by Lönnrot and first published in 1835, had great symbolic value for nation building, and in general folklore played a major role in the construction of the Finnish people as a nation (Anttonen 2005, 83, 170, Stark 2006a, 136–137). Collecting epic and lyric poetry, fairy tales, charms, proverbs, riddles etc. became one of the cornerstones of the Finnish Literature Society, alongside publishing, collecting books and manuscripts and advancing Finnish studies in general.

From the 1840s newspapers began to publish requests for collecting folklore. At the outset, the people who noted down oral lore and ethnographic data tended to be students or academically trained scholars, but especially from the 1870s onward, self-taught lay collectors also joined the ranks.[1] Just who were these individuals seeking to supply the archives with this wealth of written materials? What were their social, educational and occupational backgrounds? Under what circumstances did they conduct their work in the field, and what significance did this activity have for them? In the present article I will examine the notions the collectors themselves entertained about the nature and importance of the material they sent to the Finnish Literature Society. The main focus of my analysis will be on two particularly active collectors, Vilho Itkonen (1872–1918) and Ulla Mannonen (1895–1958), who, each in their own way, challenged the underlying ideologies of collecting oral tradition. Finally, I will review the question of authenticity in folklore, as well as the role of "undesirable" materials from the vantage point of present-day research.

Lay Collectors and Academic Researchers

Alongside a vast amount of folklore material, the archives of the Finnish Literature Society house autobiographical accounts of lay collectors and their letters to the archives. There are also copies of letters sent to the collectors by the academic researchers responsible for the collecting work at the Society. I have studied some 1600 letters from 90 lay collectors and about 30 autobiographies, mainly from the end of the 1800s to the late 1940s.[2] They provide valuable insights into the views of non-professional collectors with regard to their own activities. Most of the letters sent to the Finnish Literature Society are short requests for paper and envelopes or for payments given in cash or books. Yet among them there is also a significant number of lengthy accounts of the day-to-day work in the field and the challenges the amateur collectors faced in soliciting material, as well as passages elucidating the collectors' motives for setting out to record folk traditions.

The letters of the lay collectors reveal a wide range of attitudes toward their academic counterparts, ranging from humility and deference to familiarity and friendliness. Although some letters betray a hierarchical relationship, others communicate an impression of equals working for a common goal. The undercurrent of the correspondence contains both the legacy of the class system, which functioned to make and reinforce the distinctions between the academics and the common people, and the rhetoric of striving for the modern ideal of a civil society, building a nation.

In the early days, women working in the field were rare exceptions, constituting approximately 5 % of the collectors at the end of the 19th century; but by the 1930s it is estimated that women formed one-third of the Finnish Literature Society's network of collectors (Mikkola 2009, 85, Näyhö 2008). The lay collectors came from a wide range of occupational and socio-economic backgrounds. The largest group consisted of people earning their living through agriculture, but there were also craftspeople, itinerant workers, merchants, clerks and schoolteachers. Some of the collectors had received no formal schooling at all. In spite of their diverse backgrounds, the collectors were united in their interest in oral traditions, reading and writing. Furthermore, nearly all of them were Finnish speakers who had been born and raised in rural areas. Because most of the collectors were engaged in farm work, the tasks of collecting folklore and writing out the field notes had to be carried out during the quieter times in the autumn and winter, in the evenings and during holidays – though even at those times fatigue and poor lighting may have hindered their efforts. The task of collecting folklore was further impeded by poor weather conditions and the difficulties presented by travelling, as well as a perennial lack of funding.

In their letters the collectors described how people in their immediate surroundings reacted to their commitment to documenting elements of traditional life. Although some of the collectors enjoyed the appreciation, sympathy and esteem of the community, others met with constant suspicion and even antagonism. Many collectors found that the young tended to sneer at the older people who acted as informants to the collectors; indeed, at times the elders were forbidden to prattle on about the old ways. Occasionally collectors were suspected of exploiting their informants; some people even imagined that big earnings were being made from the lore they provided. In traditional rural society, writing down folklore was something which did not belong to the natural order of things. Interestingly, even though the lay collectors were participants in the local culture from which they collected the traditions, their literary pursuits set them apart from their own people, observing their own milieux with an outsider's gaze.

In their letters and autobiographies, amateur collectors explained what had motivated them to write down folk traditions. While some simply found it a stimulating pastime, others pursued their work with an enthusiasm that verged on the professional. The rewards – whether in the form of books or cash – were far from exorbitant, but they did mean recognition and thus provided an incentive to go on with the work. Still more important for the collectors was the idea of seeing their own notes as bound in volumes on the shelves of the archive, which gave them the sense of that they were contributing to something permanent. In addition to the idea of rescuing fragments of antiquity from oblivion, patriotism and a commitment to cherishing one's local area figure prominently in the ideological motives underlying folklore collection. The Finnish Literature Society also actively encouraged these ideals in their requests and manuals aimed at amateur fieldworkers.

Folklore collecting can be seen as an arena made up of two sets of actors: the ordinary people who wrote down the data and the representatives of the cultural and academic elite who organised the work and subsequently analysed the material that was sent to the archives. This educational and social gap serves, at least in part, as an explanation for the amateur collectors' incessant need to ponder the significance of the materials they sent to the archives. These reflections were also connected to discussions about the "authenticity" of folklore. From the standpoint of folklore research, the criteria for the authenticity of the data were the following: age, collectiveness, distribution, orality, the aesthetic value of the material and the reliability of the collecting method. When considering views expressed in the 19th and early 20th century about the authenticity of folklore materials, we are forced to draw our conclusions using relatively scattered observations taken from various sources. The establishment of the Folklore Archives at the Finnish Literature Society in the 1930s further served to systematise the classification of data with regard to its authenticity and scientific value. Archivists carefully screened newly received folklore materials to ensure that no items deemed spurious or to have come from unreliable sources were mixed up with the so-called authentic data.[3] Even though the great majority of collectors appeared to have embraced the collecting ideals, there were individuals such as Vilho Itkonen and Ulla Mannonen who contested the conventions set by the researchers regarding the folklore which warranted salvation – not to mention its authenticity and interpretation.

Vilho Itkonen's Theosophical Views on Folk Traditions

Vilho Itkonen was born into a family of crofters in Heinävesi, in the province of Savo, in 1872.⁴ Itkonen's mother died before he had reached his first birthday. Although he gave the impression in his texts that he had received no formal education, Itkonen had apparently attended elementary school for some time. As an adult, Itkonen travelled to towns throughout Finland, earning his living in various ways; at times he had no work at all. He managed to supplement his income by collecting folklore. He also wrote for newspapers and published critical broadsheet ballads under the penname of Mooses. Itkonen was a theosophist who advocated temperance and socialism. During the periods of Russian oppression he was arrested and imprisoned on numerous occasions for political reasons; in 1918, during the Civil War, he was sent to the prison camp in Tampere, where he died of an illness. According to the official records, he was an unmarried father of two children at the time of his death (*War Victims in Finland 1914–1922*).

Itkonen collected folklore from the 1890s to the 1910s and also sent his poems and other writings to the Finnish Literature Society. He was interested in social issues as well as in innovations in technology and science. His letters and other writings convey a belief that his ideas would persist as a legacy for future generations: "If a scientist versed in the study of the soul should ever rummage through these archives, may he be the one to discover my thoughts", he wrote to E. A. Tunkelo (1870–1953), Secretary of the Society, in 1911.⁵

In 1910, the Finnish Literature Society received a 20-page manuscript entitled *Uusi tapa tutkia kylätaikureita* ("A new way to study village magic-workers"), in which Itkonen presented a theosophist approach to the study of folk beliefs (see also Stark 2006a). Itkonen's criticism of academic scholars contains no hint of inferiority or servility. After reading travel accounts by earlier researchers, Itkonen denounces these writers for their contempt of folk beliefs, which manifests itself in the writers' disgust and condemnation of the actual practitioners of magic. In other words, earlier collectors had approached the wizards, witches and magicians with condescension, supposedly out of "mercy". According to Itkonen, the academic fieldworkers had clearly regarded themselves as "superior beings", which prevented them from them from grasping the deepest essence of folk knowledge – for no practitioner of folk magic would ever trust a disrespectful collector. Itkonen himself recounts a long-standing interest in the topic, beginning in his childhood, from his personal experiences of telepathy and omens.

Itkonen's argumentation places folklore research, founded in the "old" human sciences, and the "new" theosophist perspective, which had its roots in the "extreme depths of eternal life", in stark contrast. According to him, the same division also presided in the press and in literature: while both continued to bemoan the flourishing of superstition among the ordinary people, they nevertheless chronicled ominous dreams come true and successful incidents of suggestion, hypnotism and spiritist séances. As far as Itkonen was concerned, practitioners of magic had not been approached with sufficient depth, because the "materialistic" researchers had been incapable of distinguishing the gold from the dross of the village magic-worker's soul. Nearing the age of forty, Itkonen writes that he is just beginning to find the best way to approach such village magic-workers. The approach requires a sensitive attitude and an appreciation of the wider body of knowledge to which these fragments of folk belief ultimately belong.

The name of Madame Blavatsky (1831–1891), whose opus *The Key to Theosophy* was translated into Finnish in 1906, recurs frequently in Itkonen's writings. A theosophical stance to life structured his view of the village magic-workers; in his mind they were the kindred spirits of holy individuals such as Jesus and Buddha. Itkonen was extremely critical of greedy priests and the "Christian doctrine of murder and persecution", but he appreciated the "spiritual teachings" of the Bible, for in his mind its eternal life was analogous to idea of reincarnation. According to Itkonen's perception, the mental basis of Finnish folk belief was "Indian-Hindu-Nazarene-spiritist-scientific" – the village magic-worker had connections, either conscious or unconscious, to these wider currents, for the secrets of all nations were in their essence fundamentally the same.

For Itkonen, the central figure of Finnish tradition was the main protagonist of the *Kalevala*, the sage Väinämöinen, who stepped aside upon the arrival of the new Lord, Jesus Christ, yet promised to return when the time was right and he once again was needed. Itkonen's view of Väinämöinen as a historical figure was not in itself exceptional: many scholars also espoused the so-called historical interpretation of the *Kalevala*, regarding the protagonists of the narrative poems as ancient Finnish heroes (Wilson 1985, 40–41, Honko 1999, XIX, Lönnrot 1999, 10, Laaksonen 2005, ix). For the nationally-minded cultural elite, the ancient ethnic religion and mythology were sacred symbols pointing to the nation's past and representing its glorious history. For Itkonen, however, Väinämöinen's covert knowledge continued to be relevant from a standpoint that was both religious and ideological. In his opinion, the time was ripe for Väinämöinen's return.

Essentially, Itkonen believed that the study of magic was "the eternal investigation of the human being", an activity based on "the law of life". In order to understand spells, the researcher had to delve deeply into the education of the practitioner of magic: under what circumstances, from whom and for what purpose had he or she learnt the necessary techniques? According to Itkonen, the village magic-worker displayed an astonishing level of erudition about the secrets of astronomy, chemistry, physics and alchemy; yet this knowledge was "unrefined", containing flawed ingredients such as black magic for perpetrating vengeful deeds. Indeed, the fundamental task of the scholar was to discriminate between precious knowledge and worthless matter; for there in "that gold was the Soul of life – God". Once the teachings of the Church, of medical science, of art and the natural sciences could be harmonised with the knowledge of the village magic-worker, the mysteries of life would be unlocked. Itkonen's espousal of theosophical thought therefore still meant that the magic-worker's tricks had to be subjected to strict scientific control.

Within the ideological framework of the cultural elite, the collecting of folklore was firmly embedded in the idea of a national future: the material housed in archives would later serve as evidence of the nation's long history. Itkonen never equated folklore with a clinging to the past; instead, for him the activity represented a new era and openness to innovation. According to Itkonen, the boundaries between the scientific and the pseudoscientific, the natural and the supernatural, were not strictly demarcated. For example, he drew parallels between wireless electricity and human telepathic communication. As Itkonen saw it, the core of tradition was formed from eternal truths that also had practical significance for the future. This stance with regard to tradition also links up with the international ethos characteristic of his argumentation. While folklore and spells were granted esteem within national ideology as part of national history, Itkonen regarded them as representations of humanity and the mysteries of humankind in a broader sense.

Ulla Mannonen and the Question of Valuable Folklore

Ulla Mannonen (1895–1958) was born into a family of small farmers in Uusikirkko, near Viipuri. In spite of the misgivings expressed by the older members of her extended family, Mannonen started school at an early age, first attending elementary school and later farming school. Her working life included a range of occupations: parlour maid in St Petersburg, shop assistant, housekeeper, ambulatory schoolteacher and milkmaid. She also claimed to have earned her wages by running a store and a café as well as numerous boarding houses. After about ten years of marriage, her husband died and she was left to raise three children on her own.

Mannonen began collecting folklore in the middle of the 1930s and became one of the most active fieldworkers who sent material to the Finnish Literature Society.[6] Her remarkable industry is evidenced by the sheer volume of her correspondence: 453 letters to the Finnish Literature Society written between 1936 and 1956. In addition, she wrote for newspapers and read her causeries aloud at hundreds of celebrations. Her book *Muistojen muruja* (*Flecks of memories*), which contains brief vignettes describing folk life in Karelia, was published in 1952. Her archive also includes an unfinished novel, in which she describes the vicissitudes of a Karelian family during the Second World War. According to Mannonen's own estimation, she wrote in the course of her life tens of thousands of pages (Mannonen 1952, 9–10).

The contributions of Ulla Mannonen were highly esteemed by the Finnish Literature Society, and she received numerous awards. Nevertheless, from time to time her activities incurred severe criticism. In a letter dated 2 February 1939, for example, she was sent the following warning:

> We have asked some of our collectors to give up collecting because their contributions contain an excess of unreliable and useless data for research; these materials will surely be tossed into the waste-paper basket, or simply lumped together with other bits of erroneous data and labelled as such.[7]

The image of her discarded contributions was not easily forgotten, and in a letter dated 6 March 1939, Mannonen asked whether her materials were now in the waste-paper basket. Although the doubts cast on the value of her efforts and the reliability of her data left Mannonen distressed and disheartened, she nevertheless described in a letter dated 12 May 1956 how the collection of folk wisdom continued to attract her as though by a magnetic force.

The national elite privileged and prized the most ancient oral traditions because these samples of collective wisdom and artistry bore witness to the extensive roots of Finnish culture. Indeed, this politicisation of age has been the subject of extensive analysis by critics of nationalism, such as Eric Hobsbawm (Hobsbawm 1989, see also Anttonen 2005, 55). From time to time, collectors were informed that the things they had documented were far too recent, and some material was even returned. In a letter dated 29 October 1936 Manninen conceded that not all the items she was sending – lyrics of ring songs – were old. She did point out, however, that the passage of time would surely age the materials, thus contesting the criteria the archives had set for the collectors.

Archival policy presented Mannonen with yet another challenge vis-à-vis her own autobiographical materials. Concerns about the true nature of tradition, that is, its communality, are reflected in the letters written by lay collectors. Though eager to share their personal memoirs, the writers continually ask about the merit and appropriateness of such documents. As a general principle, personal memoirs were not of the primary interest of the archive. Despite this, Mannonen persisted in sending accounts of her childhood and photographs of her surroundings – which, having acquired a camera of her own, she had begun to document. The archives were not always pleased with the material she sent. In a letter from 23 June 1939 Mannonen was asked only to send 'ethnographically relevant' photographs, such as pictures of her informants. Mannonen tried to comply with these instructions, but remarked in her letter that her photographs might prove to be ethnographically valuable in the future. In the 1930s folklore research was entirely historically oriented, and no attention was paid to the idea of tradition-in-progress: documenting one's own time was not seen relevant (Knuuttila 1994, 17). From today's perspective, Mannonen was obviously right: her photographs reflected contemporary reality, but in time they did become documents of ethnographic interest (C.f. Sinisalo 1981, 16).

The guidelines provided by the archives underscored the importance of precision, of making notes "exactly according to what the folk say", "with no retelling or embellishment" (Mustonen 1936, 5, Haavio 1935, 3, 1936, 3, 1937, 8). Lay collectors assured archive employees of the authenticity of their data by underlining their commitment to the values of honesty and respect for the truth (see also Peltonen 1996, 102). And so did Mannonen. Just as the writers of the Scriptures were believed to be divinely inspired faithfully to convey God's message, the recorder of folk tradition emerges in her reasoning as a means by which the ancient wisdom of the folk is transported from the oral into the written form. When documenting the old traditions for the archives – as opposed to newer or more personal documents – Mannonen conformed wholeheartedly to the principles set down by the archives.

Was it necessary to preserve accurately every utterance from the mouths of the folk? Many collectors believed that their fundamental task as recorders of folklore was simply to separate the wheat from the chaff – that is, to capture the authentic traditional elements in the stream of their informants' speech. Such discernment was also, at least implicitly, expected of the staff at the archive. The authenticity of recorded folklore was further guaranteed by only using materials obtained from narrators who had not acquired their traditional knowledge from books (Haavio 1935, 3, 1936, 3, 1937, 8). In a letter sent from the Archives and dated 17 February 1939, doubts were cast on the authenticity of a tale of an elk hunt. According to the letter, Mannonen's informant had clearly learned the narrative from a book. The next day Mannonen wrote a response claiming that her 82-year-old informant had not read anything in her life but hymnbooks, the Catechism and the history of the Bible. Her explanation failed to convince Martti Haavio, the director of the archives, however, and on 20 February 1939 he informed Mannonen that a similar tale had been published in the journal *Kotiseutu*; he also added that men of science had the expertise to determine the authenticity of any given text. It is no wonder that Mannonen constantly articulates concern over the worthiness of the materials she has sent: "One speaks in one way, another in another way, which of these then has value?" (20 January 1937).[8]

According to Seppo Knuuttila, the question of authenticity in the history of folklore collection has always turned on the question of the narrator's literacy skills. Even well into the 20th century, both the scholarly and popular imagination held that the illiterate people, the folk, "the last rune-singers", were the bearers of originality and the authentic messengers of antiquity (Knuuttila 1994, 126). Such a view makes it easy to appreciate Mannonen's need to underline her informants' lack of formal education: "They are all simple people, from the deepest strata of the folk, and I do not believe that any of them have added anything of their own" (20 January 1937).[9]

The notion of folklore collection as a shared national effort emerges as a rhetorical strategy in the correspondence between the representatives of the archives and the self-taught collectors of folklore. What is more, this effort was organically connected to the idea that each amateur collector represented above all his or her own home region and province. Local and national arguments coexist in Mannonen's texts – but not without tension. Time after time, Mannonen asserted that the rationale behind her collecting was to defend the *honour* of her home region, the Karelian Isthmus. She broadly presents her views on Karelianness and the status of Karelians within the larger framework of Finnishness. As Mannonen saw it, Karelians were misunderstood and undervalued by the rest of the Finnish population, even though Karelians were exceptionally "Finnish" compared with western Finns, who were suspiciously predisposed to things Swedish.

When Mannonen's contributions to the archives were criticised, she was left with the feeling that the western Finnish gentlemen of the Finnish Literature Society had failed to grasp the circumstances under which the people of the eastern parts of the country lived (7 December 1938, 6 March 1939). The Second World War and the painful experiences of evacuation and resettlement further coloured Mannonen's perception, making her statements even more exalted and polemical. In a letter dated 19 September 1940, Mannonen stated her conviction that the prevailing goal of the elite was to eradicate Karelian culture. In her view, the aloofness to the plight of the Karelians arose from Finnish envy of the Karelians, for it was their home locale which was the cradle of ancient Finnish culture. For Mannonen, the core of Finnishness was represented in the Kalevalaic world, whose origins in Karelia were an unassailable fact. Martti Haavio's studies, in which the influences of western Finnish tradition on Kalevala-metre poetry are discussed (Haavio 1933, 283–286), appeared to Mannonen as an envious attempt to wrest from Karelians their rightful position as a part of Finnish culture and nation (15 February 1941).

How Does What Is Deemed Worthless Attain Value?

In his *Tradition through Modernity* (2005), Pertti Anttonen considers the ways in which historical reality as depicted by archival authority has obscured the collectors' quotidian use of power; in other words, the collectors who sifted through the materials sent to the archives had the power to choose whose voice would be heard and how. From the point of view of the nationalistic interests of the archives, the collector's task was to select and collect the kind of material laden with symbolic value for the nation. The choices made influenced which cultural representations came to stand for the traditional and were thus granted epistemic value as belonging to the scientific category of folklore (Anttonen 2005, 39, 53, 57, 87). Despite official attempts to collect representations consonant with national ideals, archival materials ultimately turn out to be unpredictable and diverse. Not all collectors embraced or even understood the ideological principles of the archive. As the examples of Itkonen and Mannonen have shown, individual collectors often had their own agenda when highlighting some issues and playing down others.

The institutional power of the archives is evinced by the archive's relationship to historical reality; after all, the materials which are eventually housed in archives come to define what is viewed as historical and what is not. This occurs either by a steady process of selection, or at the very least, through guidelines and instructions which act as a filter, discouraging in advance the arrival of any spurious materials. The instructions and feedback given to collectors constituted part of a subtle use of control, which ultimately led to the creation of a body of materials with historical significance (Mikkola 2009, 109). Later generations of researchers may be grateful that collectors did not always heed the directions they were given. Indeed, the value of "undesirable" items resides in the rough edges they add to the impression of the past produced by adherence to archival principles. For example, not all of the texts sent by Vilho Itkonen and Ulla Mannonen were necessarily wanted, but having ended up in the archives they gradually turned into documents about the ideals and forms of life of a certain time.

During each historical period attempts are made to build up the archival holdings with prevailing scientific ideals in mind. Discussions about the "authenticity" of the materials have, through the constructivist understandings of knowledge, been given a new light, for from this vantage point all folklore is socially constructed and in this regard no traditional items are more "authentic" or more "invented" than any other. Yet another issue – which invariably turns on a political argument – is the relationship between generic status and time, for each era holds certain folklore genres in higher and others in lower regard (Anttonen 2005, 106–107). The study of culture and tradition is always in a state of flux, which is to say that each new era inevitably involves a desire to traditionalise the old on the one hand and the necessity to see the past from a new historical perspective on the other. The value and reliability of archival materials are viewed largely through the scientific lenses of their beholder. Tuulikki Kurki has shown that from the perspective of collecting materials for archives, the concept of *potential information* is apt in the case of problematic data. The research questions themselves determine whether the materials can function as sources of knowledge – that is, whether they answer the questions posed by the research (Kurki 2002, 23, 2004, 72).

The interpretation of any folkloric material inevitably involves the use of power by the researcher, who assesses the reliability and value of the data. From the vantage point of today we are able to re-assess the once questionable and even controversial contributions of Itkonen and Mannonen. Itkonen's writings offer a rare glimpse into the intellectual progress of a largely self-taught man from the working class. The archived documents of his efforts to put his thoughts into words allow today's researchers to witness how he interpreted the new religious and political ideologies of his day and then incorporated his views into the work of recording traditions. Mannonen's ways of challenging the archival ideals of folklore collection also offer glimpses of day-to-day life and individual experiences the historical value of which has grown over time. As self-taught collectors of tradition, both Itkonen and Mannonen, albeit each in their own fashion, contested the hegemonic concepts and roles of the national elite offered to them by the collecting organisation. These exceptional individuals are indispensable, for they enrich and diversify our image of the past. At the same time, their contributions underscore the dimension of variability added to the archives with the passage of time: once deemed worthless, many contributions to the archives have now acquired new value.

Notes

1 The number of lay collectors increased dramatically after the establishment of the Folklore Archives in the Finnish Literature Society in the 1930s. The new Folklore Archives became the headquarters for the organisation of the collection of folklore through various means, for example, with the aid of a network of collectors across the country. At its most extensive, the network included some one thousand people from different parts of Finland (Peltonen 2004, 211–212, Pöysä & Timonen 2004, 222, 230–231).
2 Most of these autobiographies are stored at the Lexical Archives of Finnish Dialects. See also Mikkola 2009.
3 The doubts cast upon the authenticity of materials are evinced by the unofficial

information that circulated among archival staff and researchers. Orally transmitted, this "hidden tradition" has travelled across generations of researchers, and I too have encountered its numerous variations while carrying out my own research (see Kuusi 1970, 300, Kurki 2004, 66). However, the cases where inauthentic material has been discovers, are relatively rare. Based on statements made by researchers from the Folklore Archives, Leena Hukkinen listed a total of 75 collectors whose collections were considered at least partially to have come from unreliable sources. According to Hukkinen, the origins of "inauthentic" folklore can be listed as follows: inappropriate collecting methods, copying of campaign prizes, the intrusive presence of the respondent's personality in the collection work as well as ignorance as to what constitutes "folk poetry" (Hukkinen 1963, see also Kurki 2004, 70).

4 According to the baptismal entry in the parish register, his name is Wilhelm Eliaanpoika, and according to the statistics in the *War Victims in Finland 1914-1922*, the name used to record his death information is Ville Eliaanpoika.
5 *Jos joku sielutieteen tutkia osuu arkistoja penkomaan, löytäköön hän, etupäässä, ajatuksiani, tusina sieluilla ei ole väliä.*
6 About Mannonen's collecting work see Mikkola 2009.
7 *Eräitä kerääjiä olemme kehoittaneet luopumaan keräyksestä siksi, että heidän keräyksissään on liian runsaasti epäluotettavaa ja tutkijoille kelvotonta ainesta, joka tietenkin siirretään paperikoriin tai liitetään epäluotettavan aineksen joukkoon ja varustetaan vastaavalla merkillä.*
8 *Yksi puhuu yhdellä tavalla, toinen toisella, mikä heistä sitten kelvannee?*
9 *He ovat kaikki; yksinkertaisia ihmisiä, kansan syvimmistä kerroksista, enkä usko että heistä kuka on omiaan lisännyt.*

Archival Sources

Personal communication from Ulla Issakainen from the Parish Office of Heinävesi on 22 Oct. 2010. Information from the Parish Register on Wilhelm Itkonen.

The Finnish Literature Society, Folklore Archives:
KV. Correspondence 1935-1959 (incl. Ulla Mannonen's correspondence, 411 items).
KV KRK. Correspondence related to the collecting campaign to celebrate the Kalevala Jubilee Year (incl. letters from Ulla Mannonen, 26 items).
KV PK. Correspondence related to the collection campaign for historical and local legends (incl. letters from Ulla Mannonen, 16 items).
Mannonen, Ulla 1952, 316-327. *Maalaiskodin tarina*. ["Story of a country home"] Karjalaisten Heimoseura ry. 1951-1952, Kotiseutu 2.

Finnish Literature Society, Literary Archives:
A1910. Mannonen, Ulla. *Hely. Kuvaus erään Koivistolaisperheen vaiheista sotavuosina 1939-1941.* [Account of a family from Koivisto during the war years 1939-1941.] 8 notebooks, 420 pp. KI. 8336a. An accompanying letter dated 18 Nov. 1948.
A1225. Itkonen, Vilho. *Elämän käsitykseni*. [My understanding of life]; with accompanying letter.
B453. Itkonen, Vilho. *Kokoelma runoja*. [Collection of poems]; with two accompanying letters.
B456. Itkonen, Vilho. *Uusi tapa tutkia kylätaikureita*. [A new approach to village magicworkers]; with three letters and two letters of testimony from acquaintances.
Vilho Itkonen's letters to the Finnish Literature Society. 86 vir. mf. p. 257, 1 letter.
Vilho Itkonen's letters to the Finnish Literature Society. 98 vir. mf. pp. 171-173, 1 letter.

Vilho Itkonen's letters to the Finnish Literature Society. 99 vir. mf. pp. 184–186, pp. 187–190, pp. 388–389, 3 letters.
Vilho Itkonen's letters to the Finnish Literature Society. 100 vir. mf. p. 583, 1 letter.
Vilho Itkonen's letters to the Finnish Literature Society. 103 vir. mf. pp. 109–119, 1 letter.
Vilho Itkonen's letters to the Finnish Literature Society. 108 vir. mf. p. 189, 1 letter.
Vilho Itkonen's letters to Kaarle Krohn. 109 [109:17–25, Hä–I].

The Lexical Archives of Finnish Dialects, Institute for the Languages of Finland:
Life stories of folklore collectors; incl. Ulla Mannonen's life story, from 1947, handwritten, about 19 pages.

Petri Lauerma

Finnish Revivalist Movements and the Development of Literary Finnish

Literary Finnish During the Swedish Reign

Although Finnish as a written language dates back to the Middle Ages, and the first printed books in Finnish appeared in the 1540s, the literary use of Finnish remained limited throughout the early-modern period for various reasons, both internal and external. Most Finns were illiterate during this period, and even if they had been able to read and write, the language used in Finnish books would have looked unfamiliar to a large part of the population.

Old Literary Finnish was almost exclusively based on western dialects, especially on south-western dialects spoken in the vicinity of Turku. In the oldest literary Finnish, for example in the language of Mikael Agricola (ca. 1510–1557), there were occasional eastern features, but such features were lost in language purification processes as early as the 17th century. The first Finnish translation of the whole Bible, from the year 1642, is much more exclusively based on western Finnish dialects than Agricola's New Testament, published nearly a hundred years earlier. The literary use of the Finnish language was quite restricted at least until the last quarter of the 18th century, with Old Literary Finnish used almost exclusively in religious and legal publications. Original Finnish culture remained on the oral level, mainly in the form of folk poetry. Some isolated attempts to produce art poetry on this basis were made, but with only very limited results. On the contrary, the whole status of Finnish began to decline, owing partly to political factors, partly to the shift in language from Finnish to Swedish. Finnish was not the language of the educated class: if you managed to get an education, you had to change your language to Swedish.[1]

With the advent of Romanticism in the last quarter of the 18th century, things began to change. The question regarding the cultural influences which changed the way Finnish was perceived is a large and complex one. During the last decades of the 18th century J. G. von Herder's (1744–1803) ideas on nationality and language led to the reappraisal of the cultural value of small nations. This sparked the collecting and publishing of old Finnish folk poems and even attempts of their scientific study, mainly thanks to H. G. Porthan (1739–1804), then professor of Latin literature and rhetoric at the Academy of Turku. Even a dictionary of Finnish was planned on the basis of materials collected by Christfrid Ganander (1741–1790); this, however, did not materialise, partly because in Porthan's generation the practical command of Finnish in academic circles had become too weak. The circle of Porthan's pupils and friends, the so-called first Åbo School, concentrated on getting inspiration from Finnish national culture, but they couldn't do much for the benefit of the Finnish language. The greatest progress was made in another direction, in the realm of the Finnish Church. The Finnish translation of the Bible was thoroughly revised in 1776 by Anders Lizelius (1708–1795), an enterprising clergyman who started using Finnish in some municipal records and also published a newspaper in Finnish, the first one ever. Unfortunately there were not enough readers for a publication of this kind, and Lizelius had to abandon the project after a year; even so, it meant progress in the use of the Finnish language.[2]

Changes During the Russian Reign

When, in 1809, Sweden lost Finland to the Russian Empire, the geopolitical situation of Finland changed. Russian granted Finland autonomy, so that Finns would not miss Swedish rule too much. One important fact was that Russia began to support attempts to develop the Finnish language, which had otherwise been in clear decline for the whole of the 18th century. This political support partly explains why Finnish developed so rapidly in the course of the 19th century. On the other hand, Russia allowed Swedish to remain the administrative language of Finland.[3]

The old Finnish literary tradition was almost immediately challenged: in 1810 and 1811, Gustaf Renvall (1781–1841) defended dissertations which laid the foundation of modern Finnish orthography, proposing several revisions to the complicated and unstable orthography of Old Literary Finnish. The practical introduction of these revisions was carried out by Jacob Judén (Jaakko Juteini, 1781–1855), who started to publish small booklets of his own poems and other works of pedagogical nature. Juteini did not want to reform orthography as much as Renvall, but he introduced some morphological innovations based on his own Tavastian dialect. In only a few years' time, Juteini was followed by neologists of eastern Finnish background: C. A. Gottlund (1796–1875), A. Poppius (1793–1866), A. J. Sjögren (1794–1855) and R. von Becker (1788–1858). These men demanded more reforms to the Finnish language; some even wanted to found a totally new literary language based on eastern Finnish dialects, an idea which sprang from the newly found riches of Finnish folk poetry, which was much better preserved in the east than in the west. The conflict emerged in the late 1810s and culminated in 1820, when von Becker launched a newspaper called *Turun Wiikko-Sanomat* in strongly (but not exclusively) eastern Finnish. This lead to the so called "War of the Dialects" in Finnish language usage, when different dialects were used alongside the more traditional literary language, eventually leading the Finnish literary language to the brink of division in the 1830s. This was prevented above all by Renvall, who in an essay published in 1837 made a strong plea for preserving the western dialects as the basis for literary Finnish, while also enriching it with eastern vocabulary and some originally eastern forms. Renvall based his suggestions on the tendencies which were prevalent in the literary use of Finnish in from around 1810, and formulated them in such a way that they received the support of the champions of both the main dialects. Later on, Elias Lönnrot (1802–1884), who originally favoured eastern dialects even though he was born in the west, took a slightly modified transitional view, following Renvall. Their joint effort largely calmed down the rivalry between eastern and western dialects.[4]

A Problem of Viewpoint and Sources

The story of how the Finnish language in the 19th century rose from oblivion – while also maintaining its unity – is usually told almost exclusively from the point of view of secular culture. This viewpoint underlines the difference between biblical Old Literary Finnish (which was based on the western dialects) and more secular Early Modern Finnish (which at its height contained even more eastern Finnish features than the present literary language), no doubt because most language developers of that era preferred eastern dialects. But at the same time the final result of these 19th-century linguistic controversies has been forgotten. In fact, modern Finnish, if we think of it as the final product of all the linguistic processes ongoing in times of Early Modern Finnish, could never have devolved into its present form if there hadn't been some other forces behind its development than those usually acknowledged. Even Rapola (1969, 106–107), a leading authority of literary Finnish in his time, seems to have wondered why the basic structure of literary Finnish remained so close to the old literary language.

If we want to find answers to this question it is obvious that we must go deeper into the linguistic sources. The chief short-coming of nearly all earlier studies in 19th-century Finnish has been that the sources used have been insufficient – if, indeed, there have been any real primary sources at all. Most of the information has come indirectly through earlier studies, and even where sources have been analysed, only famous secular publications have been studied, while little known and forgotten works have truly remained forgotten. Only secular literature has been studied because it has been tacitly supposed that there had been no linguistic innovations in religious literature whatsoever, and that all processes of renewal must therefore have begun in the realm of secular literature. Unfortunately for this viewpoint, literature was still for the most part religious in the first half of the 19th century, which means that most of the literature published during this period has been excluded as research material. There are two further areas, both equally vast, which have also gone for the most part unstudied: broadsides and unpublished literature. In view of this it is obvious that many of the previous studies of 19th-century Finnish tell only part of the story.

The Role of the Church and the Birth of Revivalist Movements

If we go back to the basics, we must remember that Finland during the time of Old Literary Finnish was a deeply Lutheran country (the influence of the Orthodox Church was restricted to the easternmost areas of Finland). Even elementary education was in the hands of the church, which tried to teach everyone to read, and basic reading skills were required before one was allowed to marry. The results of this training were not always totally convincing – in many cases the catechism was merely learnt by heart and no real reading skills ever developed – but by the 18th century some form of rudimentary literacy was common throughout the nation.[5] This laid the foundations both for higher education – where and when this was possible – and for a deeper spiritual life. The latter, however, soon led to conflicts with the rather stiff and formal official form of Christianity.

The Pietists criticised the church for its formal and cold religiosity and demanded the right to personal decision and a Christian way of life. These ideas came to Finland mainly from German Pietism, but also partly (through literary contacts) from English Puritanism. Only official Christianity as practiced in the Lutheran (or Orthodox) Church was allowed, and all religious literature with leanings elsewhere was forbidden and free religious meetings were strictly prohibited, yet revivalism of the Pietist type began to have organized forms in the 18th century. There were other kinds of groups, too. In the first half of the century there was a small separationist group in Ostrobothnia which was eventually sent into exile. Later the so-called Ostrobothnian Mystics, who cherished the teachings of Jakob Böhme (1575–1624), worked in secrecy, circulating their translations in manuscript form only (c.f. e.g. Luukkanen 1994–1995). In the mid-18th century the revivalist rising in southwestern Finland began to have even ecstatic forms. Under the guidance of clergyman Abraham Achrenius (1706–1769), who had been influenced by German-type Pietism, the revivalism in this area moved in a more conventional direction. At the end of the 18th century a revivalist movement called Prayerism emerged from this basis.[6]

At the turn of the 19th century revivalism was rising in quite another part of Finland, in northern Savo. It took some decades, however, until a new kind of revivalist movement called Awakenism truly emerged under the leadership of Paavo Ruotsalainen (1777–1852). By this time the Prayerist type of revivalism had been introduced in eastern Finland by Henrik Renqvist (1789–1866). These two men became the leaders of the most important revivalist groups in the first half of the 19th century, when revivalist movements sprang up among the common people, while at the same time a nationalist awakening was stirring in educated circles.[7]

Renqvist, Prayerism and the Importance of Book Publishing

Henrik Renqvist, a clergyman, writer and book publisher, born Henrik Kukkonen, came from a peasant family in the distant parish of Liperi in northern Karelia, but managed to attend the Kuopio trivial school. After experiencing a religious awakening, Renqvist came into contact with religious organisations such as the Evangelical Society in Stockholm and their leaders. Renqvist also met the Scotsman John Paterson (1776–1855), who visited Turku in the year 1812 and inspired Finns to found a Finnish Bible Society for promoting the Bible. These contacts led Renqvist to concentrate his activity on publishing and circulating religious literature, even after he had eventually finished his theological studies in Turku and become a clergyman.

Because the books Renqvist published were aimed at the common people, they were in the kind of language which they would understand, the language of the Bible, even though it was in many ways dated. This is the reason why Renqvist is seldom mentioned in the standard histories of Finnish, and even when he is mentioned it is generally to stress the old-fashioned nature of his language (e.g. Lehikoinen & Kiuru 1998, 72). But if we ignore Renqvist, we also ignore how common illiteracy still was among the people who joined the revivalist groups – even some of the leaders of local revivalist groups were originally illiterate – and how important it was that some individuals, in particular clergymen joining the revivalists, began to organise more efficient literacy education, even employing new ways of teaching, such as the Bell-Lancaster method (Lauerma 2001, 574–576).

This was the starting point for the work of men like Renqvist, who made the acquirement of books possible even to those who lived in remote areas of the countryside, far from bookshops (Laine & Perälä 2005). And as for the nature of the language used in the publications that Renqvist wrote, translated or published, it is paradoxically their very linguistic conservatism that makes Renqvist so important. By contributing books in rather old-fashioned language, Renqvist formed an opposing force to neologists like Gottlund, who wanted to liberate written Finnish from its previous traditions.

The old-fashioned nature of Renqvist's language has, however, been somewhat exaggerated. Renqvist's orthographic conservatism is easy to recognise, but already on the morphological level there are some eastern Finnish features in his language. This should not be at all surprising, since Renqvist came from this area. Traditional western features are still dominant in his language, however.[8] By creating and circulating books which were close both in content and style to previous religious literature, revivalist clergymen like Renvall not only activated their own command of Finnish, which in these circles was clearly improving,[9] but they managed to reactivate the tradition of Old Literary Finnish. The common people, whose contacts with the literary type of language had been very limited, did not create a written language of their own from scratch on the basis of their spoken dialects, but rather adapted the old literary language at least as the basis of their own literary attempts. Nordlund (2007) has stressed that even the people who had received no formal education clearly tried to write standard language rather than dialect in their writing efforts, though the results also contained dialectal features. Later on, the literary language started to change also in religious usage, not only because of the pressure caused by the quicker development of secular Finnish at that time, but also because of processes inherent in the linguistic culture created by the revivalist groups.

Paavo Ruotsalainen, Awakenism and the Oral Culture of Revivalist Movements

The culture of the revivalists was originally more oral than written, not only because illiteracy was so common, but also because the Christian tradition which had prevailed in Finland for centuries had never relied solely on written material; it was usual for the word to be transmitted orally, by preaching, praying and singing. Because of this tradition, even those revivalists who were unable to read could nevertheless preach and teach the Bible.

It is another question how this situation affected the rather complicated and for most Finns already difficult Old Literary Finnish. Where contact with the literary tradition was mostly only oral, those features of the literary tradition which were merely visual could not survive. In Old Literary Finnish there were still "silent letters" and sounds which were spelt in several different ways but pronounced the same. When people learnt not only to read but also to write, in circumstances where the amount of literature was rather limited, the spoken form of the language tended to have a strong effect on the written form. This contributed to the simplification of the orthography which was taking place, especially through the first half of the 19th century. And where orally transmitted religious tradition was affected by features of local dialects, even the morphology and syntax began to change.

These processes can be followed by examining private and handwritten materials like the letters of Paavo Ruotsalainen, covering the time from the late 1820s to his death in 1852.[10] This material, forming one of the most important revivalist documents in Finland, is of a special nature, however. Ruotsalainen, lacking formal education, was able to read, but his writing abilities were quite limited, so he did not write his letters himself but dictated them to scribes. There are a number of special problems in this kind of material, but even from dictated letters you can see how the old language based on the Bible and the western dialects had begun to evolve in new directions. The orthographical variation in these letters is considerable, mirroring the varying abilities and intentions of Ruotsalainen's scribes. In some letters the eastern Finnish phonetical characteristics, no doubt typical of Ruotsalainen's own language, have been preserved quite well. In most cases, however, scribes have normalised the dialect, which has brought to the text both phonological and morphological features which were too literary for Ruotsalainen to have used them (Lauerma 2008b, 74–82).[11]

Syntactically, Ruotsalainen's letters vary from meticulously recorded free speech to a decidedly literary type of language. This reflects the fact that many letters have been copied and re-copied, which was common practice in 19th-century Pietistic circles (e.g. Kukkonen in Ruotsalainen 1977, 15). Revivalist culture activated thus not only the reading but also the writing skills of its members in a way which led to a more standardised form of literary expression, where both the old-fashioned literary features and overtly dialectal forms tended to be replaced with more novel and acceptable variants (Lauerma 2008b, 82–84).

Letters were not the only way Paavo Ruotsalainen took care of his fellow revivalists' spiritual lives. Ruotsalainen was also a keen traveller who kept contact also with those who lived far away. The verb *reisuta* ("to travel") is in fact strikingly common in Ruotsalainen's letters (Lauerma 2008b, 74), even though travelling was not common – and not always even permitted – in those days. Rural culture in Finland, as elsewhere, was originally very local; people had contact only with the local centres of the parishes, very seldom with more distant places. Revivalism was the first movement which broke the chains of that immobility. Revivalists organised meetings attended by people from other villages, parishes and eventually even from other parts of Finland. And when people gathered, different dialects came into contact and mingled, especially after the original awakening began in the 1830s to spread from Savolax to Ostrobothnia (Lauerma 2001, 575–576).

Glimpses of Ostrobothnian Revivalism: Kemelli and Ingman

In 1831–1832 revivalism reached the Kalajoki region on the coast of northern Ostrobothnia. One of its new followers was Klaus Kemelli (1805–1832), a local chaplain who had become famous as a poet and a translator of Bellman. Before his early death, Kemelli managed to translate *De Imitatione Christi* by Thomas à Kempis. The book was published posthumously in 1836 under the title *Kristuksen Seuraamisesta*. In this book Kemelli abandons the language and style of Old Literary Finnish, which was still used in religious literature, and writes using many features from the dialects of Central Ostrobothnia and Oulu (Lauerma 2001, 561–567).[12]

Kemelli's translation became very popular, especially in Ostrobothnia. Anders Wilhelm Ingman (1819–1877), a contemporary theologian and translator of the Bible, claimed that leading local parsons abandoned the old religious language and started using the language people spoke around them in their sermons, after the model of Kemelli. Certain poetical and vernacular traits found in some religious writers by the late 1830s can be seen to have been influenced by Kemelli's language rather than by Lönnrot's Kalevala, published in 1835, though they may also have arisen independently in cases like the sermons of revivalist leader Nils Gustaf Malmberg (1807–1858), praised for their rich language and command of expressions found in different dialects. Kemelli, however, was the first author who showed that it was acceptable to use partially dialect-based language even in religious literature. This opened the gates to linguistic innovations previously restricted to secular literature only, especially after Renvall's plea in 1837 (Lauerma 2001, 573–574). From the 1840s, even Renqvist started to modernise the language in his books to a certain extent (cf. endnote 8).

More progress was seen in Ingman's own works. Together with Frans Oskar Durchman (1813–1880) and aided by some men close to Kemelli, Ingman translated Luther's *Der Kirchen-Postille* ("A collection of Church Homilies"), which was published as *Kirkko-Postilla* in two parts 1848–1851. The language of this work reveals some features typical of southern or northern Ostrobothnian dialects, as well as some stylistic features familiar from Kemelli's language, but above all the language of this book shows how close to secular literature the religious language had come in its development (Lauerma 2001, 571–572).[13]

In the next decade, Ingman was given the task of revising the language of the Finnish Bible. The Lizelius version of the Bible was published in a revised edition in 1853, but the revisions were almost exclusively restricted to the orthography (Rapola 1965, 79, 82, 83, 95) with one morphological change, the adaptation of the inessive ending with geminate *s* (Lauerma 2004, 164). Ingman's linguistic alterations in his Bible revision are quite conservative, particularly if one compares them with his previous Luther translation. In the vocabulary and the style of especially some parts of the Old Testament, which Ingman worked through last, there are, however, features of Kalevala style such as extended alliteration, which in Ingman's case is a legacy more from Kemelli than from Lönnrot.[14] This aroused indignation, and Ingman's version of the Bible, the so-called *Koetusraamattu* ("A Trial Bible"), published in 1857–1859, was never officially accepted, though it became rather popular. The disapproval was partly political. Ingman turned against Nils Gustaf Malmberg, the leader of the Awakenist branch of revivalism, and the Awakenists consequently turned their back on Ingman's literary work. Later on, Ingman, who became a professor of exegetics, grew alienated from Awakenism, but his interest in the development of literary Finnish remained active, leading him finally to a bitter controversy with August Ahlqvist (1826–1889), professor of Finnish language. All this has caused the memory of Ingman to fade, though his work formed an important link between earlier Ostrobothnian revivalism and later Bible revisions.

Conclusions and New Movements

The legacy of the 19th-century revivalist movements to the development of literary Finnish is twofold, activating the tradition of Old Literary Finnish among the previously semi-literate rural population of especially eastern and northern areas, but also encorporating into it linguistic innovations of the secular literature. These processes proceeded hand in hand with the general development of written Finnish, mirroring not only the growing literacy, but also the impact of the very same dialects.

Though revivalism began in westernmost Finland already in the 18th century, this does not seem to have affected Old Literary Finnish very deeply, because the revivalists of western Finland used dialects which resembled the accepted (dialectally western) literary language of that time. The later work of the "Ostrobothnian Mystics" could have had more influence, but due to political and religious restrictions they had to work secretly, and their influence was therefore less obvious. Their work, however, may partly explain the important role of relatively distant Ostrobothnia in the development of literary Finnish in the next century. The northern dialects started to influence literary Finnish a little later (from the last years of the 1820s onwards, when books were printed and a weekly newspaper started to appear in Oulu) than the eastern dialects did (nearly a decade earlier), but the impact of northern dialects managed to level out the differences between the old western type and the most radical eastern type of linguistic usage. It should be remembered that Lönnrot, who had worked in the northern areas, was also influenced by some features of these dialects in his own language.

It is hardly a coincidence that the extending of the dialectal background of the literary language followed a geographical pattern similar to that of the revivalist movements. The spreading of revivalism to eastern Finland through leaders like Renqvist and Ruotsalainen activated the use and knowledge of western-based Old Literary Finnish among the east Finnish common people. On the other hand, the growing literacy among the rural common people whose own dialects differed strongly from the old biblical language also guaranteed that the old literary language could not remain unaffected, especially when the rich oral culture of revivalist groups started to have an influence of its own. When the Awakenist-type of revivalism spread into central and northern (and later especially to southern) Ostrobothnia, the northern dialects had their share in this development, especially after Kemelli's example made the use of dialectal language acceptable to revivalists. This line of development continued in Ingman's work and finally in the later revisions of the Bible. All this supported the prevailing tendencies of secular language development which largely led to the survival of only those (diachronically) eastern Finnish features which were also in use in northern dialects. This finally explains why so few eastern Finnish features survived into modern literary Finnish (Lauerma 2008a, 370).

In the latter part of the 19th century the revivalist movements could no longer have the same impact on linguistic development. The situation and inner state of the movements had also changed. The Prayerist movement gradually became marginalised. The activities in the Awakenist movement were – after Ruotsalainen's death and Malmberg's disgrace – for a long time quite subdued. The evangelical movement, which had separated from Awakenism as early as in the 1840s, was, however, growing, and spreading also to the Swedish-speaking coastal areas (e. g. Murtorinne 2000, 115–121).[15] From the 1860s on in the far north, originally in Swedish Lapland, there emerged yet another new revivalist movement called Laestadionism. Especially in its northern areas of origin, this movement helped its members to become more literate and – outside the borders of Finland – also clearly supported the preservation of both the Finnish and the Sami languages. No wonder that this revivalist movement had, though later, a role in the establishment of new literary variants of Finnish, such as *meänkieli* (lit. "our language"). This new literary language based on Finnish dialects spoken in Swedish Lapland preserves many linguistically archaic features, not only because of limited contacts with standard Finnish, but also because of uninterrupted use of old religious books and translations stemming from the 19th century (like the oeuvre of Laestadius) and even farther back (the old Finnish Bible translation of 1776 is still actively used).[16] In this way *meänkieli* also gives a hint of the kind of regionally based literary languages that could have emerged on Finnish soil too, if the impact of revivalist movements had not eventually coincided with both the dialectal and intentional development of literary Finnish in a way that finally led to the preservation of an undivided, but only moderately revised, literary Finnish.

Notes

1. On Old Literary Finnish e.g. Ikola 1962, c.f. Häkkinen 1994 and 1998; on Agricola's language e.g. Magoun 1967, on Finnish dialects Hormia 1978. The literature on the Finnish literary language is written almost exclusively in Finnish, especially larger treatises (of which Rapola 1965 and Häkkinen 1994 are the most eminent, though there is new information also in text books such as Lehikoinen & Kiuru 1998 and Pulkkinen 1972). In view of this, I have focused the research literature used in my present article to smaller studies published in English, German or Swedish and to those Finnish articles which have a summary in one or another of these languages.
2. On the Finnish language in the 18th century e.g. Häkkinen 1995 and 2006; on Herder's influence c.f. also Riikonen 2006; on Porthan Ikola 1983.
3. On language politics in Finland during the autonomy e.g. Klinge 1985.
4. On the development of Finnish literary language in the first half of the 19th century Häkkinen 1994, 447–449 and 1998; Lauerma 2004; on Lönnrot Häkkinen 2002; on Renvall Lauerma 2005.
5. On popular education and literacy in Finland e.g. Mäkinen 1997, 61–67, 445; c.f. Luttinen 1984.
6. On the beginnings of revivalism and its background e. g. Laasonen 2000, 268–279; Murtorinne 2000, 77–90. There is a shorter presentation of Finnish church history in German (Heininen & Heikkilä 2002, on revivalism cf. especially 131–136, 150–160), but not in English. Some brief descriptions of revivalism are to be found in works like Sinnemäki 1973, 15–16.
7. On Renqvist and Ruotsalainen and their times e.g. Murtorinne 2000, 90–102.
8. In my studies on the orthographical and morphological change of Early Modern Finnish (Lauerma 2007 and 2008a, revised and enlarged edition 2012) I have followed the progress encountered in all substantial printed books published from 1800 to 1843 (of religious books until 1848). Thus I have studied some basic changes also in Renqvist's books, though based on short samples only. Renqvist maintains the old orthography with its *x*:s, *tz*:s and more frequent use of voiced stops until 1843, thus reflecting the revision made in the Finnish Hymn Book version of 1841, though in the Bible these changes were made as late as 1852–1853. Morphologically some clearly eastern features, like the allative endings with *llen*, are characteristic to Renqvist's books from 1830s on, but from the 1840s on he seems to abandon the 3rd pers. imperfect and conditional plural ending *vat, vät*, which he has occasionally used in his books, in favour of the traditional ending with *t* only. On the other hand, the personal endings *mma, mmä* and especially *tta, ttä* of 1st and 2nd pers. plural were in at least partial use in Renqvist's books from the beginning, nor did they disappear later.
9. Lauerma 2006; on the language choice among the clergy c.f. Saari 2001.
10. These letters have been published in various editions (the most recent one, Ruotsalainen 2005, is by Elenius; Ruotsalainen 1977 is a selection in English made by Kukkonen).
11. E.g. the letter *x* is used also in some late letters, reflecting how the different scribes confuse the chronological changes in the material. The *tz*-digraph (instead of later *ts*) is, however, practically unknown in Ruotsalainen's letters. This is explainable chronologically (in the published Finnish literature *tz* was already rare in the 1820s), but this may also tell how alienating the *tz*-grapheme could have been to the speakers whose own pronunciation would have been *ts* or more probably *tt* or *ht*. On one hand, there are orthographical features like gradational forms with *d*, which can only be scribal solutions (there is no *d* in eastern Finnish dialects). Morphologically, a feature of this type is the old western-type inessive ending with *sa, sä* (in eastern dialects *ssa, ssä*). On the other hand, letters reveal also forms like

pronominal accusative endings with *t*, which were only rarely used in the first half of the 19th century (especially in religious language) and whose origin must therefore be in the dialect used by Ruotsalainen or his scribe.

12 Orthographically Kemelli already follows modern conventions which were just breaking through in the religious literature of the 1830s, but there are far more colloquialisms than in the average secular literature of that time. Even *d* is sometimes missing and *ht* and *tt* (in prolative also *t*) are used instead of *ts*. The forms of the negation verb begin with *e*, as in eastern dialects, and there are also features typical of geographically very restricted areas, like instances of special gemination. The abessive ending is with geminated *t*, as is typical of northern dialects. There are also some instances of accusative ending *t* in plural personal pronouns. The 3rd pers. plural ending is *vat*, *vät* also in the imperfect and conditional. In some cases Kemelli seems to follow the norms of (secular) literary language instead of dialectal usage: e.g. inessive case is rarely without double *s*. It is in any case noteworthy that some features like the allative ending with final *n* and the endings of 1st and. 2nd pers. plural with end vowel *a*, *ä*, which were not uncommon at the time but disappeared later from literary Finnish, seem to be missing in Kemelli's language.

13 In this translation of Luther's sermons there are illative forms with *h* (typical of Ostrobothnian dialects, but slowly disappearing from literary language) and abessive endings with geminate *t*, which were in the religious prose published in 1848 typical of only the works of northern writers (c.f. Lauerma 2008a, 363 footnote 10). Orthographically the work is more standardised than Kemelli's Thomas à Kempis translation of 1836, but morphologically slightly more conservative (there seem to be no accusative endings with *t*).

14 In the Bible revised by Ingman in 1857–1859, the forms of the negated verb begin with *ä*, the abessive ending is with single *t* and the ending of 3rd pers. plural of imperfect and conditional is only *t* instead of *vat*, so the revision appears more western and traditional than the Luther translation of Ingman and his friends in 1848 or the work of Kemelli published in 1836. The neglect and even ignorance of Ingman's work is seen from the fact that all major treatises on Finnish literary language seem to confuse Ingman's Bible edition of 1857–1859 with those Bible translations which he published in his later years, 1868–1877, and which on the whole show undeniably exaggerated use of alliteration.

15 There seem to be no linguistic studies on the language of Fredrik Gabriel Hedberg (1811–1893), the founder of the evangelical movement, except some remarks on the choice between Finnish and Swedish in his activities (Schmidt 1948, 37, 172–174, 253, 271, 277–280, 305; some reinterpretations and comparisons are made in Lauerma 2006). Because Hedberg's earliest Finnish works reveal certain middle Ostrobothnian features (he was born in Saloinen near Raahe, in the same area as Kemelli), it is possible that his work also formed a channel by which certain northern dialectal features were absorbed in the gradually standardising literary language.

16 On the impact of Laestadionism on varieties of Finnish spoken in northern Sweden e.g. Winsa 1998, 106–109.

Lea Laitinen & Taru Nordlund

Language from Below?
Indexing Identities in the Writings of Common People in 19th-Century Finland

In the present article, various linguistic approaches will be applied to texts written by common people in Finland in the 19th century, and some recurring linguistic features found in these texts will be analysed. Writings of self-educated, non-elite people have predominantly been an object of study in historical sociolinguistics, which, like other fields of study, attempts to look at events *from below*. In recent years, sociolinguistics has been extended in two directions. In one of them, specific features of language have been interpreted at a micro level, from an interactional point of view. In the other, their use as a means of creating linguistic identities and socio-cultural meanings has been analysed with tools originating in linguistic anthropology. Our aim is to illustrate the possibilities that these two approaches open up for the study of the self-educated writers' language and their texts, using as our data a number of corpora of letters.

In describing the language of self-educated writers, we will first discuss the terms *intended standard* and *audience design* as well as *stylistic rupture* and *pre-textual gap*. The former two concern the intentions of the sender of the message, whereas the latter two focus on the point of view of the recipient; both these approaches are easily guided by the point of view of *from above*, however. Following the discussion of these concepts, we will examine formulae taken from the standard language which the self-educated writers used as a resource for making meaning but which have often been characterised in research from the perspective of the educated classes. Finally, we will address the question of how the linguistic structures that index local and national communities were standardised, and how this process is reflected in the language of self-educated common people.

Theoretical Starting Points

Language is a social phenomenon. This basic tenet of sociolinguistics lies in the premise that social factors influence the ways language varies and changes. These principles are also present in historical sociolinguistics, which focuses on earlier speech communities. Human languages have not, in the course of their history, been crucially different from the languages of today. Languages have always been spoken in speech communities, and the use of language has always been socially meaningful (Nevalainen & Raumolin-Brunberg 2003, 22). Traditionally, sociolinguists have used spoken language as their data. Among other things, they have looked into the ways in which the age, profession or social status of the speakers influence their language use. Recently, there has been more and more research on language used in interaction and on the possibilities speakers have to reflect different identities through utilising various linguistic features (Omoniyi & White 2006, 1–2). These kinds of issues can be studied from written data as well. Research has shown that it is in speech that changes typically start, however, whereas stability is one of the basic properties of written language, which has often been consciously standardised. In fact, one of the main aims of 19th century nationalistic language ideology was to create a standard language with a minimum of variation (Paunonen 2006; Kroskrity 2003a).

Letters are a common form of data for historical sociolinguistics. Letters represent interaction across time and distance, and as texts they have often been formed to mimic the course of spoken interaction (Fitzmaurice 2002, 38). In addition, with respect to their linguistic features, they often resemble spoken language more than other texts. Letters are suitable data for the study of self-educated writers as they have a fairly clear overall structure and many fixed formulae. Through them it is possible to trace the writers' background, for example, and to study writing as a social practice (Laitinen & Nordlund 2012).

The language of the lower classes with little or no schooling has usually been compared to spoken language such as local dialects and to the standard languages that were developed partly on the basis of vernaculars. Standardisation was carried out by the literate upper classes in the 19th century to meet nationalistic goals (cf. Vandenbussche 2007, Nordlund 2005, 2007.) The relations between vernacular and standard languages and their history is currently being studied within linguistic anthropology, which used to focus predominantly on the lexis and grammar of "exotic" languages used in "unwritten" cultures and to collect traditional narratives of local communities. Subsequently, the semiotic-functional approach has led anthropologists study the pragmatic or indexical meanings of linguistic structures tied to the context of the speech event (Silverstein 2003, Pressman 1994, Kroskrity 2003b, Woolard 2008). Indexical meanings also lead a linguist to analyse the reflexivity and the metapragmatic level of language – the way in which language refers to itself and creates itself in the course of verbal interaction – and to study the limits of the speakers' linguistic awareness. Here, typical topics of research are discourses and ideologies, their relations to the institutions of power as well as the linguistic formation of national, local, ethnic or multilingual identities in different kinds of communities (e.g. Blommaert & Verschueren 1998, Kroskrity 2003a, Lucy 2003, Silverstein 1998, 2007).

Texts by self-educated writers are highly relevant objects of research when discussing 19th century linguistic and national ideologies, being located at the interface of many dichotomies: in the border area between lower and higher classes, local and national identities, free and standardised language as well as oral and written expression. Of course, the form of language always varies from situation to situation, and the way in which the self-educated wrote was influenced by the recipient and by the speech community they happened to belong to or identify themselves with, among other things.

The Language of the Self-educated and the Intended Standard

Looking at what kinds of language variety the self-educated have aimed at in their writing, researchers in different countries have come to very similar conclusions. It has been observed that the writers did not use their own local variant but were aiming instead at some kind of standard through the use of forms and structures belonging to the public language: a so-called *intended standard*. This term refers to a variant used in the functions of the standard which does not fulfil all its formal criteria (Vandenbussche 2004, 30).[1] We will illustrate this phenomenon with some business letters from 1812–1828 (for more thoroughgoing discussion, cf. Nordlund 2005, 2007). These letters were sent by eastern Finnish farmers to the Bergbom trading house in Oulu, on the west coast Finland, concerning the trade of agricultural products such as butter, tar and hides (cf. Kauranen 1999). Here is one example:

(1)
1   Hyvin Kunioitettava Herra Patr(...) ja Herr Hantels manen
2   Minä Rukoilisin Kaicein Nöyrimästi Jos mahtollinen olis Että Tietusta Nijtä minun wähiä
3   asioitani minä Nijn Kuin Yxi Teitän Nöyrä Palvelianne Tahtoisin Tietusta Kuinga on sen
4   anters Lintuisen asian Kansa ongo se   Tullud oikeuten Etein Eli Ei mohoxen Pitäiäsä Ja
5   Käräiä Paikasa Nyd wimesesä syys Käräiäsä sillä minä olen Ne Kiria Lähettänyd oikialla
6   aialla mohoxein
7   Sixi Toisexi minä Rukoilisin Että annaisitte Tietä mitä Makxa Tänä Talvena Woi: ja Tali ja
8   Nahka värki ja Läsci ja Rawas Sika Eli mikä Tavara Kuin maasa Kävis Tänä Talvena =
9   minä Rukoilen Kaikcein Nöyrimästi Herr Patron olkad Nijn Hywa ja wastakad Tämän
10 Kirien Päällen minä Nijn Totta Kuin Herra Elä Olen maxava Teitän welkanne ja
11 waiwanne mitä Te Kulutatte Näisä asioisa: Eimitän Tällä Kerralla wain Tuhannen palion
12 Terveysi
13 annettu Liexasta sinä 9. päiwä Desem: 1816.
14 Matts Pakarin

1   Most Respectful Mr Patr-- and Mr Merc hant
2   I Would Beg Most Humbly If it were possible to Inquire after my minor matters
3   As A Humble Servant of Yours I would like to Inquire
4   After anters Lintuinen's case if it has been Brought To justice Or Not in

          the Parish of muhos
5   in the District Court Sessions during autumn as I have sent
          Those Documents
6   in due time to muhos
7   and Another Thing I would Beg That you let me Know the Price of
          Butter, Tallow and
8   Hides and Fat and Pork That is what kind of Commodity is Needed
          This Winter
9   I Beg you Most Humbly Mr Patron please answer
10   This Letter as Truly as Lord Lives I Will pay back Your loan
11   and the trouble that you have in These matters: Nothingelse This time
          but Thousands of
12   Greetings
13   from Lieksa the 9. day Decem: 1816.
14   Matts Pakarin(en)

Example 1 shows in many ways how eastern Finnish farmers were aiming at writing old literary Finnish, so-called *Biblical Finnish*, which had been developed on the basis of western dialects during the time Finland formed part of the Swedish kingdom (ca.1540–1809) and was heavily influenced by Swedish. In this letter there are several Swedish features, such as the adpositional structure found in lines 9–10 *wastakad Tämän Kirien Päällen* (Sw. svara *på brevet* "answer [on] this letter"), and the use of an indefinite and a definite article: line 3 *Yxi Teitän Nöyrä Palvelianne* (Sw. *en* ödmjukast tjänare av Er, "*a* most obedient servant of Yours") and line 13 *sinä 9. päiwä Desem: 1816* (Sw. den 9. Dagen, "*the* 9th day"). In present day language these are all considered to be against non-standard. The farmers who sent the letters did not usually know Swedish themselves but had learned it only indirectly, which can be seen by how they spelled proper names, for example. There are also many features of Biblical language which originate in western Finnish dialects, as in (1), line 4 the local case form *Pitäiäsä* instead of *Pitäjässä* ("in the parish").

It is noticeable that there are hardly any features from the farmers' own vernacular functioning as *indicators* of dialectal variation (Labov 1971), or as *first-order indexes* of membership in the local speech community (Silverstein 2003). Instead, in order to position themselves in a suitable way in the transaction, these eastern writers formulated the style of their business letters with features from Biblical Finnish. These kinds of linguistic forms which show stylistic variation and signal the identity adopted by the speaker in the speech situation are called *markers* (Labov, *op. cit.*) or *second-order indexes* (Silverstein, *ibid.*).

The written or literary tradition behind the letters of the eastern Finnish farmers becomes particularly conspicuous when their language is compared to the letters that the so-called Forest Finns, descendants of Finnish emigrants to Sweden and Norway, were sending to the linguist and folklorist Carl Axel Gottlund in Finland at about the same time. The Forest Finns' ancestors had moved from eastern Finland to central Scandinavia in the 16th and 17th centuries and had lived for a long time isolated from Finnish culture. There were naturally Swedish loan words in these 19th century letters, but also consistently eastern Finnish and even more extensive features of spoken vernaculars, which were often presented in the letters with phonetic spelling (Nordlund 2007, Laitinen & Nordlund 2008). When the letters by the eastern Finnish farmers living in the Grand Duchy of Finland and those of the Forest Finns of central Scandinavia are compared with each other, some differences can be noticed between their solutions in language use and possibly even between their linguistic awareness. The farmers who lived in the tradition of Biblical Finnish knew what written language looked like and attempted to follow this tradition. The Forest Finns of Scandinavia had hardly any experience of written Finnish and no public model such as Biblical Finnish to go by in producing their own texts.

(2)
1   Hyvin Kunioitettava Herra C:A: Gottlund
2   Minä Tykkeän paljon hyvin kuin mä Suomenkielisiä kirjoja saisin; Van *teällä* on niin
3   harva joka niitä taita Lukea, *Van Ejkös nuo tok taitas oppia*! Lähätä heita kuitenkiin,
4   kyllä minä heista Rahat talven ajkaan kahvoaan *Koarloistahaan*. –
5   N̄ Nyt luulen, etta me tuulemmä kokoon Reholtassa huomen aamulla, niin saame
6   yli tehta, jos tahtoivat panna Rahoja Suomen Tidninkihiin. –
7   Saanotaan että anti Porka on saanut Rukiinsa jalleen Sater Pekalta.
8   Öijerissä sina 22 p: Novemb kuussa 1821.
9   *Puavo* Räisäinen.

1   Most Respectful Mr. C.A. Gottlund
2   I would really Love to get Finnish books; But here are so
3   few (people) who are able to Read them. *But Wouldn't those probably learn!* Send them
4   anyway, I'll charge the Money in winter time in *Karlstad*. –
5   Now I think that we'll come together in Revholt tomorrow morning, so we can
6   work over time (?) if they wanted to pay Money for the Finnish Newspaper. –
7   They say that Antti Porkka has received his Rye again from Pekka Säteri.
8   In Öijer the 22 day November 1821
9   *Paavo* Räisänen

This letter by a Forest Finn called Paavo Räisänen has in its date (line 8) the same kind of definite article as the preceding letter: *sinä 22. p: Novemb kuussa 1821* ("the 22th day in November 1821"). On the other hand, there are many phonetic features of Savolax dialect that can be taken as indicators of the membership of the writers in their own community. For example, the long vowel *ää* is represented by the diphthong *eä* (line 2) in *teällä* (standard Fi *täällä* "here"), and the long vowel *aa* as *oa* (line 4) in the place name *Koarloistahaan* (pro *Kaarloistaan*-; cf. Sw. place name *Karlstad*) and in the proper name *Poavo* (line 9 pro *Paavo*). An example of eastern Finnish dialect syntax is the exclamation *Van Eijkös nuo tok taitas oppia!* ("But surely they would learn to read!") in line 3, where apart from the form of negative question *ei-kös* ("not-if") there is also the particle *tok* "surely" and the pronoun *nuo* "those". What is also missing in the language of the Forest Finnish letters is perhaps the most distinctive grammatical feature of standard Finnish – the convention dating back to the 16th century to refer to 3rd person human beings with the pronoun *hän* "s/he".[2] The self-educated writers that lived within the area of Finland aimed at following this written language norm at least in their official letters (cf. Laitinen 2009). In the spoken vernacular and in present day informal spoken language, a person is quite generally referred to with the 3rd person pronoun *se* "s/he; it",[3] whereas the pronoun *hän* has a function of its own, i.e. it is logophoric (Laitinen 2005). Finnish grammarians noted this division of labour between these pronouns already in 19th century syntax. The next example is taken from one of these grammars (Setälä 1883).

(3)
Se sano, että kyllä *hän* tiätää mitä se tekee
S/he$_1$ said that surely s/he$_1$ (the same person) knows what s/he$_2$ (another person) is doing

The index ($_1$) in the English translation marks the fact that the pronoun *hän* refers to the same person as the pronoun *se* in the main clause. The latter *se* refers to a different person, marked with an index ($_2$). In other words, the task of the pronoun *hän* is to indicate that the speaker has said something about her/himself in particular: it is an index of the participation status in the speech event.[4] In narratives, *hän* often conveys the perspective of the main character. The next example is from a letter in 1842 by the self-educated Mats Matinpoika Varilainen to his brother Anders Warilainen (Warelius), who had risen to the literate class. Here, the pronoun *hän* refers to the main protagonist in the story, the neighbour's hired man ($_2$), from whose point of view the situation is narrated, while the pronoun *se* is used of the old man ($_1$), who is only treated as an object of observation.

(4)
1   (…) nin isändä eli faari oli kans kohta minun peräsäni lähtenu kylän toisalle päin, tappelua
2   haastaman nin ojansun drengi oli näyttäny että voima ja urholisutta oli naapurisa ette sitä
3   tarvitte kauka hake, mutta ei *hän* sendä kovin pidelly sillä *hän* katto meijän faarin nin ylön
4   ette *se* olisi *hänen* käsisänsä kestäny (…).

(…) so the master or old man$_1$ had also gone soon after me to the village the other direction, to pick a fight, so the hired man$_2$ of Ojansuu had shown that there is strength and bravery next door, that you don't have to search for it far away, but he$_2$ (*hän*) didn't at least handle [him$_1$] badly, because he$_2$ (*hän*) looked down on our old man so that he$_1$ (*se*) couldn't cope in his$_2$ (*hän*) hands (…).

In Standard Finnish *hän* distinguishes human beings unambiguously from other entities irrespective of context, whereas in the vernacular the referent is not necessarily a human being. The narrator can refer with it also to speechless persons like babies or animals when s/he is interpreting their motives, thoughts or understandable behaviour in some event. This difference could be characterised as a difference between "world views" in written and spoken Finnish, if we stayed on the level of the denotative code, in semantic meanings, which are context independent (cf. Silverstein 1998, 422). It is more important to note, however, that in the written language, the meaning of *hän* is purely semantic whereas in spoken language it gets its meaning pragmatically, depending on the conditions of the narrated speech event.

The logophoric *hän* belonged to the language spoken by the Forest Finns. Examples such as the following (5) were still attested in the latter half of the 19th century from the last speakers of this variety of Finnish.

(5)
Ne sae papin$_1$ sinne, van *se*$_1$ sano, jotta *hän*$_1$ ei taija tehä mitää. Pappi$_1$ ei jelpan(n)na mitää; *se*$_1$ ol' sluutti (Mägiste 1960: 125).

They managed to have the priest there but he (*se*) said that he (*hän*) cannot do anything. The priest did not help; he (*se*) was finished.

In the letters received from the Forest Finns by Gottlund, this kind of division of labour between the pronouns *se* and *hän* was also observed, as Mari Myllynen (2010) has shown. Thus, this contrast must have existed in the Finnish vernacular from the 16th century. Example (6) is from 1822 (Myllynen op. cit. 52):

(6)
Minä olin puupoista Huitkernitä puhutelu, ja se pyysi minun Kieriutaman *Hänen Estän*. *Hän* tahtois tietoa, toko yhtään protokoliia tahika Raia Kierioa löytys, joka selitäis Kuinka Loava Huitkernin mehtä oli Kuin se wuona 1649 weroilen pantin, (…).

I did speak with Puupoinen$_1$ from Hvitkärn, and he$_1$ (*se*) asked me to write on his$_1$ (*hänen*) behalf. He$_1$ (*hän*) would like to know, if there could be found any protocol or boundary minutes that would explain how big the wood of Hvitkärn was when it was taxed (...).

The phonological and morphological features as well as the grammar of person show that the Forest Finnish writers did not aim at the Finnish standard but wrote the kind of language that they used in speaking. In other words, the language of the letters indicated their membership in the local speech community. They were, however, also encouraged to do this by Carl Axel Gottlund, who in his own writings used a variety adapted from the eastern Finnish dialects,[5] and in this case the choice could be interpreted as a (second-order) index of their orientation to the discourse of the letter; the concept *intended standard* might therefore mean aiming at Gottlund's variety. The recipient of the text – his position and the variety he himself would use – was relevant when the self-educated writers adopted the linguistic form of their texts.

Audience Design and Textual Expectations

In the letters sent by the Savolax farmers to the Bergbom trading house, written language is discernible throughout, and not just in the linguistic detail: with respect to their genre, they were letters, which means that they obeyed the essential conventions of letter writing. In addition, they represented the style of official letters to business associates. They were written in a respectful manner, and the conventions of politeness closely resembled those of Swedish business letters of the period:

(7)
(Finnish) *Minä Rukoilisin Kaicein Nöyrimästi* Jos mahtollinen olis Että Tietusta Nijtä minun wähiä asioitani.
I would Beg Most Humbly If it were possible To Inquire for These minor matters of mine.

(Swedish) *Jag skulle be ödmjukast* att Herr Handelsman vore af den godheten och skulle skrifva.
I would beg most humbly that Mr. Merchant would be so kind as to write.

From the point of view of the eastern Finnish farmers, Mr. Bergbom the merchant was an important person and a valuable business associate. The letters reflected the social inequality between the writer and the recipient. The concept *intended standard* implicitly suggests that the speaker or writer takes into consideration the recipient. It is thus closely connected with *audience design*:[6] from the resources available to them, the writers choose the means suited to the current situation and adapt their style in accordance with the recipient (Bell 2001, 139–140).

As shown above, the style and variety of language used by the Forest Finns in their letter was adapted to suit the recipient, Carl Axel Gottlund. In example (8), the polite form of request addressed to Gottlund greatly resembles the formulations in (7), where the performative form ("I am asking"; see the next section) acts as an introduction to the 3rd person form used in address ("that Sir / He would like to do something"). This polite form of address may have been familiar to the writer from the surrounding Swedish and Norwegian culture. Otherwise, the style in the Finnish letters is clearly more familiar and closer to spoken language than in the business letters to Bergbom; in the letters sent in the early 19th century, respectful forms of address and closing formats were often missing. In that sense, the letter in (8) bears a closer resemblance to the letters between equals in the 19th century than to the business letters written by the farmers.

(8)
Barltden den 22. Aprill 1826.
Herra gottlundi!
Minä olin tulossa Tukullmin, wan kuin minä puhutelin Maaherroa Niin hän Lupaisi tehänsä kaik mittä kuninkas pyytä, Ja Mitä Hän ei pyytä sitä hän ei taita tehtä. *Nyt minä pyyän Herroa että hän teke niin hyvin ja krono prinsiltä kysy* tokko nämä Ruunun viliat on kuninkallta köyhillen jälken annetuxi tullut. (...)
Antti Porkka

Mr. gottlund!
IwascomingtoStockholm,butwhenIspoketotheGovernorSohePromisedtodoanything the king asks, And What He doesn't ask that he cannot do. *Now I am asking the Sir if he would be so kind and ask the crown prince* if this Crown corn is given by the king to the poor. (...)
Antti Porkka

When the speaker adapts his language or code according to the recipient, he simultaneously anticipates an answer. The concept *audience design* is thus connected to the dialogical nature of language (Bell 2001, 143–144). In this section, we will approach texts by self-educated writers from the listeners' point of view, focusing on the reception of the message and on the social evaluation of the language used in a communicative situation. The letters by these farmers can be characterised as institutional in that they have a specific function, recognised by both the sender and the recipient. It is typical of such texts to be fixed in form and wording. Various guides to letter and document writing published in the 19th century had a standarqising effect on texts with a specific institutional purpose, such as legal or financial documents. From a functional point of view, business letters by self-educated farmers also fulfilled their function e.g. as invitations for tenders, announcements or enquiries concerning joint transactions. The function of text (9) is also clear; this excerpt was discussed in Iisalo's (1992) research on literacy among sailors in Uusikaupunki, a town on the west coast of Finland. The letter concerns the granting of permission which Klara Packalen sent to her son, who had gone to sea:

(9)
tämän kauta annan minä luan minun pojalleni Johan Henrik Packalinilla että hän ensitulevan suven alla ja edespäin saa merellä mennä, joska joku hänellä kysyä antaa
Udesta kaupungista se 13 päivä Huhtikuta 1863
Klara Packalen

through this [paper] I permit my son Johan Henrik Packalin to go to sea before next summer and after, if someone asks him
From New town (Uusikaupunki) the 13th day April 1863
Klara Packalen

The text by Klara Packalen is clearly an institutional letter of permission, and it follows the structure presented in a guide to document writing published a couple of years later by Jaako Länkelä (1865): it states 1) about whom something is testified (the writer's son Johan Packalen), 2) what is testified about him (that he may go to sea), 3) when does this testimony take place (in Uusikaupunki April 13th 1863) and 4) who is testifying (Klara Packalen, Johan's mother). The writer is clearly familiar with the social conventions and is to some extent aware of the linguistic choices she is making. Iisalo (*op.cit.*) characterised texts of this kind as linguistically and stylistically primitive, and similar evaluations of texts by self-educated writers have been presented in the scholarly literature every now and then. The texts are considered to fulfil the requirements of well-formedness in some respects but not altogether, as if they had attempted to imitate a certain genre but succeeded only in part. This feature of text by self-educated writers associated with a stumbling style or one that is not entirely suited to the context has been called *stylistic rupture* or *breakdown* (cf. e.g. Vandenbussche 1999, 53, 2007).[7] The term usually refers to a text which starts with a formula well suited to the situation but subsequently collapses, as it were, and does not keep up the style or register all the way through.

The farmers are also typically – although not always – more formal and formulaic in the introductory and closing lines of their letters. But this is only one part of the picture, as the business letter itself as a genre can display internal variation. This can be illustrated by looking at the different types of directives used in the Bergbom business letters (cf. Nordlund 2007). The invitations for tenders of the letters are usually quite similar in their structure and have several expressions of politeness, as in example 10a, where the request greatly resembles that of example 8. But when concrete practical guidance is offered, for example about paying or writing a letter, the writers typically use the plain imperative mood (10b), which is the 2nd person directive form without address terms.

(10)
a. *toivon ~ rukoilen nöyrimmästi* että herra Patruul olisi niin hyvä että kirjoittaisi, mitä maksaa leiviskä voita
I wish / beg humbly that Mr. Merchant would be so kind as to write to me what a pound of butter costs

b. *laittakaa* raha postiin ja kirje kiinni sinetillä
send the money by post and seal the letter

This kind of variation can be thought of as stylistic: after all, it is likely that it is precisely in official business acts that the writers would have a ready-made model to follow; since the correspondence was bidirectional, the writers may have used the letters they received from the trading house as their models. One could also describe it as topic driven: certain topics were discussed in certain ways and different directives were used in different kinds of activity types. Directives also differ according to what is being requested. It would be stylistically improper, for example, to use highly deferential forms in relatively unproblematic requests, such as *I would beg most humbly that Mr. Merchant be so kind as to seal the letter.

The stylistic variation in self-educated texts has also been described as hybridity. The texts often have traces of different genres, especially from religious texts, which were the texts most familiar to the writers. Preaching style was present in both letters and factual texts, and emigrant letters were for example often interspersed with quotes from the Bible, excerpts from hymnbooks and proverbs. Similar observations have been made of letters written by Scottish and German emigrants (Dossena 2007, Elspaß 1999). Hybridity has been approached from the point of view of genre awareness. Untrained writers are not as aware of different genres or their characteristics as are trained writers or those who have more contact with written culture. The resources available for literary production could be limited due to lack of schooling, with the borrowing from other genres as a likely option. In this sense, the writers of emigrant letters can be compared with learners of a new language who grow to the mastering of different genres bit by bit as they acquire the language (Kalliokoski 2006, 256, 262).

There was stylistic variation within a text as a whole when the writers used ready-made formulae and expressions in building their texts. According to Stephan Elspaß (2005, 180–181, 2012, 56), the initial and final formulae, Biblical quotations and fixed phrases functioned as building blocks with the help of which even a weaker writer could produce a full text. The image is somewhat unbalanced. As remarked by Silverstein (2003, 193–194), any indexical sign carries both presuppositions of the "appropriateness" of its usage in the context as well as contextual entailments, i.e. performative or "creative effects" in context. In the following section, we will show that the Finnish emigrants used this kind of formulation in a creative way for specific (meta-)pragmatic and textual functions.

Performativity of Immigrant Letters and the Rise of a Group Style

At the turn of the 20th century, approximately 400,000 people left Finland to emigrate to North America (Kero 1996, 54–55). Millions of letters crossed the ocean, a large number of which have been preserved in archives (Kero 1985). Many emigrants took up the pen for the first time in their lives to keep in contact with relatives and friends that were left behind. Emigrant letters offer interesting material for the study of identity building among self-educated writers. When taking to writing they had many kinds of linguistic resources available. As examples 7–10 above have shown, they had, as members of Finnish written culture, the possibility to make use of the expressive resources of the clerical and administrative language combined with their own vernacular. We will now illustrate the use of these different resources in the letters by taking up some recurrent performative formulae in the emigrant letters, which the writers used to create their own expressions for the maintenance of the interaction and the exchange of information.[8]

Performatives are linguistic expressions which describe the speaker's current speech acts and create new states of affairs. Those performatives that have a fixed format are used in different kinds of rituals, such as baptisms or weddings (Austin 1962, Agha 2007). They have the verb in the 1st person, such as the *I inform* in example (11). The letters to the emigrants about the news back home often begin with an explicit performative formulation:

(11)
(…) ja ilmoitan että nyt on oikia posti konttuuri täälä Jumpin talossa ja nyt tulee kaikki kirjeet tänne ettei tarvite porista noutaa oli mitä tahansa (J. Heinonen 10.3.1890)
(…) and [I] inform that there is a real post office here in the house of Jumppi and now all letters come here so that we need not pick up anything from pori

The explicit performative formulations in the emigrant letters resemble the structures of administrative language, which was familiar to the common people, as both local and state statues, announcements and orders were read aloud in the church every Sunday from the 16th century onwards (Villstrand 2008). Written notifications performed the function of oral mass media, whereby the communications and the orders of the king, later of the emperor, or the local administrator were spread to the common people (Tommila 1983, Reutersvärd 2001). In the following notification by the king of Sweden (12), given in Finnish, the 1st person form *me* "we" represents the so called royal plural:

(12)
An edict from Gustav II Adolf, King of Sweden in 1628:
Me Gustaff Adolph Jumalan armosta Ruotzin, Göthin ia Wendin, Cuningas, Suriförsti Suomen Maalle, Eestin maalle ja Carelin, Herra Ingermannin maalle etc. *Teemme tiettäväxi, että* (…).⁹

We, Gustaf Adolph, by the grace of God, the King of Sweden, Göta and Wendi, the Grand Duke for Finland, Estland and Karelia, the Overlord for Ingermanland, etc., *Make*$_{1PL}$ known [to you my subjects] *that* (…).

The members of the correspondence network made use of the formulae of the administrative language. They did not copy them mechanically, however, but combined the resources of spoken and written language in their letters. With the help of these performative structures two worlds were distinguished: the epistolary world and the world in which the events described in the letters took place. For this purpose the writers used the performative constructions of the old institutional written language on the one hand, and, on the other, the alternative structures of Finnish-language person marking.

In Finnish, person can be expressed both with the person suffix on the verb (e.g. 1st person singular *ilmoita-n* "I let know") and with a personal pronoun (e.g. *minä* "I"), so it is possible to tell about the events and situations of the speaker through two linguistic constructions: either by using just the verb with a person ending or by using both the pronoun and the verb. In the course of standardisation in the 19th-century these alternatives were separated into different varieties of language. In the Grand Duchy of Finland, which became an autonomous part of Russia in 1809, a new national written standard, ultimately modern Finnish, was in the process of being developed. In this variety, the plain verb alternative (*ilmoitan*) was recommended, while the construction with the pronoun (*minä ilmoitan*) belonged to the spoken vernacular[10] and to the old Biblical Finnish used in the Swedish kingdom in 1540–1809. Similar use of the pronoun is obligatory in Swedish grammar as well (cf. *jag tillkännagifver* "I let know"). In the 19th century, the new standard language distanced itself from all these varieties with respect to the use of the personal forms.

It is interesting to see how the letters of self-educated emigrant writers exploited all three varieties of Finnish: the performative formulations of the old Biblical Finnish as well as the personal forms of the vernacular and of the new standard. With these alternatives, they made a meaningful distinction in their double role of maintaining the written interaction (the so-called *writing self*) and as the protagonist in the story (the *narrative self*), whose acts, experiences and states they described in their letters. Example 13 will illustrate this state of affairs:

(13)
Rakas Weljeni Wilhem Kangas
Täsä lähestyn sinua Muutamalla sanalla ja ilmoitan että Minä olen terve ja voinu hyvin jota samaa toivoisin sinun ja kaikkien omaisieni saavan nauttia siälä synnyin Maasa *ja saan Ilmoitta* että Minä olen saanu kuulla surusia sanomia siältä kehuvat siälä hirveasti raivoovan Rupulin joka viäpi tu hansia tuanen tuville (...). (Antti Kangas 1882)

My dear brother Wilhelm Kangas
[I] *hereby approach you with a few words and inform* that I am healthy and have been feeling well and hope that you and all my relatives there in my native country have also enjoyed the same *and* [I] *may inform* that I have come to hear sad news from there and they tell that there is an epidemic of diarrhea that kills thousands of people (...).

On the level of interaction, in performing the world of writing, the subject pronoun is missing (*lähestyn sinua* (...) *ja ilmoitan* "[I] approach you (...) and inform"), but on the narrative level in telling the news it is present (*minä olen terve*; *minä olen saanu kuulla* "I am healthy; I have come to hear"). Thus, the formulae used in these letters cannot be seen as empty "envelopes" (Lyons 2010, 175–184), but rather had textual and (meta)pragmatic functions of their own. The writers combined the person form that followed the new standard with the old performative formulae, thereby constructing in their letters a space for the metapragmatic event of writing which was separate from the narrated events of the outside world (cf. Jakobson 1971, 133). While the performatives were maintaining the ongoing interaction, they also organised the delivery of information in the textualised event-structure of the letters. The grammatical and textual practice that was created in this way can be taken as presenting a local *group style*. As Eckert (2008, 46) points out, style is a category of content and of ideology: each stylistic move in a local practice is a result of an act of interpreting the social world and its meanings. This idea is corroborated by the observations we will make below on the letters written by literate writers.

The Linguistic Resources of the Literate Classes

Analysing texts by the educated upper classes of society on a par with those of self-educated people brings the formation of social meanings in the 19th-century context more clearly into light. As stated above, the meanings of indexical linguistic elements are constantly being negotiated during the interaction, and are influenced by the background and the normative expectations of both the speaker and the recipient (see also Coupland 2001, 197–204). But the creation of meaning is also influenced by the broader language community and its socio-cultural norms of usage. We will now show examples from the letters of two representatives of the intelligentsia, Elias Lönnrot and August Ahlqvist.

In Finland, the educated classes wrote mainly in Swedish until the 19th century; Swedish was used in official contexts as the language of administration, teaching and higher culture. Swedish was the predominant written language, whereas Finnish, "the language of the people", was for the most part used orally.[11] During the 19th century its domain was extended, as it gradually came to be used in administration and as the language of schooling, art and scholarship. Part of the educated classes began to use Finnish even in their personal texts, such as letters to the family or close friends and colleagues. Unlike self-educated writers, who mostly needed only a few textual genres, educated writers produced different kinds of texts for different recipients.[12] For example, Lönnrot and Ahlqvist, who both came from humble backgrounds but eventually became professors of Finnish language, wrote personal correspondence in Finnish and even formal Finnish letters to recipients who were socially their superiors. On the other hand, they also wrote letters in Swedish, both official and personal, to their Swedish-speaking relatives.

The presence or absence of performative formulations in Lönnrot's and Ahlqvist's letters clearly depended on the recipient. They occurred in two contexts. First of all, they were used, both in Finnish and in Swedish, in letters addressed to recipients who were socially superior. Example 14 is the beginning of a letter by the 19-year-old August Ahlqvist to Elias Lönnrot, who was then 43 and worked as a district physician and was preparing an edition of the Kalevala:

(14)
Ylistettävä Herra Tohtori! Mennä kesänä Karjalasta kerääni runot, sadut ja arvoitukset *saan* tässä Herra Tohtorille nöyrimmästi *lähettää*. Syy siihen, että ovat näin kauan minun hallussani viipyneet, on ollut osaksi mielessäni kytevä toivo, saada ne uudesta kirjoitetuksi ja parempaan järjestykseen laitelluksi, (...).
(Ahlqvist 15.6.1845)

> Most Revered Sir Doctor! [I] *may* here most humbly *send* Sir Doctor the poems, fairy tales and riddles I collected last summer in Karelia. The reason for [them] remaining so long in my possession has been the smouldering hope in my mind to have them written anew and better systematised, (...).

Second, Lönnrot and Ahlqvist used old formulae when they wrote to self-educated common people. Example 15 is from a letter by Lönnrot to his brother Henrik Johan Lönnrot, a tailor and self-educated writer who acted as a scribe in his home village (Anttila 1985, 36).

(15)
Muutamilla radeilla saan tietä antaa, että olemma voineet hyvin kaikki. Calle oli suvella 4 viikkoa täällä kotona, vaan on nyt taas Kuhmon papin edessä lukemassa 10 penik. täältä. Talvella *taidan minä tulla* Helsinkiin ja sinne kotiakin. (Lönnrot 18.9.1835)

With a few lines [I] may$_{1.Sg}$ let [you] know that we are all doing fine. During the summer Calle stayed here at home for 4 weeks but now he is again studying under the direction of Kuhmo's priest 10 miles away from here. In the winter I will$_{1.Sg}$ probably come to Helsinki and home to you, too.

On the lexical level ("with a few lines"; "I may let know"), the letter begins with one of the most popular old formulations. It is also worth pointing out that Lönnrot uses exactly the same meaningful system of person forms as the self-educated writers (cf. example 13). Both Ahlqvist and Lönnrot knew the style of the self-educated writers and consequently used the same conventions in their letters to them. In the letters to socially equal colleagues, close friends and small children these formulae were missing, however – they were not needed.

Audience design was, then, the principle observed by both the self-educated lower class and the literate upper class. Members of the Finnish upper class, who were used to writing, had of course more resources at their disposal than the self-educated common people. They could change both language (from Finnish to Swedish) and code (from familiar or intimate to deferential or distant register) according to the recipient. With respect to language policy, however, these two groups were coming closer to each other, as the old estate society was being transformed into a nation in the 19th-century and the Finnish vernacular to a common national language. The self-educated writers and the Finnish literary elite were in fact in same position as users of the written language: as it was in the process of establishing itself as an official language,[13] the mere fact of writing in Finnish created and strengthened this new standard and thereby helped in constructing the new nation. In the final section, we will see how the concepts of local and national language community found their place in the written idiom of the self-educated common people.

Identification with the Local and National Language Communities

Three kinds of language communities can be distinguished: global, national and local. The globalisation phenomenon as we know it today had begun already in the social, political and economic changes of the 19th century (Blommaert 2010, 13–15), but, above all, the 19th century was the time of national movements. Both the global and the national language communities are institutional results of socio-political processes. The "locality" of a language community, on the other hand, is relational, i.e. seen in relation to other communities. It becomes for a group of people an assumed property of self-ascriptions of having a particular "culture". They see their membership in the group as a positive thing (Silverstein 1998, 403–404.)

Ironically, both national states and imperial regimes tend to borrow expressions from the local communities in order to create an illusion that the hegemony they exercise is necessary for them (Silverstein *ibid.*). In 19th-century Finland, the language of the majority, the vernacular spoken by the common people, was elected as the "nation's mother tongue". This involved starting a massive language reform, however, in order to make the national standard suitable for the cultural needs of the elite as well.

In this section we look at three kinds of grammatical constructions having the 1st person plural form as the modifier – i.e. phrases expressing common "possessive" relations like "our land", "our village", "our people" or "our language". They express the relationship of the speaker and his/her reference group to some shared object. In Finnish, this type of relation can be expressed in three different ways. For example, the construction "our land, our country" can be translated as follows:[14]

(a) *meidän maa+mme*   (b) *meidän maa*   (c) *maa+mme*
our land + 1.Pl our land   land + 1.Pl

In the first alternative (a), the 1st person plural is marked twice: it includes both the possessive pronoun *meidän* "our", and the possessive suffix *mme* ("of ours") attached to the noun *maa* "land". In the second alternative (b), only the pronoun *meidän* "our" modifies the noun *maa* "land", and in the third alternative (c), the same function is expressed through the suffix *mme* alone. In the 19th century, these alternative possessive constructions were standardised to mean the identification of the speaker to either national or local communities (Laitinen 2008, 2010).

Since the construction (a) *meidän maamme* was perceived as influenced by Swedish grammar, it was restricted in the 19th century to emphatic uses only. In Biblical Finnish during the period of Swedish rule (ca. 1540–1809), the construction was by far the most frequent 1st person possessive construction. It is illustrated in 16 by an excerpt of the king's text. In statutes, this kind of a phrase with the royal plural always referred to the Swedish kingdom, the global territory of the plurilingual community.

(16)
Että yxi Partija, jonga waikutus Hallituxen päälle, ja tarkoitus että kukistaa kaiken Kuningan wallan ja järjestyxen olisit aiwan ilmeiset, kiukutzelisit *meidän maasamme*. (1794, Kustaa IV Adolf)[15]

That one Party, whose influence on Government, and purpose to overthrow all Royal power and order would be quite apparent, would act ill-tempered *in our land*.

The variant (b), *meidän maa*, was mainly used as an expression of local relations. It appeared in the written language in 18th-century guidelines published for the common people, where, as in the text of Per Gadd (example 17), it refers to concrete land or soil. At the same time, however, this is one of the rare examples from the period of Swedish rule where the area of Finland is referred to as a separate unit of its own.

(17)
Krydimaan yrtit, joita *meidän massa* kaswatetaan, ne owat ruan ja elannon awuxi tarpeelliset, osittain juurten ja lehtein, osittain palko-kaswandoin ja siemenden tähden. (Pietari Gadd 1768)[16]

The herbs of the herb garden that are grown *in our land*, they are necessary for food and maintenance, partly for their roots and leaves, partly for their legumes and seeds.

In the 19th century, this variant, (b) *meidän maa*, was restricted to the vernacular. It referred exclusively to local relations, like the field, home and its inhabitants, or to the village community to which the speaker belonged (cf. Judén 1818), and it was recommended that it be avoided in the written language (von Becker 1824). By the middle of the 19th century, however, it was considered suitable in a news item which announced the publication of the Swedish language poem *Vårt land* ("Our country") by the national poet Johan Ludvig Runeberg (18).

(18)
"*Meidän maa*, laulu Runebergiltä" (*Suometar* 1847)
"*Our country*, a song by Runeberg"

Later, the poem was to become the national anthem of Finland, and the dozens of translations into Finnish soon established its title as the variant (c) *Maamme*, "Our Country". Among others, the self-educated translator, janitor Johan Léman, used this form in 1854.[17] As the use of the possessive suffix was seen as a specifically Finno-Ugrian way of expressing possessive relations, the third variant (c) became the standard form during the 19th-century, and began to become stabilised particularly in those ideological connections where national concepts were of relevance. Many native Finnish-speaking men of influence – especially Elias Lönnrot and August Ahlqvist (example 19) – still often used the vernacular variant in national contexts as well, e.g. such phrases as *meidän maa* "our country", *meidän kieli* "our language" and *meidän kansa* "our people, our nation". In his Finnish grammar, A. W. Jahnsson pronounced the phrase *meidän maa* "our country" to be a suitable expression when referring to the homeland of the speaker (example 20).

(19)
Mutta ei sentähden Ruotsin kieltäkään tarvitse pois heittää; osata sitäkin pitää *meidän maassa* vielä, ja osata myös säännöllisesti kirjoittaa, jota real-koulussa ei näy opetetun. (Ahlqvist 1859)[18]

But one need not throw away the Swedish language either; one still has to know it *in our country*, and also write regularly, which seems not be the case in the intermediate school.

(20)
Meidän maassa on paljo köyhiä: i vårt land (i det land, där den talande bor) finnes mycket fattiga. (Jahnsson 1871)
There are many poor people *in our country* (in the country in which the speaker lives).

Even if such grammatical constructions express fairly abstract relations, Finnish speakers were at least to some extent aware of their potential meaning in the 19th century. It has been assumed that people are most aware of words that refer to concrete objects, specifically to living and personal referents (Silverstein 1981). According to Joseph Errington, pragmatically the most salient ones would be the personal pronouns, which refer to the participants in the speech situation and can develop ideological or metalinguistic meanings (Errington 1985, 294–297). The variant (b), *meidän maa*, is a good example of this type of form, and it would have been suitable as a construction that refers to the whole national entity formed by the grand duchy of Finland. Even the self-educated writers gradually adapted to the new standard norm of 19th-century Finnish, however, and used variant (c). Examples 21 and 22 are from a manuscript of the self-educated labourer Nikolai Herranen dating from 1889.[19] Example 21 refers concretely to the land and soil which the writer is tilling and cultivating. It represents the vernacular construction with which one expresses the belonging to a location and its local community. Example 22 discusses the Finnish area as a national entity.

(21)
Hartiani on köyristynyt, ja käteni vapisee Ahran kanssa ikäni taistellessani, perkaten soita ja rämeitä pelloksi *meidän niukassa maassa* ja kylmässä pohjolan povessa, (…).

My shoulder is bent and my hand is quailing as I struggle with the plough, clearing the bog and swamp into field *in our barren land* and the cold bosom of the north (…).

(22)
Mutta vilpun Isä oli toimekas ja uuttera mies, huolimatta niistä nälkä vuosista ynnä muista rasituksista, jotka silloin *maatamme* ahdisti.

But Vilppu's father was an active and hard-working man, in spite of the famine years and other strains that troubled *our land* at that time.

In the vernacular, variants like (c) usually referred to abstract entities like "our friendship(s)", "our faith(s)" distributively, i.e. referring to each individual of the "we-group" separately. From the point of view of a self-educated writer these "national constructions" took their place in the group of abstract entities, and thereby the national identity was conceptualised as an individual rather than a collective relation.

The standardisation of Finnish in the 19th century meant simplifying the indexical grammar of the vernacular and making the language community more homogeneous. The meaning potential of variant (b) was restricted to marginal contexts in the standard language, predominantly to expressions belonging to the sphere of children (*meidän äiti* "our mother", *meidän koulu* "our school", etc.). On the other hand, this construction is still frequent in the 21st century. In written texts, it can be used to show the closeness of national institutions to the writer. For example, the former president of the republic, Tarja Halonen, is frequently referred to in texts on the internet as *meidän Tarja*, as if she belonged to the immediate local community of the writers.

Discussion: From below or from above?

In this article, we have focused on the context dependent, indexical (pragmatic) meanings of linguistic expressions, and especially linguistic signs that refer to the participation in a communicative event, belonging to a group, membership in a speech community, identity, cultural or local ties, attitudes and ideologies. At the same time we have also discussed theoretical concepts used in linguistic research on texts by self-educated writers.

We have pointed out that the notion *intended standard* is directly related to another key notion, *audience design*, which again describes the textual practices of the Finnish-speaking educated class as well. The concepts *stylistic rupture* and *intended standard* have been used precisely in the kind of research that aims at an interpretation relying on *from below* ideology, i.e. studying the history of a language looked at from the lower social classes. In actual practice these concepts easily represent the ideology of *from above*, as the yardstick of the lower-class writers' texts tends to be the stylistic purity that follows the ideals of the standard language. Blommaert (2008, 17, 198) sees the problem of the approach from above to be that the texts are not being looked into from the point of view of their own meaning making. As we all have experienced, even a researcher with a lot of goodwill ends up with normative or subjective interpretations without careful socio-cultural and historical analysis (cf. Silverstein 1998, 422–423).

The interpretation of texts is always influenced by the perspective adopted by the researcher. A present day linguist will always have difficulties in getting rid of the socio-cultural expectations about the structure of a good text that he or she has acquired as a member of his or her own speech community. Many of the texts by 19th-century self-educated writers were consciously addressed to the audience of the time, to a field larger than their immediate circle. Common people sent their texts to the Finnish Literature Society with the purpose of getting them published. So, their context of interpretation could be, in addition to the writer's own intentions and the lenses used by the linguist, also the 19th-century sociolinguistic community and the atmosphere of linguistic ideology, which can be unravelled with the help of contemporary comments and values. The business letters of farmers also moved from one social environment to another originating in eastern Finnish villages and arriving at a distant trading house in the town of Oulu. It is not possible to trace directly the value attached to them by Bergbom the merchant, but something may be read into the fact that he did not save copies of his own letters to the farmers:[20] the business relation essential in the lives of the farmers played after all a small part in the transactions of the mighty businessman.

We have also presented a case study on more personal letters – emigrant letters which although sent across the ocean, were not intended for an audience wider than the writers' closest relatives and friends. In the performative formulae used in the letters, we found stylistic features that were jointly composed by the writers. Making use of the syntactic alternatives of the Finnish personal forms, the writers created a metapragmatic space which enabled them to build their own writer identities, maintain interaction and organise the telling of news. They formed the stylistic practices of their own group style using resources from three different linguistic varieties shared in their local community: old Biblical Finnish, new standard Finnish and their own dialect. Thus the process of creating new stylistic practices cannot be described as either *from above* or *from below*, but *from common ground*. The view of the texts of self-educated writers as hybrids can be seen as an example of the erasure of their own voice as well. If one just tries to reconstruct the intertextuality of the text and trace back its possible literary models, what is left out is a discussion of what kind of intentions the writer may have had with his or her linguistic choices. For example, choosing a certain kind of religious style in letters dealing with illness or death is a cultural choice, but it is also the writer's meaningful act, which serves his/her purpose in the current interaction.

Notes

1 The term is based on German literature that discusses workers' language (*Arbeitersprache*). The original term is *intendiertes Hochdeutsch* (Vandenbussche 2006).
2 The Finnish pronoun *hän* ("s/he") and its plural equivalent *he* ("they") do not mark gender.
3 In literary Finnish, the pronoun *se* and its plural equivalent *ne* are demonstrative pronouns ("it" resp. "they"), that are not used of human beings; in spoken language,

they can refer to both living and non-living entities, even to human beings.
4   Cf. the Greek word *logos* "speech, word, thought". Logophoric pronouns are known from many languages in oral cultures, e.g. in West Africa (Hagège 1974) as well as in the Saami languages (Laitinen 2002). In Icelandic, Japanese and English the logophoric function is expressed by reflexive pronouns ("self", "own").
5   To begin with, Carl Axel Gottlund's native language was Swedish, as it was for the majority of the 19th-century educated Finnish people. For a long time, the Finnish elite disapproved of his liberal stance to the development of the Finnish written language, whereas it was appreciated by even those peasants who were speakers of the western dialects (Kuuliala 1939). In Sweden and Norway Gottlund had a strong influence on language policy, and he is still respected for that: he e.g. sent Finnish literature and newspapers to the Forest Finns, as can be seen in the letter quoted in example (2).
6   The corresponding term in conversation analysis is *recipient design*.
7   In German research literature the term *Stilzusammenbruch* has been used (Vandenbussche 2006, 448).
8   As our data we use the correspondence between Frans Oskar Heinonen and Josefiina Heinonen, altogether 45 letters from 1887–1898. Frans Oskar Heinonen emigrated from Merikarvia, Satakunta to North America in 1887, and in addition to the couple, letters were written by their close friends and relatives. (For a more detailed analysis, cf. Laitinen & Nordlund 2012)
9   The corpus of 17th-century laws and statutes, Institute for the Languages of Finland. http://kaino.kotus.fi/korpus/vks/teksti/lait/ahf1600.xml#s16, as of 10.2.2011.
10 The mere verb variant has its own contexts and meaningful functions both in the vernacular and in current spoken language (Hakulinen 2001, Duvallon & Chalvin 2004). About the history of the written norm cf. Strellman 2005.
11 The two languages had different contexts of use; in linguistics, a situation like this is called *diglossia*. The situation of the eastern Finnish peasants can be described as double diglossia, because on the national level there was a division of labour between Finnish and Swedish, but on the local level the vernacular varied with Biblical Finnish (Nordlund 2007, 235).
12 There were, of course, exceptions among the self educated as well, e.g. socially active persons, who left behind many kinds of texts: letters, sermons, polemics or literary manuscripts. See Kauranen (2005) and Kauranen & Myllynen (2006) for lists of references.
13 Finnish language was given the rights of an official language in 1863: they were supposed to take full effect by 1883.
14 In the descriptions of the constructions the abbreviation Pl stands for Plural and the plus-sign points to the beginning of the suffix.
15 The corpus of 18th century statutes, Institute for the Languages of Finland. http://kaino.kotus.fi/korpus/vks/teksti/lait/as1700.
16 The corpus of old Biblical Finnish, Institute for the Languages of Finland. http://kaino.kotus.fi/korpus/vks/teksti/varia/gadd1768.
17 Finnish Literature Society, Literary Archives.
18 A letter from Ahlqvist to his brother 6. 8.1859. (http://kaino.kotus.fi/korpus/1800/teksti/ahlqvist/kirjeet1845-1889.xml#s643.)
19 N. Herranen, 1899: *Tilppu Vipusen elämä kerta* ("A Biography of Tilppu Vipunen"). Manuscript, Finnish Literature Society, Literary Archives.
20 Personal communication by Kaisa Kauranen.

Bibliography

Abrahams, Roger D. 1993a: After New Perspectives. Folklore Study of the Late Twentieth Century. *Western Folklore* 52: 379–400.
Abrahams, Roger D. 1993b: Phantoms of Romantic Nationalism in Folkloristics. *Journal of American Folklore* 106: 1–37.
Agha, Asif 2007: *Language and Social Relations*. Cambridge: Cambridge University Press.
Ahlqvist, A. 1982 [1845–1889]: *Kirjeet*. http://kaino.kotus.fi/korpus/1800/meta/ahlqvist/kirjeet1845–1889_rdf.xml
Anttila, Aarne 1985: *Elias Lönnrot. Elämä ja toiminta*. Helsinki: SKS.
Anttonen, Pertti J. 2005: *Tradition through Modernity. Postmodernism and the Nation-State in Folklore Scholarship*. Studia Fennica Folkloristica 15. Helsinki: SKS.
Apo, Satu 2001: *Viinan voima: näkökulmia suomalaiseen kansanomaiseen alkoholiajatteluun ja -kulttuuriin*. Helsinki: SKS.
Austin, J. L. 1962: *How to do Things with Words*. Oxford & New York: Oxford University Press.
Bacconnier, Gérard, Minet, André & Soler, Louis (eds.) 1985: *La plume au fusil. Les poilus du Midi à travers leur correspondance*. Toulouse: Privat.
Bakhtin, Mihail 1994 [1981]: *The Dialogic Imagination*. Ed. Michael Holquist. Austin: University of Texas Press.
Bakhtin, Mikhail 1984. *Problems of Dostoyevsky's Poetics*. Ed. and transl. by Caryl Emerson. Minneapolis: University of Minnesota Press.
Barton, David 1991: The Social Nature of Writing. In David Barton & Roz Ivanič (eds.), *Writing in the Community*. Newbury Park, London & New Delhi: Sage, 1–13.
Barton, David 2000: Researching Literacy Practices. Learning from activities with teachers and students. In David Barton, Mary Hamilton, & Roz Ivanič (eds.), *Situated Literacies. Theorising Reading and Writing in Context*. London & New York: Routledge, 167–179.
Barton, David 2007 [1994]: *Literacy. An Introduction to the Ecology of Written Language*. Malden, MA: Blackwell.
Barton, David 2010: Vernacular Writing on the Web. In David Barton & Uta Papen (eds.), *The Anthropology of Writing. Understanding Textually-Mediated Worlds*. London & New York: Continuum, 109–125.
Barton, David & Hamilton, Mary 1998: *Local Literacies. Reading and Writing in one Community*. London & New York: Routledge.
Barton, David & Hamilton, Mary 2000: Literacy practices. In David Barton, Mary Hamilton, & Roz Ivanič (eds.), *Situated Literacies. Theorising Reading and Writing in Context*. London & New York: Routledge, 7–15.
Barton, David & Hamilton, Mary 2005: Literacy, Reification and the Dynamics of Social Interaction. In David Barton & K. Tusting (eds.), *Beyond Communities of Practice. Language, Power and Social Context*. Cambridge: Cambridge University Press, 15–35.
Barton, David, Hamilton, Mary & Ivanič, Roz (eds.) 2000: *Situated Literacies. Theorising Reading and Writing in Context*. London & New York: Routledge.
Barton, David & Papen, Uta (eds.) 2010a: *The Anthropology of Writing. Understanding Textually-Mediated Worlds*. London & New York: Continuum.
Barton, David & Papen, Uta 2010b: What is the Anthropology of Writing? In David Barton & Uta Papen (eds.), *The Anthropology of Writing. Understanding Textually-Mediated Worlds*. London & New York: Continuum, 3–32.
Baynham, Mike & Prinsloo, Mastin (eds.) 2009: *The Future of Literacy Studies* (Palgrave Advances in Linguistics). New York: Palgrave Macmillan.

Becker, Reinhold von 1824: *Finsk Grammatik.* Åbo.
Bell, Alan 2001: Back in Style: Reworking Audience Design. In Penelope Eckert & John R. Rickford (eds.), *Style and Sociolinguistic Variation.* Cambridge: Cambridge University Press, 139–169.
Benhabib, Seyla 1995: Die Quellen des Selbst in der Zeitgenössischen Feministischen Theorie. *Die Philosophin* 11: 12–32.
Benhabib, Seyla 1997: "Jagets källor" i modern feministisk teori. In Ulla M. Holm, Eva Mark, & Annika Persson (eds.), *Tanke, känsla, identitet.* Göteborg: Anamma, 123–149.
Besnier, Niko 1993: *Literacy, Emotion and Authority. Reading and Writing on a Polynesian Atoll.* Cambridge: Cambridge University Press.
Blasco Martínez, Rosa Maria & Rubalcaba Pérez, Carmen 2003: *Para hablarte a tan larga distancia. Correspondencia de una familia montañesa a ambos lados del Atlántico, 1855–1883.* Santander: Estudio.
Blommaert, Jan 2008: *Grassroots Literacy. Writing, Identity and Voice in Central Africa.* London & New York: Routledge.
Blommaert, Jan 2010: *The Sociolinguistics of Globalization.* Cambridge: Cambridge University Press.
Blommaert, Jan & Verschueren, Jef 1998: The Role of Language in European Nationalist Ideologies. In Bambi Schieffelin, Kathryn A. Woolard & Paul V. Kroskrity (eds.), *Language Ideologies. Practice and Theory*, 189–210.
Blomqvist, Håkan 2006: *Nation, ras och civilisation i svensk arbetarrörelse före nazismen.* Stockholm: Södertörns högskola.
Brandt, Deborah & Clinton, Katie 2002: Limits of the Local. Expanding Perspectives on Literacy as a Social Practice. *Journal of Literacy Research* 34: 337–356.
Bristol, James & Marotti, Arthur 2000: Introduction. In James Bristol & Arthur Marotti (eds.), *Print, Manuscript, Performance. The Changing Relations of the Media in Early Modern England.* Columbus: Ohio State University Press, 1–32.
Burguière, André 2009 [2006]: *The Annales School. An Intellectual History.* Transl. Jane Marie Todd. Ithaca, NY: Cornell University Press.
Burke, Peter 1978: *Popular Culture in Early Modern Europe.* London: Temple Smith.
Burke, Peter 2004: *What is Cultural History?* Cambridge: Polity Press.
Burnett, John, Vincent, David, & Mayall, David (eds.) 1984–1989: *The Autobiography of the Working Class. An Annotated, Critical Bibliography 1–3.* Brighton: Harvester.
Caffarena, Fabio 2001: *Le Terre Matte e il Caro Paese. Epistolario di guerra dell'alpino Emanuele Calosso, 1915–1918.* Finale Ligure: Comune di Finale Ligure.
Caffarena, Fabio 2005: *Lettere dalla Grande Guerra: Scritture del quotidiano, monumenti della memoria, fonti per la storia. Il caso italiano.* Milan: Unicopli.
Chartier, Roger 2007: The Printing Revolution. A Reappraisal. In Sabrina Baron and Eric Lindquist (eds), *Agent of Change. Print Culture Studies After Elizabeth L. Eisenstein.* Cambridge, MA: University of Massachusetts Press, 397–408.
Christiansen, Palle Ove 1995: Culture and Contrasts in a Northern European Village. Lifestyles among Manorial Peasants in 18th-Century Denmark. *Journal of Social History* 29 (2): 275–294.
Cobb, Richard 1972: *Reactions to the French Revolution.* London: Oxford University Press.
Cochet, Annick 1985: *L'Opinion et le Moral des Soldats en 1916, d'après les archives du contrôle postal.* 2 vols. Unpublished 3e cycle thesis. Université Paris X – Nanterre.
Corbin, Alain 1998: *Le monde retrouvé de Louis-François Pinagot. Sur les traces d'un inconnu, 1798–1876.* Paris: Flammarion.
Coupland, Nikolas 2001: Language, Situation, and the Relational Self. In Penelope Eckert & John R. Rickford (eds.), *Style and Sociolinguistic Variation.* Cambridge: Cambridge University Press, 185–210.
Croci, Federico 1992: *Scrivere per non morire. Lettere della Grande Guerra del soldato*

bresciano Francesco Ferrari. Genova: Marietti, Fiori secchi. Preface by Antonio Gibelli.

Croci, Federico & Bonfiglio, Giovanni 2002: *El baúl de la memoria. Testimonios escritos de inmigrantes italianos en el Perú*. Lima: Fondo editorial del Congreso del Perú.

Darnton, Robert 2000. An Early Information Society. News and the Media in Eighteenth-Century Paris. *American Historical Review* 1: 105: 1-35.

Davíð Ólafsson 2002: Að æxla sér bækur með penna. Miðlun Íslandingasagna á 19. öld í handritum og prentuðum bókum. In *2. íslenska söguþingið 2002. Ráðstefnurit I*. Reykjavík: Sagnfræðistofnun Háskóla Íslands, Sagnfræðingafélag Íslands & Sögufélag, 193-211.

Davíð Ólafsson 2008: *Wordmongers. Post-Medieval Scribal Culture and the Case of Sighvatur Grímsson*. Ph.D. dissertation from the University of St Andrews. http://research-repository.st-andrews.ac.uk/handle/10023/770.

Davíð Ólafsson 2010: Textinn á tíma fjöldaframleiðslu sinnar: Rannsóknir á handritamenningu síðari alda. *Saga* XLVIII: 61-97.

Davis, Natalie Zemon 1983: *The Return of Martin Guerre*. Cambridge, MA: Harvard University Press.

Davis, Natalie Zemon 2007: *Trickster Travels. A Sixteenth-Century Muslim between Worlds*. London: Faber.

Dondeynaz, Rosalba 1992: *Selma e Guerrin. Un epistolario amoroso, 1914-1920*. Genova: Marietti-fiori secchi.

Dossena, Marina 2007: As This Leaves Me at Present. Formulaic Usage, Politiness, and Social Proximity in Nineteenth-Century Scottish Emigrants' Letters. In Stephan Elspaß et al. (eds.), *Germanic Language Histories 'from Below' (1700-2000)*. Berlin: Walter de Gruyter, 13-29.

Driscoll, M. J. 1997: *The Unwashed Children of Eve. The Production, Dissemination and Reception of Popular Literature in Post-Reformation Iceland*. Enfield Lock, England: Hisarlik Press.

Driscoll, M. J. 2003: Fornaldarsögur Norðurlanda. The Stories that Wouldn't Die. In Á. Jakobsson, A. Lassen, & A. Ney (eds.), *Fornaldarsagornas struktur och ideologi*. Uppsala: Uppsala universitet, 257-267.

Driscoll, M. J. 2005: Late Prose Fiction (*lygisögur*). In Rory McTurk (ed.), *A Companion to Old Norse-Icelandic Literature and Culture*. Oxford: Blackwell, 190-204.

Driscoll, M. J. 2007: Skanderbeg. An Albanian Hero in Icelandic Clothing. In Judy Quinn, Kate Heslop, & Tarrin Wills (eds.), *Learning and Understanding in the Old Norse World. Essays in Honour of Margaret Clunies Ross*. Turnhout: Brepols, 421-446.

Driscoll, M. J. 2012: "Um gildi gamalla bóka". Magnús Jónsson í Tjaldanesi und das Ende der isländischen Handschriftenkultur. In J. Glauser & A. K. Richter (eds.), *Text, Reihe, Transmission. Unfestigkeit als Phänomen skandinavischer Erzählprosa 1500-1800*, Beiträge zur Nordischen Philologie XLII. Tübingen, Basel: Francke, 255-282.

Duvallon, Outi & Chalvin, Antoine 2004: La réalisation zéro du pronom sujet de premiére et de deuxiéme personne du singulier en finnois et en estonien parlé. *Linguistica Uralica* XL (4): 270-286.

Eckert, Penelope 2008: Variation and the indexical field. *Journal of Sociolinguistics* 12 (4): 453-476.

Edlund, Ann-Catrine 2003: Från avskrift till egen textproduktion - två ångermanländska visböcker från 1930-tal. In Lars-Erik Edlund et al. (eds.), *Ord i Nord. Vänskrift till Lars-Erik Edlund 16 augusti 2003*. Umeå: Umeå universitet, 33-50.

Edlund, Ann-Catrine 2005: Samverkan över vetenskapens gränser. Några reflektioner om metod utifrån en språkvetares samarbete med en zoolog respektive en konstnär. In Boel De Geer & Anna Malmbjer (eds.), *Språk på tvärs. Rapport från ASLA:s höstsymposium Södertörn 11-12 nov 2004*. Uppsala: Association suédoise de linguistique appliqueé, 71–79.

Edlund, Ann-Catrine 2007: *Ett rum för dagen. En studie av två kvinnors dagboksskrivande i norrländsk jordbruksmiljö.* Umeå: Kulturgräns norr.

Edlund, Ann-Catrine 2008: Visboken – en deltagare i flera skriftpraktiker. In Gunnar Ternhag (ed.), *Samlade visor. Perspektiv på handskrivna visböcker.* Uppsala: Kungl. Gustav Adolfs Akademien för svensk folkkultur, 51–68.

Edlund, Ann-Catrine & Sundström, Maria 2007: Sex dagböcker genom två betraktare. *Västerbotten* 1: 22–28.

Edlund, Lars-Erik 2005: Från Håvåsen till Sapientia Duce. Nils Jönsson och hans skrivande 1877–1882. In Björn Melander (ed.), *Språk i tid. Studier tillägnade Mats Thelander på 60-årsdagen.* Uppsala: Uppsala universitet, Institutionen för nordiska språk, 325–335.

Ehrnrooth, Jari 1992: *Sanan vallassa, vihan voimalla. Sosialistiset vallankumousopit ja niiden vaikutus Suomen työväenliikkeessä 1905–1914.* Helsinki: Suomen Historiallinen Seura.

Elspaß, Stephan 2005: *Sprachgeschichte von unten. Untersuchungen zum geschriebenen Alltagsdeutsch im 19. Jahrhundert.* Tübingen: Max Niemeyer.

Elspaß, Stephan 2012: Between Linguistic Creativity and Formulaic Restriction. Cross-Linguistic Perspectives on Nineteenth-Century Lower Class Writers' Private Letters. In M. Dossena & G. Del Lungo Camiciotti (eds.), *Letter Writing in Late Modern Europe.* Amsterdam & Philadelphia: John Benjamins, 45–64.

Errington, Joseph 1985: On the Nature of the Sociolinguistic Sign: Describing the Jananese Speech Levels. In Elizabeth Mertz & Richard J. Parmentier (eds.), *Semiotic Mediation.* Orlando, FL: Academic Press, 287–310.

Ezell, Margaret J. M. 1999: *Social Authorship and the Advent of Print.* Baltimore & London: The Johns Hopkins University Press.

Fairclough, Norman 2003: *Analysing Discourse. Textual Analysis for Social Research.* London: Routledge.

Febvre, Lucien 1982: *The Problem of Unbelief in the 16th Century. The Religion of Rabelais.* Cambridge, MA: Harvard University Press, first published in 1942.

Fet, Jostein 2003: *Skrivande bønder: Skriftkultur på Nord-Vestlandet 1600–1850.* Oslo: Det Norske Samlaget.

Finnur Sigmundsson (ed.) 1950–1951: *Úr fórum Jóns Árnasonar.* Reykjavík: Hlaðbúð.

Finnur Sigmundsson 1966a: Guðmundur Bergþórsson skáld. In Jón Guðnason (ed.), *Merkir Íslendingar. Nýr flokkur,* vol. 5. Reykjavík: Bókfellsútgáfan, 75–87.

Finnur Sigmundsson 1966b: *Rímnatal,* vol. II. Reykjavík: Rímnafélagið.

Fitzmaurice, Susan 2002: *The Familiar Letter in Early Modern English.* Amsterdam: John Benjamins.

Franzina, Emilio 1987: L'epistolografia popolare e i suoi usi. *Materiali di lavoro* 1-2: 21–63.

Freeman, Mark Philip 1993: *Rewriting the Self. History, Memory, Narrative.* London & New York: Routledge.

Fur, Gunlög Maria 2006: *Colonialism in the Margin. Cultural Encounters in New Sweden and Lapland.* http://www.brill.com/colonialism-margins

Gawthrop, Richard & Strauss, Gerald 1984: Protestantism and Literacy in Early Modern Germany. *Past and Present* 104 (1): 31–55.

Geertz, Clifford 1991: Tjock beskrivning. För en tolkande kulturteori. *Häften för kritiska studier* 3: 13–33.

Geertz, Clifford 1993 [1973]: *The Interpretation of Cultures. Selected Essays.* London: Fontana Press.

Gelbart Rattner, Nina 1987: *Feminine and Opposition Journalism in Old Regime France. Le Journal des Dames.* Berkeley & London: University of California Press.

Gemelli, Agostino 1917: *Il nostro soldat. Saggi di psicologia militare.* Milan: Treves.

Gibelli, Antonio 1987: Pratica della scrittura e mutamento sociale. Orientamenti e ipotesi. *Materiali di lavoro* 1–2: 7–20.

Gibelli, Antonio 1991: *L'Officina della Guerra. La Grande Guerra e le trasformazioni del mondo mentale.* Turin: Bollati Boringhieri.

Gibelli, Antonio 2000: C'era una volta la storia dal basso… In Quinto Antonelli & Anna Iuso (eds.), *Vite di carta.* Naples: L'Ancora, 159–175.

Gibelli, Antonio 2002: Emigrantes y Soldados. La escritura como práctica de masas en los siglos XIX y XX. In Antonio Castillo Gómez (ed.), *La conquista del alfabeto: Escritura y clases populares.* Gijón: Trea, 194–196.

Gillen, Julia & Hall, Nigel 2010: Edwardian Postcards. Illuminating Ordinary Writing. In David Barton & Uta Papen (eds.), *The Anthropology of Writing. Understanding Textually-Mediated Worlds.* London & New York: Continuum, 169–189.

Ginzburg, Carlo 1980: *The Cheese and the Worms. The Cosmos of a Sixteenth-Century,* transl. J. & A. Tedeschi. London: Routledge Kegan Paul.

Gísli Gunnarsson 1987: *Upp er boðið Ísland. Einokunarverslun og íslenskt samfélag 1602–1787.* Reykjavík: Örn og Örlygur.

Gísli Sigurðsson & Vésteinn Ólason (ed.) 2004: *The Manuscripts of Iceland.* Reykjavík: The Árni Magnússon Institute in Iceland & University of Iceland Press.

Glauser, Jürg 2005: Romance (Translated *riddarasögur*). In Rory McTurk (ed.), *A Companion to Old Norse Icelandic Literature and Culture.* Oxford: Blackwell, 372–387.

Goody, Jack 1968: Introduction. In Jack Goody (ed.), *Literacy in Traditional Societies.* Cambridge: Cambridge University Press, 1–26.

Graff, H. J. 1987: *The Legacies of Literacy. Continuities and Contradictions in Western Culture and Society.* Bloomington: Indiana University Press.

Grenadou, Ephraïm 1980 [1966]: *Grenadou, paysan français (propos recueillis par Alain Prévost).* Paris: Rombaldi.

Grímur M. Helgason 1973: Handritasafn Einars Guðmundssonar á Reyðarfirði. In *Landsbókasafn Íslands: Árbók 1972*: 153–161.

Grímur M. Helgason 1979: "Af skrifuðum skræðum er allt gott": Þáttur af skiptum Jóns Sigurðssonar og Jóns Borgfirðings. In: *Landsbókasafn Íslands. Árbók 1978*: 53–65.

Grímur M. Helgason 1988: Jón Jónsson í Simbakoti og handrit hans. In: *Landsbókasafn Íslands. Árbók 1986*: 58–64.

Grotenfelt, N. Karl 1931: *Joroinen I. Muistojulkaisu pitäjän 300-vuotisjuhlaan 6.8.1931.* Joroinen: Joroisten pitäjän 300-vuotisjuhlatoimikunta.

Grotenfelt, N. Karl, Grotenfelt, Erik & Grotenfelt, Kustavi (eds.) 1917: *Ätten Grotenfelt. Anteckningar för släkten.* Lovisa: N. B. Grotenfelt.

Guðmundur Sigurður Jóhannsson et al. (ed.) 1981–1999: *Skagfirskar æviskrár 1850–1890.* Sauðarkrókur: Sögufélag Skagfirðinga.

Guðvarður Már Gunnlaugsson 2005: Manuscripts and palaeography. In Rory McTurk (ed.), *A Companion to Old Norse–Icelandic Literature and Culture.* Oxford: Blackwell, 245–264.

Gunnarsson, Britt-Louise 1995: Varför skriver Erik? Synpunkter på John Svenskes avhandling "Skrivandets villkor". *Språk och stil* 5 (N.F.): 153–175.

Gödel, Vilhelm 1897–1900: *Katalog öfver Kongl. Bibliotekets fornisländska och fornnorska handskrifter.* Stockholm.

Haavikko, Ritva 1998: Kirjoittavat lapset. Huomioita kirjailijaksi kasvamisen psykologisista ja sosiaalisista edellytyksistä. In Henni Ilomäki, Ulla-Maija Peltonen & Hilpi Saure (eds): *Salaamatta. Kirjallisia muistikuvia ja löytöjä.* Helsinki: SKS, 187–218.

Haavio, Martti 1933: Suomalainen muinaisrunous. In Gunnar Suolahti et al. (eds.), *Suomen kulttuurihistoria I. Heimoyhteiskunnan ja katolisen kulttuurin aika.* Jyväskylä & Helsinki: K. J. Gummerus, 280–354.

Haavio, Martti 1935: *Kalevalan riemuvuoden kilpakeräys. Keruuopas.* Helsinki: SKS.

Haavio, Martti 1936: *Tarinaopas.* Helsinki: SKS.

Haavio, Martti 1937: *Kotiseudun aarreaitta.* Helsinki: SKS.

Hagége, Claude 1974: Les pronoms logophoriques. *Bulletin de la Société de Linguistique*

de paris LXIX 1 : 287–310.
Hakulinen, Auli 2001: Minimal and non-minimal answers to yes–no questions. *Pragmatics* 11: 1–16.
Halldór Hermannsson 1929: *Icelandic manuscripts*, Islandica XIX. Ithaca, NY: Cornell University Press.
Haraldur Bernharðsson 1999: *Málblöndun í sautjándu aldar uppskriftum íslenskra miðaldahandrita*. Reykjavík: Málvísindastofnun Háskóla Íslands.
Harrison, Dick 2007: *Slaveri – en världshistoria om ofrihet. 1500 till 1800*. Lund: Historiska media.
Heath, Shirley Brice 1983: *Ways with Words. Language, Life, and Work in Commuities and Classrooms*. New York: Cambridge University Press.
Heath, Shirley B. & Street, Brian V. 2008: *On Ethnography. Approaches to Language and Literacy Research*. New York: Teachers College Press.
Heininen, Simo & Heikkilä, Markku 2002: *Kirchengeschichte Finnlands*. Übersetzt von Matthias Quaschning-Kirsch. Göttingen: Vandenhoeck & Ruprecht.
Helgi Haraldsson 1948: Höfundur Njálu. *Tíminn* 9–10 April.
Helgi Magnússon 1990: Fræðafélög og bókaútgáfa. In Ingi Sigurðsson (ed.), *Upplýsingin á Íslandi. Tíu ritgerðir*. Reykjavík: Hið íslenzka bókmenntafélag, 183–215.
Hermann Pálsson 1962: *Sagnaskemmtun Íslendinga*. Reykjavík: Mál og menning.
Hitchcock, Tim 2004: A New History from Below. *History Workshop Journal*, 57: 294–299.
Hobsbawm, Eric 1989 [1983]: Introduction: Inventing Traditions. In Eric Hobsbawm & Terence Ranger (eds.), *The Invention of Tradition*. Cambridge: Cambridge University Press, 1–14.
Honko, Lauri 1999: Pitkän eepoksen laulaja. In *Kalevala taikka vanhoja Karjalan runoja Suomen kansan muinosista ajoista*.1835 julkaistun Kalevalan laitoksen uusi painos. Helsinki: SKS, VII–XX.
Hormia, Osmo 1978: *Finska dialekter. En översikt*. Lund: Liber Läromedel.
Howard, Ursula 1991: Self, Education and Writing in 19th-Century English Communities. In David Barton & Roz Ivanič (eds.), *Writing in the Community*. Newbury Park, London & New Delhi: Sage, 78–108.
Hreinn Benediktsson 1965: *Early Icelandic Script, as Illustrated in Vernacular Texts from the Twelfth and Thirteenth Centuries*. Reykjavík: Manuscript Institute of Iceland.
Hughes, S. 2005: Late Secular Poetry. In Rory McTurk (ed.), *A Companion to Old Norse-Icelandic Literature and Culture*. Oxford: Blackwell, 320–337.
Hukkinen, Leena 1963. Epäaito kansanperinne. Esitelmä prof. Hautalan johtamassa suomalaisen ja vertailevan kansanrunoudentutkimuksen seminaarissa 4.2.1963. Kansanrunoustieteen opinnäytetyö, Helsingin yliopisto. S131.
Häggman, Kai 1994: *Perheen vuosisata*. Helsinki: Suomen Historiallinen Seura.
Häkkinen, Kaisa 1994: *Agricolasta nykykieleen. Suomen kirjakielen historia*. Helsinki: WSOY.
Häkkinen, Kaisa 1995: Suomen kieli 1700-luvulla [Sammanfattning: Finska språket på 1700-talet. E. Summary: The Finnish language in the 18th century.] In Päivikki Kallio, Irma Savolainen & Sinikka Vainio (eds.), *Helsinki 1700*. Narinkka. Helsinki: Helsingin kaupunginmuseo, 109–130.
Häkkinen, Kaisa 1998: Suomen kirjakielen kehitys [E. Summary: The development of the Finnish literary language.] In Arja Koskinen & Eira Söderholm (eds.), The Baltic-Finnic Minorities of the Barents Area and the Literary Language: Papers from the Symposium held in Tromsø June 13th–15th 1997. *Nordlyd. Tromsø university working papers on language & linguistics* 26: 15–26.
Häkkinen, Kaisa 2002: Lönnrot as a linguist. *Journal of Finnish Studies* 6 (1–2): 27–40.
Häkkinen, Kaisa 2006: Suomen kielitieteen nousu 1700- ja 1800-lukujen vaihteessa [E. Summary: The rise of comparative linguistics at the beginning of the nineteenth century.]. In Sakari Ollitervo & Kari Immonen (eds.), *Herder, Suomi, Eurooppa*.

Helsinki: SKS, 291–311, 544–545.
Hästesko, F.A. 1931: *Suomen nuorisoseuraliikkeen historia*. Porvoo: WSOY.
Iisalo, Taimo 1992: *Merimies piirsi nimensä. Havaintoja Uudenkaupungin seudun merimiesväestön kirjoitustaidosta 1800-luvulla*. Turku: Turun yliopiston kasvatustieteiden tiedekunta. Julkaisusarja A:152.
Ikola, Osmo 1962: Entwicklungszüge in der Ausbildung der Finnischen Schriftsprache. *Ural-Altaische Jahrbücher* 34: 8–19.
Ikola, Osmo 1983: Porthan as a linguist. *Academia Scientiarum Fennica Yearbook* 1983–1984, 117–130.
Jahnsson, A. W. 1871: *Finska Språkets Satslära. För läroverkens behof*. Helsingfors.
Jakob Benediktsson 1981: Den vågnende interesse for sagaliteraturen på Island i 1600-tallet. *Maal og minne*, 157–170.
Jakobi-Mirwald, Christine 2004: *Das mittelalterliche Buch. Funktion und Ausstattung*, Stuttgart: Reclam.
Jakobson, Roman 1971 [1957]: Shifters, Verbal Categories, and the Russian Verb. In *Selected Writings of Roman Jakobson. Vol 2. Word and Language*. The Hague & Paris: Mouton & Co, 130–147.
Jensen, H. (ed.) 1983: *Eiríks saga víðförla*. København: Editiones Arnamagnæanæ B 29.
Jóhann Gunnar Ólafsson 1956: Magnús Jónsson í Vigur. *Skírnir* CXXX: 107–126.
Johansson, Egil 1976: International Symposium for Literacy, Persepolis, Iran, 3–8 September 1975. In Egil Johansson (ed.), *Folkbildning och samhällsutveckling. Pågående projektarbete 1976*. Umeå.
Johansson, Egil 1977: *The History of Literacy in Sweden in Comparison with Some Other Countries*. Umeå: Umeå University.
Johansson, Egil 1981: The History of Literacy in Sweden. In H. J. Graff (ed.), *Literacy and Social Development in the West. A Reader*. Cambridge: Cambridge University Press, 151–182.
Johansson, Ella 1996: "Imber och mamma gjorde lite av varje". Kvinnor, män och tid i en bondedagbok från 1920-talet. In Roger Jacobson & Britta Lundgren (eds.), *Oväntat. Aspekter på etnologisk kulturforskning*. Stockholm: Carlsson, 111–123.
Jón Guðnason 1961–1966: *Dalamenn. Æviskrár 1703–1961*. Reykjavík: Jón Guðnason.
Jón Helgason 1955: *Kvæðabók úr Vigur. AM 148, 8vo*, Íslenzk rit síðari alda, 2. flokkur. 1. bindi B. Kaupmannahöfn: Hið íslenzka fræðafélag.
Jón Helgason 1958: *Handritaspjall*. Reykjavík: Mál og menning.
Jón Karl Helgason 1998: *Hetjan og höfundurinn. Brot úr íslenskri menningarsögu*. Reykjavík: Mál og menning.
Jón Sveinsson 1913: Drög til skólasögu I. Akranes. *Skólablaðið* 7 (5): 68–72.
Jónas Jónasson 1975: *Íslenzkir þjóðhættir*. 3rd edition. Reykjavík: Ísafold.
Judén, Jac. 1818: *Försök till utredande af finska språkets grammatik*. Wiborg: Cedervaller.
Kairamo, Aimo 1986: *Ponnistuksien kautta vapauteen. Sosialidemokraattinen nuorisoliike. Osa I. 1906–1922*. Helsinki: Sosialidemokraattisen nuorison keskusliitto & Nuorten puolesta keskusliitto.
Kalliokoski, Jyrki 2006: Tekstilajin taju ja toisella kielellä kirjoittaminen. In Anne Mäntynen, Susanna Shore, & Anna Solin (eds.), *Genre – tekstilaji*. Helsinki: SKS, 240–265.
Karlsson, Anna-Malin 2006: *En arbetsdag i skriftsamhället. Ett etnografiskt perspektiv på skriftanvändning i vanliga yrken*. Stockholm: Språkrådet och Norstedts Akademiska förlag.
Karpio, Vihtori 1938: *Raittiuden Ystävät 1883–1933*. Jyväskylä & Helsinki: K. J. Gummerus.
Kauranen, Kaisa 1999: *Rahvas, kauppahuone esivalta. Katovuodet pohjoisessa Suomessa 1830-luvulla* Historiallisia tutkimuksia 204. Helsinki: Suomen Historiallinen Seura.
Kauranen, Kaisa 2005: Luettelo kansankirjoittajista, heidän aineistoistaan ja käymäs-

tään kirjeenvaihdosta. Finnish Literature Society, Literary Archives.
Kauranen, Kaisa 2006: Kansanihmisten käsikirjoitukset SKSn arkistoissa. *Elore* 13 (2) 1–15. http://www.elore.fi/arkisto/2_06/kau2_06.pdf.
Kauranen, Kaisa 2007: Did Writing Lead to Social Mobility? Case Studies of Ordinary Writers in Nineteenth-Century Finland. In Martyn Lyons (ed.), *Ordinary Writings, Personal Narratives. Writing Practices in 19th and Early 20th-Century Europe.* Bern: Peter Lang, 51–68.
Kauranen, Kaisa 2009a: Menneisyyden muistiinpanojen kirjo. In Kaisa Kauranen (ed.), *Työtä ja rakkautta. Kansanmiesten päiväkirjoja 1834–1937.* Helsinki: SKS, 6–21.
Kauranen, Kaisa 2009b (ed). *Työtä ja rakkautta. Kansanmiesten päiväkirjoja 1834–1937.* Helsinki: SKS.
Kauranen, Kaisa & Myllynen, Mari 2006: Luettelo kansankerääjien käsikirjoituksista 1831–1910. Finnish Literature Society, Folklore Archives.
Kauranen, Kaisa & Virtanen, Maria 2010: Sivistyksen ihanne torppari Kustaa Braskin elämässä ja teksteissä. In Kirsti Salmi-Niklander, Sami Suodenjoki & Taina Uusitalo (eds.), *Lukeva ja kirjoittava työläinen.* Helsinki: Työväen historian ja perinteen tutkimuksen seura, 48–79.
Kaye, Harvey J. 1984: *The British Marxist Historians. An Introductory Analysis.* Cambridge, UK: Polity.
Kero, Reino 1985: Kultaa vuolemassa ja "kolia" kaivamassa – siirtolaiskirjeitä Pohjois-Amerikasta Suomeen. In Eero Kuparinen (ed.), *Maitten ja merten takaa. Vuosisata suomalaisia siirtolaiskirjeitä.* Turku: Turun Historiallinen Yhdistys, 9–135.
Kero, Reino 1996: *Suureen länteen: Siirtolaisuus Suomesta Pohjois-Amerikkaan. Suomalaisen siirtolaisuuden historia 1.* Turku: Siirtolaisuusinstituutti.
King, Kathryn R. 1994: Jane Barker, Poetical Recreations, and the Sociable Text. *English Language History* 61 (3): 551–570.
Klemens Jónsson 1930: *Fjögur hundruð ára saga prentlistarinnar á Íslandi,* Reykjavík: Félagsprentsmiðjan.
Klinge, Matti 1967: *Ylioppilaskunnan historia. Toinen osa 1853–1871.* Porvoo: WSOY.
Klinge, Matti 1985: Finska språket i Finland under 1800-talet. De nordiske skriftspråkenes utvikling på 1800-tallet 2. Behovet for og broken av skrift i 1800-tallets forvaltning, næringsliv og privatkommunikasjon. *Nordisk språksekretariats rapporter* 6: 7–24. Oslo: Nordisk språksekretariat.
Knuuttila, Seppo 1994. *Tyhmän kansan teoria. Näkökulmia menneestä tulevaan.* Helsinki: SKS.
Kristín Geirsdóttir 1979: Fáein alþýðleg orð. *Skírnir* 153: 5–41.
Kristín Geirsdóttir 1990: Hugleiðing um fornsögur. *Skírnir* 164: 34–55.
Kristín Geirsdóttir 1995: Hvað er sannleikur? *Skírnir* 169: 399–422.
Kristín Sigfúsdóttir 1949: *Rit Kristínar Sigfúsdóttur I.* Reykjavík: Ísafold.
Kristleifur Þorsteinsson 1935–1938: *Héraðssaga Borgarfjarðar.* Reykjavík: Útgáfunefnd & Mýra- og Borgarfjarðarsýsla.
Krook, Ragnar 1949: *Vasa Svenska Lyceum 1874–1949.* Vaasa: Svensk-österbottniska samfundet.
Kroskrity, Paul V. 2003a: Regimenting Languages. Language Ideological Perspectives. In Paul V. Kroskrity (ed.), *Regimes of Language. Ideologies, Polities, and Identities.* School of American Research Press. Santa Fe, New Mexico. Oxford: James Currey, 1–34.
Kroskrity, Paul V. 2003b: Language Ideologies in the Expression and Representation of Arizona Tewa Ethnic Idenitity. In Paul V. Kroskrity (ed.), *Regimes of Language. Ideologies, Polities, and Identities.* Santa Fe: School of American Research Press & Oxford: James Currey, 329–360.
Kuismin [former Makkonen], Anna 2010: Hänen itsensä kertomana. 1800-luvun kansanihmiset ja oman elämän kirjoitus. *Lukeva ja kirjoittava työläinen.* Ed. Kirsti Salmi-Niklander, Sami Suodenjoki and Taina Uusitalo. Väki Voimakas 23. Työväen

historian ja perinteen tutkimuksen seura, 21–47.

Kuismin [former Makkonen], Anna 2011, Building the Nation, Lighting the Torch: Excursions into the Writings of the Common People in Nineteenth-Century Finland. *Journal of Finnish Studies* 16 (1): 5–24.

Kurki, Tuulikki 2002. *Heikki Meriläinen ja keskusteluja kansanperinteestä*. Helsinki: SKS.

Kurki, Tuulikki 2004. Tekstit kansanrunousarkiston liepeillä. In Tuulikki Kurki (ed.), *Kansanrunousarkisto, lukijat ja tulkinnat*. Helsinki: SKS, 65–90.

Kuuliala, Viljo–Kustaa 1939: *Toimellinen talonpoika. Kotiseutukuvaus*. Talonpoikaiskulttuurisäätiön julkaisuja 1. Jyväskylä & Helsinki: K. J. Gummerus.

Kuusi, Matti 1970: Anni Lehtosen runousoppi. *Virittäjä* 74: 293–303.

Kålund, Kristian 1888–1894: *Katalog over Den arnamagnæanske Håndskriftsamling*. København.

Kålund, Kristian 1900: *Katalog over de oldnorsk–islandske Håndskrifter i Det store kongelige Bibliotek og i Universitetsbiblioteket*. København.

Köll, Anu Mai (ed.) 2005: *Kommunismens ansikten. Repression, övervakning och svenska reaktioner*. Höör: Brutus Östlings Bokförlag Symposion.

Laaksonen, Pekka 2005: Viides Kalevala. In *Kalevala. Lyhennetty laitos. Tärkeimmillä selityksillä koulujen tarpeeksi varustanut Elias Lönnrot*. Helsinki: SKS, VII–XX.

Laasonen, Pentti 2000: *Finlands kyrkohistoria II. Åren 1593–1808*. Översättning från finskan Bill Widén. Skellefteå: Artos.

Labov, William 1971: The Study of Language in its Social Context. In Joshua A. Fishman (ed.), *Advances in the Sociology of Language. Vol. 1*. The Hague: Mouton & Co, 152–216.

Laine, Tuija & Perälä, Anna 2005: *Henrik Renqvist julkaisijana ja kirjakauppiaana 1815–1866*. [Zusammenfassung: Henrik Renqvist als Herausgeber und Buchhändler 1815–1866.] Suomen kirkkohistoriallisen seuran toimituksia 198. Helsinki: Suomen kirkkohistoriallinen seura.

Laitinen, Lea 2002: From Logophoric Pronoun to Discourse Particle. A Case Study of Finnish and Saami. In I. Wischer & G. Diewald (eds.), *New Reflections on Grammaticalization*. Amsterdam & Philadelphia: John Benjamins, 327–344.

Laitinen, Lea 2005: *Hän*, the third speech act pronoun in Finnish. In Ritva Laury (ed.), *Minimal Reference. The Use of Pronouns in Finnish and Estonian*. Helsinki: SKS, 75–106.

Laitinen, Lea 2007: Meidänkö maassa? *Yliopisto* 12/2007.

Laitinen, Lea 2008: Maamme – meidän maa. *Virittäjä* 112: 84–114.

Laitinen, Lea 2009: Kesytöntä kirjoitusta vai kesytettyä puhetta? Itseoppineiden tekstit tutkimuskohteena. In Jyrki Kalliokoski, Tuija Nikko, & Saija Pyhäniemi (eds.), *The Diversity of Speech and Writing. AFinLA Yearbook 2009*, 43–78.

Laitinen, Lea 2010: Kylä, kirkko ja kuningas. Omistusrakenteiden kielipolitiikka Ruotsin ajan suomessa. In Hanna Lappalainen, Marja-Leena Sorjonen, & Maria Vilkuna (eds.), *Kielellä on merkitystä. Näkökulmia kielipolitiikkaan*. Helsinki: SKS, 369–402.

Laitinen, Lea & Nordlund, Taru 2008: Kansankirjoittajat kaksisataa vuotta sitten. In Tiina Onikki-Rantajääskö & Mari Siiroinen (eds.), *Kieltä kohti*. Helsinki: Otava, 218–232.

Laitinen, Lea & Nordlund, Taru 2012: Performing Identities and Interaction through Epistolary Formulae. In Marina Dossena & Gabriella Del Lungo Camiciotti (eds.), *Letter Writing in Late Modern Europe*. Amsterdam & Philadelphia: John Benjamins, 65–88.

Laitinen, Marja 1992: Mikkelin yhdistyselämän historia. In *Mikkelin maalaiskunnan kirja*. Mikkeli: Mikkelin maalaiskunta ja maaseurakunta, 471–508.

Larsson, Bo 1992: *Svenska bondedagböcker. Ett nationalregister*. Stockholm: Nordiska Museet.

Larsson, Bo & Myrdal, Janken 1995: *Peasant Diaries as a Source for the History of Mentality*. Stockholm: Nordiska Museet.

Lassila, Pertti 2008: *Syvistä riveistä. Kansankirjailija, sivistyneistö ja kirjallisuus 1800-luvulla*. Helsinki: Gaudeamus.

Latour, Bruno 1998: *Artefaktens återkomst. Ett möte mellan organisationsteori och tingens sociologi*. Stockholm: Nerenius & Santérus.

Latour, Bruno 2005: *Reassembling the Social. An Introduction to Actor-Network-Theory*. Oxford: Oxford University Press.

Lauerma, Petri 2001: Klaus Kemelli ja varhaisnykysuomen unohdetut uudistajat. *Virittäjä* 105: 4: 561–579. [E. Summary: Klaus Kemelli and the unknown reformers of Early Modern Finnish.]

Lauerma, Petri 2004: Aluemurre vai murteiden yhdistelmä – keskustelu kirjakielen perustasta 1800-luvun alkupuolella. In Katja Huumo, Lea Laitinen, & Outi Paloposki (eds.), *Yhteistä kieltä tekemässä. Näkökulmia suomen kirjakielen kehitykseen 1800-luvulla*. Helsinki: SKS, 136–176.

Lauerma, Petri 2005: Gustaf Renvall suomen kirjakielen standardoijana. [E. Summary: Gustaf Renvall and the standardisation of the Finnish literary language in the 19th Century.] *Sananjalka* 47: 119–157.

Lauerma, Petri 2006: Kolmen heränneen kielivalintoja. In Taru Nordlund, Tiina Onikki-Rantajääskö, & Toni Suutari (eds.), *Kohtauspaikkana kieli: näkökulmia persoonaan, muutoksiin ja valintoihin*. 367–385. Helsinki: SKS.

Lauerma, Petri 2007: Vieraiden grafeemien väistyminen varhaisnykysuomesta etenkin Jakob Johan Malmbergin tuotannon valossa. [E. Summary: The abandonment of foreign graphemes in Early Modern Finnish with special reference to Jakob Johan Malmberg's works.] *Virittäjä* 111: 3: 322–345.

Lauerma, Petri 2008a: Varhaisnykysuomen morfologinen etääntyminen vanhasta kirjasuomesta etenkin Jakob Johan Malmbergin tuotannon valossa. [E. Summary: Morphological divergence of Early Modern Finnish from Old Literary Finnish with particular reference to the works of Jakob Johan Malmberg.] *Virittäjä* 112: 3: 355–381.

Lauerma, Petri 2008b: Paavo Ruotsalaisen kirjeiden kielestä. [E. Summary: On the language of Paavo Ruotsalainen's letters.] *Sananjalka* 50: 73–86.

Lauerma, Petri 2012: *Kristityn vaellus varhaisnykysuomen merkinnässä. Jakob Johan Malmbergin suomennosten kielellinen kehitys 1800-luvun kirjasuomen murroksessa*. Kotimaisten kielten keskuksen verkkojulkaisuja 31. Helsinki: Kotimaisten kielten keskus. http://scripta.kotus.fi/www/verkkojulkaisut/julk31/

Laurila, Vihtori 1956: *Suomen rahvaan runoniekat sääty-yhteiskunnan aikana. I osa. Yleiset näkökohdat*. Helsinki: SKS.

Lehikoinen, Laila & Kiuru, Silva 1998 [1989]: *Kirjasuomen kehitys*. Helsinki: Helsingin yliopiston suomen kielen laitos.

Leino-Kaukiainen, Pirkko 2007: Suomalaisten kirjalliset taidot autonomian kaudella. *Historiallinen aikakauskirja* 105 (4): 420–443.

Lejeune, Philippe 1989: *On Autobiography*. Ed. and with a foreword by Paul John Eakin. Transl. by Katherine Leary. Minneapolis: The University of Minnesota Press.

Lerner, Daniel 1963: Toward a Communication Theory of Modernization. In Lucian W. Pye (ed.), *Communications and Political Development*. Princeton: Princeton University Press.

Le Roy Ladurie, Emmanuel 1966: *Les Paysans du Languedoc*. 2 vols. Paris: Imprimerie Nationale.

Le Roy Ladurie, Emmanuel 1972: *Times of Feast, Times of Famine. A History of Climate since the Year 1000*. Transl. by Barbara Bray. London: Allen & Unwin.

Le Roy Ladurie, Emmanuel 1980 [1978]: *Montaillou. Cathars and Catholics in a French Village, 1294–1324*. Transl. by Barbara Bray. Harmondsworth, UK: Penguin.

Liikanen, Ilkka 1995: *Fennomania ja kansa. Joukkojärjestäytymisen läpimurto ja*

Suomalaisen puolueen synty. Helsinki: Suomen Historiallinen Seura.
Liljewall, Britt 1995: *Bondevardag och samhällsförändring. Studier i och kring västsvenska bondedagböcker från 1800-talet.* Göteborg: Historiska Institutionen i Göteborg.
Liljewall, Britt 2001: *Självskrivna liv. Studier i äldre folkliga levnadsminnen.* Stockholm: Nordiska museets förlag.
Liljewall, Britt 2002: 'Self-written lives' or Why did peasants write autobiographies? In Klaus-Joachim Lorenzen-Schmidt & Bjørn Poulsen (eds.), *Writing Peasants. Studies on Peasant Literacy in Early Modern Northern Europe.* Gylling: Landbohistorisk selskab, 210–238.
Lindmark, Daniel 1990: *Läs- och skrivkunnigheten före folkskolan. Historisk läskunnighetsforskning i nordiskt och internationellt perspektiv.* Umeå: Forskningsarkivet, Umeå Universitet.
Lindmark, Daniel 1994: *Pennan, plikten, prestigen och plogen.* Umeå: Institutionen för religionsvetenskap, Umeå universitet.
Lindmark, Daniel (ed.) 1998: *Alphabeta Varia. Orality. Reading and Writing in the History of Literacy. Festschrift in honour of Egil Johansson on the occasion of his 65th Birthday March 24, 1998.* Album Religionum Umense 1. Umeå: Umeå University.
Lindmark, Daniel 2004: *Reading, Writing and Schooling. Swedish Practices of Education and Literacy, 1650–1880.* Umeå: Institutionen för litteraturvetenskap och nordiska språk.
Lockridge, Kenneth A. 1974: *Literacy in Colonial New England. An Enquiry into the Social Context of Literacy in the Early Modern West.* New York: Norton.
Loftur Guttormsson 1981: Læsefærdighed og folkeuddannelse 1540–1800. In Mauno Jokipii & Ilkka Nummela (ed.), *Ur nordisk kulturhistoria. Läskunnighet och folkbildning före folkskoleväsendet. 18. Nordiska historikersmötet, Jyväskylä 1981. Mötesrapport III.* Jyväskylä: Studia Historica Jyväskyläensia 22 (3), 123–191.
Loftur Guttormsson 1987: Bókmenning á upplýsingaröld: Upplýsing í stríði við alþýðumenningu. In Þuríður J. Kristjánsdóttir (ed.), *Gefið og þegið: Afmælisrit til heiðurs Brodda Jóhannessyni sjötugum.* Reykjavík: Iðunn, 247–289.
Loftur Guttormsson 1989: Læsi. In Frosti F. Jóhannsson (ed.), *Munnmenntir og bókmenning, Íslensk þjóðmenning VI.* Reykjavík: Þjóðsaga, 117–144.
Loftur Guttormsson 1990: The Development of Popular Religious Literacy in the Seventeenth and Eighteenth Centuries. *Scandinavian Journal of History* 15 (1): 15–35.
Loftur Guttormsson 1992: Farskólahald í sextíu ár (1890–1950). Nokkrir megindrættir. *Uppeldi og menntun* 1 (1): 207–222.
Loftur Guttormsson 2008: Fræðsluhefðin. Kirkjuleg heimafræðsla. In Loftur Guttormsson (ed.), *Almenningsfræðsla á Íslandi 1880–2007*, vol. 1. Reykjavík: Háskólaútgáfan, 21–35.
Lorenzen-Schmidt, Klaus-Joachim & Poulsen, Bjørn (eds.) 1992: *Bäuerliche Anschreibebücher als Quellen zur Wirtschaftsgeschichte.* Neumünster: Wachholtz.
Lorenzen-Schmidt, Klaus-Joachim & Poulsen, Bjørn (eds.) 2002: *Writing Peasants. Studies on Peasant Literacy in Early Modern Northern Europe.* Kerteminde: Landbohistorisk Selskab.
Love, Harold 1993: *Scribal Publication in Seventeenth-Century England.* Oxford: Clarendon Press.
Lovie, Jacques (ed.) 1981: *Poilus Savoyards (1913–1918. Chronique d'une famille tarentaise.* Chambéry.
Lucy, J. A. 2003: Reflexive Language and the Human Disciplines. In J. A. Lucy (ed.), *Reflexive Language. Reported Speech and Metapragmatics.* Cambridge: Cambridge University Press, 9–32.
Lúðvík Kristjánsson 1980–1986: *Íslenzkir sjávarhættir.* Reykjavík: Menningarsjóður.
Lúðvík Kristjánsson 1989: Minnisblöð Sigurðar Lynge á Akranesi. *Árbók Landsbókasafn Íslands.* Nýr flokkur 15: 14–16.

Luettelo Suomen teosofisen seuran jäsenistä syysk. 1:pnä 1911. 1911. Helsinki: Kirjapaino-osakeyhtiö Sana.

Luttinen, Rauno 1984: Läs- och skrivkunnighet i Finland före folkskolväsendet. In *De nordiske skriftspråkenes utvikling på 1800-tallet 1. Skolens og lese- og skrivefärdighetens betydning for de nordiske skriftsspråkenes utvikling på 1800-tallet.* Nordisk språksekretariats rapporter 4. Oslo: Nordisk språksekretariat, 78–87.

Luukkanen, Tarja-Liisa 1994–1995: Pilatuxen breivit ja apostolien kilvoitukset – Pohjanmaan mystikot kristinuskon historian alkulähteillä. [Zusammenfassung: Die Briefe des Pilatus und das Bemühen der Apostel – die ostbottnischen Mystiker an den Quellen der Geschichte des Christentums.] *Suomen kirkkohistoriallisen seuran vuosikirja* 84–85, 89–99.

Luukkanen, Tarja-Liisa 2005: *Sääty-ylioppilaasta ensimmäisen polven sivistyneistöön. Jumaluusopin ylioppilaiden sukupolvikehitys ja poliittis-yhteiskunnallinen toiminta 1853–1918.* Helsinki: SKS.

Lyons, Martyn 2003: French Soldiers and Their Correspondence. Towards a History of Writing Practices in the First World War. *French History* 17 (1): 79–95.

Lyons, Martyn 2008: *Reading Culture and Writing Practices in Nineteenth-Century France.* Toronto: University of Toronto Press.

Lyons, Martyn 2008: Why and How did Workers Write and Publish their Autobiographies in 19th century Europe? *Language and the Scientific Imagination. Proceedings of the 11th Conference of the International Society for the Study of European Ideas (ISSEI).* http://hdl.handle.net/10138/15287

Lyons, Martyn 2010: *History of Reading and Writing in the Western World.* Basingstoke, U. K: Palgrave and Macmillan.

Lyons, Martyn 2012: *The Writing Culture of Ordinary People in Europe, c. 1860–1920.* Cambridge: Cambridge University Press.

Länkelä, Jaako 1867 [1865]: *Asioimiskirjain tekemisen johdatus. Kansa-, pyhä- ja maanviljelyskouluin ynnä yksityisten tarpeeksi.* Published by the writer.

Lönnrot, Elias 1999. Esipuhe. In *Kalevala taikka vanhoja Karjalan runoja Suomen kansan muinosista ajoista.* 1835 julkaistun Kalevalan laitoksen uusi painos. Helsinki: SKS, 1–28.

Magnús H. Árnason 1961: *Ljúfa vor. Bernskuminningar og eyfir3kir þættir.* Akureyri: Prentsmiðja Björns Jónssonar.

Magoun, Francis P. Jr. 1967: *Mikael Agricola's Gospel according to St Mark.* Ed. with foreword, an outline of the language, glossary and appendix. Helsinki: SKS.

Makkonen, Anna (ed.) 2002: *Karheita kertomuksia. Itseoppineiden omaelämäkertoja 1800-luvun Suomesta.* Helsinki: SKS.

Makkonen, Anna 2005: *Kadonnut kangas. Retkiä Ida Digertin päiväkirjaan.* Helsinki: SKS.

Manninen, Antti 1856 [1863]: *Taito ja Toimi. Lyhykäinen käsikirja Talouden hoitajille.* Helsinki: P. Tikkanen.

Marchi, Clelia 1992: *Gnanca na busia, 1912–1985.* Pieve Santo Stefano: Mondadori.

Martínez Martín, Laura 2006: 'Cartas Migrantes'. La correspondencia de una familia de asturianos en Chile (1874–1932). Unpublished preliminary thesis, Universidad de Alcalá de Henares.

McKinnell, John 1978–1979: Saga Manuscripts in Iceland in the Later 18th Century. *Saga-book* XX: 131–136.

Melander, Björn 1999: *Vetenskap och underhållning. Den allmännyttiga uppsatsen i den svenska almanackan från 1749 till 1990.* Lund: Lunds universitet, Institutionen för nordiska språk.

Mikkola, Kati 2009: *Tulevaisuutta vastaan. Uutuuksien vastustus, kansantiedon keruu ja kansakunnan rakentaminen.* Helsinki: SKS.

Mitchell, S. A. 1991: *Heroic sagas and ballads.* Ithaca, NY: Cornell University Press.

Mordenti, R. 2001: *I libri di famiglia in Italia, 2, Geografia e storia.* Rome: Edizioni di

Storia e Letteratura.

Muir, Edward 1991: Introduction. In Edward Muir & Guido Ruggiero (eds.), *Microhistory and the Lost Peoples of Europe. Selections from* Quaderni Storici. Baltimore: Johns Hopkins University Press.

Munck, Thomas 2004: Literacy, Educational Reform and the Use of Print in Eighteenth-Century Denmark. *European History Quarterly* 34: 275–276.

Murtorinne, Eino 2000: *Finlands kyrkohistoria* III. *Autonomins tidevarv 1809–1899*. Översättning från finskan Bill Widén. Skellefteå: Artos.

Mustonen, O. A. F. 1936 [1885]: *Taikanuotta eli opas taikojen kerääjille*. Helsinki: SKS.

Myllynen, Mari 2010: Kuultua, luultua ja kunnioitettua. *Hän-* ja *he-*pronominien funktiot metsäsuomalaiskirjeissä 1820–1870. Unpublished Master's Thesis in Finnish. University of Helsinki.

Mägiste, Julius 1960: Vermlannin sammuvaa savoa. Kielennäytteitä vuosilta 1947–51. Helsinki: SKS.

Mäkinen, Ilkka 1997: *"Nödvändighet af LainaKirjasto". Modernin lukuhalun tulo Suomeen ja lukemisen instituutiot*. [E. Summary: "The Necessity for the Lending Library". The Introduction of the Modern "Desire to Read" into Finland and the Institution of Reading]. Helsinki: SKS.

Mäkinen, Ilkka 2007: Kirjoitustaidon leviämisen herättämiä epäluuloja 1800-luvun Suomessa. *Historiallinen aikakauskirja* 105 (4): 402–419.

Nevalainen, Terttu & Raumolin-Brunberg, Helena 2003: *Historical Sociolinguistics*. London: Longman/ Pearson Education.

Nilsson, Anders & Pettersson, Lars 1992: *Education, Knowledge, and Economic Transformation. The Case of Swedish agriculture 1800–1870*. Lund: Lund University.

Nilsson, Anders & Svärd, Birgitta 1994: Writing Ability and Agrarian Change in Early 19th-Century Rural Scania. *Scandinavian Journal of History* 19: 251–274.

Nordlund, Taru 2005: Miten ja miksi kansa alkoi kirjoittaa? Suomalaisten talonpoikien kirjeitä 1800-luvun alusta. In Sirpa Huttunen & Pirkko Nuolijärvi (eds.), *Tahdon sanoa. Kirjoituksia kielen ja perinteen voimasta*. Helsinki: SKS, 51–79.

Nordlund, Taru 2007: Double Diaglossia. Lower Class Writing in 19th Century Finland. *Multilingua – Journal of Cross-Cultural and Interlanguage Communication* 26 (2–3): 229–246.

Numminen, Jaakko 1961. *Suomen nuorisoseuraliikkeen historia I. Vuodet 1881–1905*. Keuruu: Otava.

Näyhö, Kristiina 2008. *Naiset perinteenkerääjinä 1800-luvun Suomessa*. Unpublished Master's Thesis in Folklore Studies, University of Helsinki.

Odén, Birgitta 1975: Läskunnighet och samhällsförändring. *Forskning om utbildning* 1: 17–31.

Oddur Björnsson (ed.) 1929–1931: *Gríma. Þjóðsögur*. Akureyri: Þorsteinn M. Jónsson.

Ólafur Halldórsson 1989: Skrifaðar bækur. In F. F. Jóhannsson (ed.), *Munnmenntir og bókmenning*, Íslensk þjóðmenning VI. Reykjavík, Iceland: Þjóðsaga, 57–89.

Ollila, Anne 1998: *Jalo velvollisuus. Virkanaisena 1800-luvun lopun Suomessa*. Helsinki: SKS.

Ollila, Anne 2002: *Aika ja elämä. Aikakäsitys 1800-luvun lopussa*. Helsinki: SKS.

Olson, David R. 1980: On the Language and Authority of Textbooks. *Journal of Communication* 30 (1): 186–196.

Omoniyi, Topo & Goodith White 2006: Introduction. In *Sociolinguistics of Identity*. London & New York: Continuum, 1–8.

Ong, Walter J. 1982: *Orality and Literacy. The Technologizing of the Word*. London & New York: Methuen.

Ottenjann, Helmut & Wiegelmann, Günter (eds.) 1982: *Alte Tagebücher und Anschreibebücher. Quellen zum Alltag der ländlichen Bevölkerung in Nordwesteuropa*. Münster: Coppenrath.

Páll Eggert Ólason 1935–1937: *Skrá um handritasöfn Landsbókasafnsins 3*. Reykjavík:

Gutenberg.
Páll Eggert Ólason 1948–1976: *Íslenzkar æviskrár frá landnámstímum til ársloka 1940*. Reykjavík: Hið íslenzka bókmenntafélag.
Paunonen, Heikki 2006: Suomen kielen ohjailun myytit ja stereotypiat. *Virittäjä* 100: 544–555.
Peltonen, Matti 1992: *Talolliset ja torpparit. Vuosisadan vaihteen maatalouskysymys Suomessa*. Helsinki: Suomen Historiallinen Seura.
Peltonen, Ulla-Maija 1996: *Punakapinan muistot. Tutkimus työväen muistelukerronnan muotoutumisesta vuoden 1918 jälkeen*. Helsinki: SKS.
Peltonen, Ulla-Maija 2004: Kalevalan riemuvuoden kilpakeruu ja hyvän kerääjän käsite. In Tuulikki Kurki (ed.), *Kansanrunousarkisto, lukijat ja tulkinnat*. Helsinki: SKS, 199–217.
Poirrier, Philippe 2008: *L'histoire culturelle. Un 'tournant mondial' dans l'historiographie?* Dijon: Presses Universitaires de Dijon. Postface by Roger Chartier.
Power, Rosemary 1984: Saxo in Iceland. *Gripla* VI: 241–258.
Pressman, Jon F. 1994: Pragmatics in the Late Twentieth Century: Countering Recent Historiographic Neglect. *Pragmatics* 4 (4): 461–489.
Procacci, Giovanna 2000: *Soldati e prigionieri italiani nella Grande Guerra*. Turin: Bollati Boringhieri.
Pulkkinen, Paavo 1972: *Nykysuomen kehitys. Katsaus 1800- ja 1900-luvun kirjakieleen sekä tekstinäytteitä*. Tietolipas 72. Helsinki: SKS.
Purcell-Gates, Victoria (ed.) 2007a: *Cultural Practices of Literacy. Case Studies of Language, Literacy, Social Practice, and Power*. Mahwah, NJ: Lawrence Erlbaum Associates.
Purcell-Gates, Victoria 2007b: Complicating the Complex. Cultural Practices of Literacy. In V. Purcell-Gates (ed.), *Cultural Practices of Literacy. Case Studies of Language, Literacy, Social Practice and Power*. Mahwah, N. J.: Routledge, 1–22
Purcell-Gates, Victoria 2007c: Comprehending Complexity. In Victoria Purcell-Gates (ed.), *Cultural Practices of Literacy. Case Studies of Language, Literacy, Social Practice and Power*. Mahwah, N. J.: Routledge, 197–216.
Pöysä, Jyrki & Timonen, Senni 2004: Kuinka ahkerat muurahaiset saivat kasvot? Henkilökohtaisen tiedon paikka arkiston keruuohjeissa. In Tuulikki Kurki (ed.), *Kansanrunousarkisto, lukijat ja tulkinnat*. Helsinki: SKS, 218–254.
Rapola, Martti 1965 [1933]: *Suomen kirjakielen historia I*. Helsinki: SKS.
Rapola, Martti 1969 [1945]: *Vanha kirjasuomi*. Tietolipas 1. Helsinki: SKS.
Rasila, Viljo 1961: *Suomen torpparikysymys vuoteen 1909. Yhteiskuntahistoriallinen tutkimus*. Helsinki: Suomen Historiallinen Seura.
Redfield, Robert 1967: *The Little Community and Peasant Society and Culture*. Chicago: University of Chicago Press.
Rehumäki, Pekka 2008: *Tasa-arvoa tanssilattialla. Käsityöväen sivistysseurat 1840-luvulta 1870-luvun alkuun*. Oulu: Oulu University Press.
Reutersvärd, Elisabeth 2001: *Ett massmedium för folket. Studier i de allmänna kungörelsernas funktion i 1700-talets samhälle*. Lund: Studia Historica Lundiensia 2.
Riikonen, H. K. 2006: J. G. Herderin tuntemus Turun Akatemian piirissä Porthanin ja Franzénin aikana. [E. Summary: Porthan and Franzén on J. G. Herder at the Turn of the Eighteenth and Nineteenth Centuries.] In Sakari Ollitervo & Kari Immonen (eds.), *Herder, Suomi, Eurooppa*. Helsinki: SKS, 265–290, 543–544.
Runcis, Maija 1998: *Steriliseringar i folkhemmet*. Stockholm: Ordfront.
Ruotsalainen, Paavo 1977: *The Inward knowledge of Christ. The Letters and other Writings*. Transl. and with introduction by W. J. Kukkonen. Publications of Luther-Agricola Society B 10.
Ruotsalainen, Paavo 2005: *Kirjeitä*. Ed. J. Elenius. Helsinki: Kirjapaja.
Russo, Matteo 1993: *Lettere dal Fronte (1916–1917)*. Eds. Sebastiano Maggio et al. Catania: Cooperativa Universitaria Editrice Catanese di Magistero.

Ruuth, Martti 1921: *Abraham Achrenius. Ajan merkki ajoiltaan. Toinen osa.* Porvoo: WSOY.
Ruutu, Martti 1939: *Savo-karjalaisen osakunnan historia II 1857–1887.* Porvoo & Helsinki: WSOY.
Saari, Mirja 2001: Språkval och språkbyte inom en prästsläkt i autonomitidens Finland. In Marianne Blomqvist, Mirja Saari & Peter Slotte (eds.), *Våra språk i tid och rum.* Meddelanden från Institutionen för nordiska språk och nordisk litteratur vid Helsingfors universitet B 21. Helsingfors: Institutionen för nordiska språk och nordisk litteratur, 198–209.
Salmi-Niklander, Kirsti 2004: *Itsekasvatusta ja kapinaa. Tutkimus Karkkilan työläisnuorten kirjoittavasta keskusteluyhteisöstä 1910- ja 1920-luvuilla.* Helsinki: SKS.
Salmi-Niklander, Kirsti 2005: Käsin kirjoitettua. 1800-luvun lopun nuoret naiset historian opiskelijoina ja tulkitsijoina. In Elina Katainen et al. (eds.), *Oma pöytä. Naiset historian kirjoittajina Suomessa 1800- ja 1900-luvuilla.* Helsinki: SKS, 75–97.
Salmi-Niklander, Kirsti 2006: Tapahtuma, kokemus ja kerronta. In Outi Fingerroos et al. (eds.), *Muistitieto. Metodologisia kysymyksiä.* Tietolipas 1008. Helsinki: SKS, 199–220.
Salmi-Niklander, Kirsti 2007a: Kokemus varoitti, halu voitti. Juho Kaksola ja 1800-luvun kirjoittavan talonpojan ajatusmaailma. In Eija Stark & Laura Stark (eds.), *Kansanomainen ajattelu.* Helsinki: SKS, 165–184.
Salmi-Niklander, Kirsti 2007b: Bitter Memories and Burst Soap Bubbles: Irony, Parody, and Satire in the Oral-Literary Tradition of Finnish Working-Class Youth at the Beginning of the Twentieth Century. *Humour and Social Protest. International Review of Social History* 52: 189–207.
Salmi-Niklander, Kirsti 2009: Pienet kertomukset, suuret merkitykset. Kerronta, identiteetti ja vuorovaikutus käsinkirjoitetuissa lehdissä. *Kasvatus ja aika* 1: 3: 7–23. http://www.kasvatus-ja-aika.fi/site/?lan=1&page_id=172
Samuel, Raphael 1975: *Village Life and Labour.* London: Routledge Kegan Paul.
Samuel, Raphael 1977: *Miners, Quarrymen and Saltworkers.* London: Routledge Kegan Paul.
Schmidt, W. A. 1948: *Fredrik Gabriel Hedberg. Den evangeliska rörelsens i Finland grundare.* Lutherska Litteraturstiftelsens svenska publikationer 1. Helsingfors: Förbundet för svenska församlingsarbetet i Finland.
Schofield, R. S. 1968: The Measurement of Literacy in Pre-Industrial England. In Jack Goody (ed.), *Literacy in Traditional Societies.* Cambridge: Cambridge University Press, 318–325.
Scott, James C. 1990: *Domination and the Arts of Resistance. Hidden Transcripts.* New Haven & London: Yale University Press.
Scott, Joan W. 1992: Experience. In J. Butler & J. W. Scott (eds.), *Feminists Theorize the Political.* London: Routledge, 22–40.
Scott, Joan W. 1999: *Gender and the Politics of History.* New York: Columbia University Press.
Seelow, Hubert 1989: *Die isländischen Übersetzungen der deutschen Volksbücher: Handschriftenstudien zur Rezeption und Überlieferung ausländischer unterhaltender Literatur in Island in der Zeit zwischen Reformation und Aufklärung.* Reykjavík: Stofnun Árna Magnússonar.
Serna, Justo & Pons, Anaclet 2000: *Cómo se escribe la microhistoria. Ensayo sobre Carlo Ginzburg.* Madrid: Cátedra/Universidad de València.
Setälä, E. N. 1883: Lauseopillisia havaintoja Koillis–Satakunnan kansankielestä. *Suomi* II: 16.
Sigfús Eymundsson (ed.) 1897: *Sagan af Skáld–Helga.* Reykjavík: Sigfús Eymundsson.
Sighvatur Grímsson 1962: Snorri Björnsson, prestur á Húsafelli. In Jón Guðnason (ed.), *Merkir Íslendingar I. Nýr flokkur.* Reykjavík: Bókfellsútgáfan, 75–87.
Sigurður Gylfi Magnússon 1993: *The Continuity of Everyday Life: Popular Culture in*

Iceland 1850–1940. Doctoral thesis, Carnegie Mellon University.

Sigurður Gylfi Magnússon 1995a: From Children's Point of View: Childhood in Nineteenth Century Iceland. *Journal of Social History* 29: 295–323.

Sigurður Gylfi Magnússon 1995b: Siðferðilegar fyrirmyndir á 19. öld. *Ný saga* 7: 57–72.

Sigurður Gylfi Magnússon 1997a: *Menntun, ást og sorg: Einsögurannsókn á íslensku sveitasamfélagi 19. og 20. aldar*. Sagnfræðirannsóknir 13. Reykjavík: Sagnfræðistofnun Háskóla Íslands og Háskólaútgáfan.

Sigurður Gylfi Magnússon 1997b: Kynjasögur á 19. og 20. öld. Hlutverkaskipan í íslensku samfélagi. *Saga* 35: 137–177.

Sigurður Gylfi Magnússon 2004: Fortíðardraumar: Sjálfsbókmenntir á Íslandi. *Sýnisbók íslenskrar alþýðumenningar* 9. Reykjavík: Háskólaútgáfan.

Sigurður Gylfi Magnússon 2005: Sjálfssögur: Minni, minningar og saga. *Sýnisbók íslenskrar alþýðumenningar* 11. Reykjavík: Háskólaútgáfan.

Sigurður Gylfi Magnússon 2010: *Wasteland with Words: A Social History of Iceland*. London: Reaktion Books / University of Chicago Press.

Sigurður Gylfi Magnusson & Davíð Olafsson 2002: 'Barefoot Historians': Education in Iceland in the Modern Period. In Klaus-Joachim Lorenzen-Schmidt & Bjørn Poulsen (eds.), *Writing Peasants. Studies on Peasant Literacy in Early Modern Northern Europe*. Gylling: Landbohistorisk Selskab, 175–209.

Sigurgeir Steingrímsson 1972: *Þúsund og einn dagur: Íslenzkar þýðingar og varðveizla þeirra*. Unpublished cand.mag. thesis. Háskóli Íslands, Reykjavík.

Silverstein, Michael 1981: The Limits of Awareness. *Sociolinguistic Working Paper 84*. Austin, Texas: Southwest Educational Development Library.

Silverstein, Michael 1998: Contemporary Transformations of Local Linguistic Communities. *Annual Review of Anthropology* 27: 401–426.

Silverstein, Michael 2003: Indexical Order and the Dialectics of Sociolinguistic Life. *Language & Communication* 23: 193–229.

Silverstein, Michael 2007 [2000]: Whorfianism and the Linguistic Imagination of Nationality. In Paul V. Kroskrity (ed.), *Regimes of Language. Ideologies, Polities, and Identities*. Santa Fe: School of American Research Press & Oxford: James Currey, 85–138.

Sinisalo, Hannu 1981: *Ihmisen ja työn kuvia. Valokuvia 1920- ja 1930-luvun kansanelämästä*. Kuopio: Kimy Kustannus oy.

Sinnemäki, Maunu 1973: *The Church in Finland*. Helsinki: Otava.

Sinor, Jennifer 2002: *The Extraordinary Work of Ordinary Writing. Annie Ray's Diary*. Iowa City: University of Iowa Press.

Slay, Desmond 1960: *The Manuscripts of Hrólfs saga kraka*. Copenhagen: Bibliotheca Arnamagnæana XXIV.

Slay, Desmond (ed.) 1997: *Mírmanns saga*. Copenhagen: Editiones Arnamagnæanæ A 17.

Smith, Sidonie & Watson, Julia 2001: *Reading Autobiography: A Guide for Interpreting Life Narratives*. Minneapolis: University of Minnesota Press.

Springborg, Peter 1977: Antiqvæ Historiæ Lepores – om renæssancen i den islandske håndskriftproduktion i 1600-tallet. *Gardar* VIII: 53–89.

Stark, Laura 2006a: *The Magical Self. Body, Society and the Supernatural in Early Modern Rural Finland*. Helsinki: Academia Scientiarum Fennica.

Stark, Laura 2006b: Kansallinen herääminen & sosiaalinen nousu maaseudulla. In Hilkka Helsti, Laura Stark & Saara Tuomaala (eds.), *Modernisaatio & kansan kokemus Suomessa 1860–1960*. Helsinki: SKS, 47–109.

Stark, Laura 2008: Maalaisrahvaan kirjoitusmotivaatio & asenteet kirjoitustaitoa kohtaan 1840–1890-luvun Suomessa. *Kasvatus & aika* 3: 49–66. www.kasvatus-ja-aika.fi.

Stefán Aðalsteinsson 1978: *Svarfdælingar*. Reykjavík: Iðunn.

Stefán Karlsson 1970: Ritun Reykjarfjarðarbókar, Excursus: Bókagerð bænda. *Opuscula*

IV, Bibliotheca Arnamagnæana XXX, Hafniæ: Munksgaard, 120–140.
Stefán Karlsson 1979: Islandsk bogeksport til Norge i middelalderen. *Maal og minne*: 1–17.
Stefán Karlsson 1998–2001: The Localisation and Dating of Medieval Icelandic Manuscripts. *Saga-book* XXV: 138–158.
Stefán Karlsson 2002. The Development of Latin Script II: In Iceland. In O. Bandle, K. Braunmuller, E. H. Jahr, A. Karker, & H.-P. Naumann (ed.), *The Nordic Languages: An International Handbook of the History of the North Germanic Languages*. Berlin & New York: Walter de Gruyter, 832–840.
Stefán Karlsson 2006: From the Margins of Medieval Europe: Icelandic Vernacular Scribal Culture. In Outi Merisalo (ed.), *Frontiers in the Middle Ages: Proceedings of the Third European Congress of Medieval Studies (Jyväskylä, 10–14 June 2003)*. Louvain-la-Neuve: Brepols, 483–492.
Steingrímur Jónsson 1989: Prentaðar bækur. In Frosti F. Jóhannsson (ed.), *Munnmenntir og bókmenning*, Íslensk þjóðmenning VI. Reykjavík: Þjóðsaga, 91–115.
Stiaccini, Carlo 2005: *Trincee di Carta: lettere di soldati della prima guerra mondiale al parroco di Fara Novarese*. Novara: Interlinea edizioni.
Stone, Lawrence 1969: Literacy and Education in England 1640–1900. *Past and Present* 42 (1): 69–139.
Storå, Nils 1985: Bondedagböckerna och den finlandssvenska allmogens skrivkonst. *De nordiske skriftspråkenes utvikling på 1800-talet* 2. Oslo: Nordisk språksekretariat, 80–94.
Street, Brian V. 1984: *Literacy in Theory and Practice*. Cambridge: Cambridge University Press.
Street, Brian V. 1993: Introduction. The New Literacy Studies. In Brian V. Street (ed.), *Cross-cultural Approaches to Literacy*. Cambridge: Cambridge University Press, 1–21.
Strellman, Urpu 2005: *Persoonapronominien liikakäyttö: normin synty ja muotoutuminen*. Unpublished Master's Thesis in Finnish. University of Helsinki.
Sumpter, Caroline 2008: *The Victorian Press and the Fairy Tale*. Basingstoke & New York: Palgrave Macmillan.
Suodenjoki, Sami 2009: Kiistämisen rajat – suutari Lindholm ja kansanomainen vastarinta varhaisessa työväenliikkeessä. In Kati Launis & Marko Tikka (eds.), *Työväki ja kokemus*. Työväen historian ja perinteen tutkimuksen seura, 67–98.
Suolahti, Gunnar 1925/1991: *Elämää Suomessa 1700-luvulla*. Helsinki: SKS.
Svenske, John 1993: *Skrivandets villkor. En studie av dagboksskrivandets funktioner och situationella kontexter utgående från Backåkers Eriks dagbok 1861–1914*. Uppsala: Institutionen för nordiska språk.
Sverrir Tómasson 2002: The History of Old Nordic Manuscripts I: Old Icelandic. In Oskar Bandle et al. (eds.), *The Nordic Languages: An International Handbook of the History of the North Germanic Languages I*. Berlin & New York: De Gruyter, 793–801.
Sæmundur Dúason 1966: *Einu sinni var I. Æviminningar*. Akureyri: Prentverk Odds Björnssonar.
Teleman, Ulf 2003: Swedish. In Ana Deumert & Wim Vandenbussche (eds.), *Germanic Standardizations. Past to Present*. Amsterdam: John Benjamins.
Tommila, Päiviö 1983: Tiedonkulku talonpoikaisyhteiskunnan aikana. *Kotiseutu* 1: 31–35.
Torfi H. Tulinius 1993: Kynjasögur úr fortíð og framandi löndum: riddarasögur og fornaldarsögur. In Vésteinn Ólason (ed.), *Íslensk bókmenntasaga* II. Reykjavík: Mál og menning, 165–245.
Torfi H. Tulinius 2005: Sagas of Icelandic Prehistory (*fornaldarsögur*). In Rory McTurk (ed.), *A Companion to Old Norse-Icelandic Literature and Culture*. Oxford: Blackwell, 447–461.

Traugott, Mark (ed.) 1993: *The French Worker. Autobiographies from the Early Industrial Era*. Berkeley: University of California Press.

Turville-Petre, E. O. G. 1953: *Origins of Icelandic Literature*. Oxford: Oxford University Press.

Vandenbussche, Wim 1999: 'Arbeitersprache' in Bruges during the 19th Century. In Helga Bister-Broosen (ed.), *Beiträge zur historischen Stadtsprachenforschung*. Wien: Edition Praesens, 49–65.

Vandenbussche, Wim 2004: Triglossia and Pragmatic Variety Choice in Nineteenth-Century Bruges. *Journal of Historical Pragmatics* 5: 1: 27–47.

Vandenbussche, Wim 2006: A Rough Guide to German Research on "Arbeiterssprache" during the 19th Century. In Hana Andrášová, Peter Ernst & Libuše Spáčilová (eds.), *Germanistik geniessen. Gedenkschrift für Doc. Dr. phil. Hildegard Boková*. Wien: Praesens Verlag, 439–458.

Vandenbussche, Wim 2007: Lower Class Language in 19th Century Flanders. *Multilingua – Journal of Cross-Cultural and Interlanguage Communication* 26 (2–3): 279–290.

Vésteinn Ólason 1989a: Bóksögur. In Frosti F. Jóhannsson (ed.), *Munnmenntir og bókmenning*, Íslensk þjóðmenning VI. Reykjavík: Þjóðsaga, 161–227.

Vésteinn Ólason 1989b: Sagnadansar. In Frosti F. Jóhannsson (ed.), *Munnmenntir og bókmenning*, Íslensk þjóðmenning VI. Reykjavík: Þjóðsaga, 372–389.

Vésteinn Ólason 2005: Family sagas. In Rory McTurk (ed.), *A Companion to Old Norse-Icelandic Literature and Culture*. Oxford: Blackwell, 101–118.

Viðar Hreinsson (ed.) 1997: *The Complete Sagas of Icelanders*, 5 vols. Reykjavík: Leifur Eiríksson.

Viikki, Raimo 2003: *Joroisten historia I. Säätyläispitäjän vaiheet esihistorialliselta ajalta kunnallisen itsehallinnon alkuun 1860-luvulla*. Joroinen: Joroisten kunta ja seurakunta.

Villstrand, Nils Erik 2008: Skriftlighet med förhinder. Den svenska statsmaktens kungörelser i finskspråkiga församlingar under 1700-talet. In Nils Erik Villstrand & Max Engman (eds.), *Maktens mosaik. Enhet, särart och självbild i det svenska riket*. Helsinki & Stockholm: Svenska Litteratursällskapet i Finland & Atlantis, 315–362.

Vovelle, Michael 1985: Histoire sérielle ou 'case studies'. Vrai ou faux dilemme en histoire des mentalités. In *Histoire sociale, sensibilités collectives et mentalités. Mélanges Robert Mandrou*. Paris: Presses Universitaires de France, 49–59.

Weber, Eugen 1976: *Peasants into Frenchmen. The Modernization of Rural France, 1870–1914*. Stanford: Stanford University Press.

White, Hayden V. 1973: *Metahistory. The Historical Imagination in Nineteenth-Century Europe*. Baltimore: The Johns Hopkins University Press.

Wilson, William A. 1985: *Kalevala ja kansallisuusaate*. Helsinki: Työväen sivistysliitto.

Winsa, Birger 1998: *Language Attitudes and Social Identity. Oppression and Revival of a Minority Language in Sweden*. Occasional Paper 17. S. l.: Applied Linguistics Association of Australia.

Woolard, Kathryn A. 2008: Why *dat* now? Linguistic-anthropological contributions to the explanation of sociolinguistic icons and change. *Journal of Sociolinguistics* 12 (4): 432–452.

Zitzelsberger, Otto J. (ed.) 1969: *The Two Versions of Sturlaugs saga starfsama. A Decipherment, Edition, and Translation of a Fourteenth-Century Icelandic Mythical-Heroic Saga*. Düsseldorf: Triltsch.

Zumthor, Paul 1972: *Essai de poétique médiévale*. Paris: Seuil.

Þorsteinn Þorsteinsson 1994: Þættir úr letursögu. Appendix to Ingi Rúnar Eðvaldsson, *Prent eflir mennt. Saga bókagerðar frá upphafi til síðari hluta 20. aldar*. Reykjavík: Hið íslenska bókmenntafélag.

Þórunn Valdimarsdóttir 1989: *Snorri á Húsafelli. Saga frá 18. öld*. Reykjavík: Almenna bókafélagið.

Åström, Anna-Maria 1981: *Torpare och statare. Gårdorganisation och lönesystem på Frugård i Jorois*. Pro gradu -avhandling vid historisk-filologiska sektionen, filosofiska fakulteten vid Helsingfors universitet. Helsinki: Helsingin yliopiston kansatieteen laitoksen tutkimuksia 8.

Åström, Anna-Maria 1989: Herrskapsfolk och underlydande. In Teppo Korhonen & Matti Räsänen (eds.), *Kansa kuvastimessa. Etnisyys ja identiteetti*. Tietolipas 114. Helsinki: SKS, 162–198.

Åström, Anna-Maria 1993: *'Sockenboarne'. Herrgårdskultur i Savolax 1790–1850*. Helsingfors: Svenska Litteratursällskapet i Finland.

Åström, Anna-Maria 1995: Savon herrasväki kansan silmin. Kuinka käsitellään vierasta, kuinka koetellaan rajoja. In Kimmo Katajala (ed.), *Manaajista maalaisaateliin. Tulkintoja toisesta historian, antropologian ja maantieteen välimaastossa*. Helsinki: SKS, 208–235.

Örn Hrafnkelsson 1997: *Stofnun Þjóðbókasafns á Íslandi. Aðdragandi og upphaf*. Reykjavík: Landsbókasafn Íslands.

Index of Names

Abrahams, Roger D. 87
Abrams, Philip 15
Achrenius, Abraham 77, 161
Africanus, Leo 15
Agha, Asif 180
Agricola, Mikael 158, 167
Aguëro, Pedro Jado 18
Ahlqvist, August 165, 182–183, 185
Aho, Juhani (Johannes Brofeldt) 115
Alkio, Santeri 86
Andersson, A. P. 39
Andersson, Anders Petter 33, 39
Andersson, Olof 35, 38, 39
Angelin, Lars Johan 39
Anttila, Aarne 183
Anttonen, Pertti 146, 152, 154, 155
Apelseth, Arne 13
Apo, Satu 81
Arndt, Johann 112
Åström, Anna-Maria 122, 127
Austin, J. L. 180

Bacconnier, Gérard 22, 24
Bakhtin, Mikhail 80, 82
Barbieri, Emilio 25–26
Barbieri, Luigi 26–27
Barbieri, Nicola 25
Barletti, Marini 57
Barton, David 40, 42, 79, 90, 92, 93, 95, 98, 99, 100
Baynham, Mike 99
Becker, Reinhold von 159, 185
Belfrage, Åke 39
Bell, Alan 176, 177
Benhabib, Seyla 91
Bergbom, Gustaf 176
Besnier, Niko 87
Björg Guðmundsdóttir 140
Björn Jónsson á Skarðsá 53

Blasco Martínez, Rosa Maria 18
Blavatsky, Madame 150
Bloch, Marc 15
Blommaert, Jan 103, 170, 184, 187
Blomqvist, Håkan 38
Böcker, C. Ch. 103
Böhme, Jakob 161
Bonfiglio, Giovanni 21
Botteri, Guerrino 18
Brandt, Deborah 95
Brask, Adam 127
Brask, Konstantin 127, 131
Brask, Kustaa 11, 120–133
Brask, Niilo 122, 131, 132
Braudel, Fernand 14
Bristol, Michael 76
Brofeldt, Pekka 115
Brynjólfur Sveinsson 53
Burguière, André 15
Burke, Peter 20, 128
Burnett, John 131

Caffarena, Fabio 26
Calosso, Emanuele 27
Carlström, Anna 39
Chalvin, Antoine 189
Chartier, Roger 40, 61
Clinton, Katie 95
Cobb, Richard 16
Cochet, Annick 24
Columni, Guido de 58
Corbin, Alain 19
Coupland, Nikolas 182
Croci, Federico 21, 28

Damsholt, Tine 13
Darius Phrygius 58
Darnton, Robert 76
Davíð Ólafsson 8–10, 47, 58, 61, 62, 64,

65, 74, 76, 129
Davis, Natalie Zemon 15
Dessilani, Damiano 27
Dondeynaz, Rosalba 18
Dossena, Marina 179
Driscoll, M. J. 8, 10, 50, 54, 57, 58, 61, 62
Durchman, Frans Oskar 164
Duvallon, Outi 189

Eckert, Penelope 181
Edlund, Ann-Catrine 8, 10–11, 93, 95–96, 97, 98, 99, 100
Edlund, Lars-Erik 100
Ehrnrooth, Jari 78
Einar Gunnar Pétursson 62
Einar Þórðarson 59
Elspaß, Stephan 179
Englund, Julia 90, 99
Erlendur Jónsson 139
Errington, Joseph 186
Eskola, Kalle 78, 81–83, 84, 86, 87, 88
Ezell, Margaret J. M. 40, 76, 79, 87

Fairclough, Norman 96, 100
Febvre, Lucien 15, 17
Ferrari, Francesco 28
Fet, Jostein 13, 107
Finnur Gíslason 54
Finnur Sigmundsson 45, 55
Fitzmaurice, Susan 170
Franzina, Emilio 23–24
Freeman, Mark 91
Fur, Gunlög Maria 38
Furet, François 14

Gadd, Per (Pietari) 185
Ganander, Christfrid 159
Gawthrop, Richard 38
Geertz, Clifford 94
Geir Vigfússon 135, 145
Gelbart Ratner, Nina 76
Gemelli, Antonio 27
Georgius Castriotus 57
Gibelli, Antonio 16, 22–24, 28
Gillen, Julia 90
Ginzburg, Carlo 17–18
Gisli Gunnarsson 140
Gísli Konráðsson 58
Gísli Sigurðsson 61
Gissur Einarsson 52
Glauser, Jürg 61
Gödel, Vilhelm 61
Goody, Jack 30
Gottlund, Carl Axel 159, 162, 172, 175–176, 189
Graff, H. J. 38
Grenadou, Ephraïm 23
Grímur M. Helgason 54, 62
Grotenfelt, family 127, 131
Grotenfelt, G. O. 122
Grotenfelt, Kustavi 131, 132
Grotenfelt, N. Karl 132
Guðbrandur Sturlaugsson á Hvítadal 58, 59
Guðmundur Bergþórsson 45, 47
Guðmundur Guðmundsson 137
Guðmundur Sigurður Jóhannsson 55
Guðny Hallgrímsdóttir 12
Guðrún Arnfinnsdóttir 140
Guðrún Ketilsdóttir 12, 134–145
Guðrún Nordal 71
Guðvarður Már Gunnlaugsson 51, 61
Guerre, Martin 15
Gunnarsson, Britt-Louise 90
Gustaf II Adolf 180
Gustaf IV Adolf 185

Haapoja, Matti 111, 118
Haavikko, Ritva 77
Haavio, Martti 152, 153, 154
Hafsteinn Sigurbjarnarson 67
Hagège, Claude 189
Häggman, Kai 77
Häkkinen, Kaisa 167
Hákon Hákonarson 55
Hakulinen, Auli 189
Hall, Nigel 91, 100
Hallbjörn á Kiðjaberg 71
Halldór Hermannsson 61
Halonen, Tarja 187
Hamilton, Mary 40, 42, 90, 92, 93, 95
Haraldur Bernharðsson 53
Harrison, Dick 38
Hästesko, F. A. 77, 116
Heath, Shirley B. 40, 100
Hedberg, Fredrik Gabriel 168
Hegel, G. W. F. 146
Heikkilä, Markku 167
Heininen, Simo 167
Heinonen, Frans Oskar 189
Heinonen, Josefiina 180, 189
Helgi Haraldsson 70
Helgi Magnússon 134
Hemberg, Israel 107, 118
Herder, J. G. von 158, 167
Hermann Pálsson 54
Herranen, Nikolai 186, 189
Hill, Christopher 15

Hitchcock, Tim 16
Hobsbawm, Eric 15, 152
Holberg, Ludvig 57
Honko, Lauri 150
Hormia, Osmo 167
Howard, Ursula 79
Hreinn Benediktsson 50
Hughes, S. 62
Hukkinen, Leena 156
Huuskonen, Pekka 106

Ihalainen, Johan 106, 116
Iisalo, Taimo 177
Ikola, Osmo 167
Illugi Jónsson 140–141
Indriði Gíslisson 58
Ingman, Anders Wilhelm 164–165, 168
Itkonen, Vilho 12, 146–151, 154, 155, 156

Jacobsson, Jesper 107
Jado Agüero, Pedro 18
Jahnsson, A. W. 186
Jakob Benediksson 53
Jakobi-Mirwald, Christine 62
Jakobson, Roman 181
Jensen, H. 60
Jóhann Gunnar Ólafsson 53
Jóhannes Jónsson 55–56, 57
Johansson, Egil 9, 30, 31, 36, 38, 89
Johansson, Ivar Lo 30, 39
Johansson, Linnéa 11, 89–98, 99, 100
Jón Borgfirðing 145
Jón Espólín 62
Jón Guðmundsson 140
Jón Guðnason 56, 58
Jón Illugisson 140–142
Jón Jónsson 140
Jón Jónsson í Simbakoti 54
Jón Karl Helgason 53, 61, 75
Jón Oddsson Hjaltalín 58–59
Jón Stefánsson 46
Jón Sveinsson 43
Jón Vídalín 43, 49
Jón Þórðarson 54
Jónas Jónasson 137–138
Jónas Rafnar 143
Joyce, James 50
Juteini, Jaakko (Jacob Judén) 159, 185

Kairamo, Aimo 77
Kaksola, Juho 78, 80, 82–83, 85–86, 88
Kallio, Kustaa 109–110, 118
Kalliokoski, Jyrki 179
Kålund, Kristian 61

Kangas, Antti 181
Kangas, Wilhelm 181
Karlsson, Anna-Malin 93, 100
Karpio, Vilhelmi 78
Kauppinen, Heikki (Kauppis-Heikki) 115, 116
Kauranen, Kaisa 11, 80, 81, 83, 106, 107, 117, 131, 132, 171, 189
Kaye, Harvey J. 14–15
Kemelli, Klaus 164, 166, 168
Kero, Reino 179
King, Kathryn 87
Kiuru, Silva 162, 167
Kivekäs, Lauri 114
Kjær, Holger 67, 75
Klemens Jónsson 52
Klinge, Matti 77, 167
Knuuttila, Seppo 152, 153
Köll, Anu Mai 38
Koskelainen, Aatu 118
Kristín Geirsdóttir 70–71
Kristín Sigfúsdóttir 67
Kristján Einarsson 59
Kristleifur Kristjánsson 43
Kristleifur Þorsteinsson 43
Krogius, Birger 101
Krogius, Lars Jr. 101
Krook, Ragnar 77
Kroskrity, Paul V. 170
Kuismin, Anna 8, 11, 116, 117, 118, 131, 132
Kukkonen, J. V. 163, 167
Kurki, Tuulikki 155, 156
Kuusi, Matti 156

Laaksonen, Pekka 150
Laasonen, Pentti 167
Labov, William 172
Laestadius, Lars Levi 166, 168
Lagerström, Gustaf Fredrik 34, 39
Laine, Tuija 162
Laitinen, Lea 8, 12–13, 83, 131, 170, 173, 174, 184, 189
Länkelä, Jaako 178
Lansing, Tereza 62
Larsson, Bo 89, 90
Latour, Bruno 95
Lauerma, Petri 12, 117, 162–168
Laurila, Vihtori 104
Lehikoinen, Laila 162, 167
Leino-Kaukiainen, Pirkko 103, 120
Lejeune, Philippe 107
Lemaire, Louis 24
Lemaire, Louise 24–25

211

Léman, Johan 106, 118, 185
Leo Africanus 15
Leppänen, Alfred 118
Lerner, Daniel 30
LeRoy Ladurie, Emmanuel 14–15
Liikanen, Ilkka 77
Liljewall, Britt 9, 32, 38, 89, 90, 102, 107, 109, 111, 115
Lindmark, Daniel 30, 37, 38
Lindqvist, Aleksanteri 106, 118
Lizelius, Anders 159, 165
Lockridge, Kenneth A. 38
Loftur Guttormsson 38, 41, 42, 43, 51, 52
Lönnrot, Elias 13, 106, 146, 150, 160, 165–167, 182–183, 185
Lönnrot, Henrik Johan 183
Lorenzen-Schmidt, Klaus-Joachim 13, 90, 99, 131
Love, Harold 40, 76
Lovie, Jacques 23
Lucy, John A. 170
Luðvik Kristjánsson 63
Luther, Martin 33, 42, 164, 168
Luttinen, Rauno 167
Luukkanen, Tarja-Liisa 77, 161
Lýður Jónsson 44, 45–46, 49
Lyons, Martyn 8, 9, 22, 79, 87, 102, 114, 115, 129, 131, 181

Mägiste, Julius 175
Magnús H. Árnason 62, 66, 67
Magnús Jónsson í Tjaldanesi 10, 50, 56–61, 62
Magnús Jónsson í Vigur 47, 49, 53–54, 56, 58
Magoun, Francis P. Jr. 167
Mäkinen, Ilkka 77, 86, 87, 103, 167
Makkonen, Anna 11, 116, 131, 132, 197
Malmberg, Nils Gustaf 164–166
Mandeville, John 17
Manninen, Antti 87
Mannonen, Ulla 12, 146, 148, 151–156
Manuelli, Gaudenzio 25, 27
Marchi, Anteo 18
Marchi, Clelia 18–19
Marie F. 23
Marotti, Arthur 76
Martínez Martín, Laura 21
Martini, Angiolina 19
Maurizio, Bernardo 26
Mayall, David 131
McKinnell, John 62
Melander, Björn 99
Menocchio (Domenico Scandella) 17–18

Meriläinen, Heikki 116
Mikkola, Kati 12, 147, 154, 155
Mitchell, S. A. 54
Mordenti, R. 18
Mossetti, Giuseppe 25
Muir, Edward 18
Munck, Thomas 43
Murtorinne, Eino 166–167
Mustonen, O. A. F. 152
Myllynen, Mari 175, 189
Myrdal, Janken 90

Näyhö, Kristiina 147
Nevalainen, Terttu 170
Nilsson, Anders 38
Nilsson, Johannes 34, 39
Niskanen, Lauri Juhana 111
Nordal, Guðrún 71
Nordlund, Taru 8, 12–13, 131, 162, 170, 171, 173, 177, 189
Numminen, Jaakko 77, 78, 86

Odén, Birgitta 31, 37, 38
Ojala, Isak 113–114, 118
Ólafur Eyjólfsson 143, 145
Ólafur Guðmundsson 59
Ólafur Halldórsson 61
Ólafur Teitsson 57
Ollila, Anne 77
Olson, David R. 37
Omoniyi, Topo 170
Ong, Walter 38
Ongari, Anselma 18
Örn Hrafnkelsson 134
Österberg, Maria 112, 119
Österberg, Matilda 112–113, 119
Ottenjann, Helmut 90

Packalen, Johan 178
Packalen, Klara 177–178
Päivärinta, Pietari 87, 110, 118
Pakarin[en], Matts 171–172
Páll Eggert Ólason 12, 55, 56, 58, 61, 134–135, 142
Panattaro, Giovanni 26
Papen, Uta 90, 92, 93, 98, 99
Paterson, John 162
Paunonen, Heikki 170
Peltonen, Ulla-Maija 152, 155
Perälä, Anna 162
Pers, Anders 35, 39
Pettersson, Lars 38
Pinagot, Louis-François 19
Poikonen, Johan 111, 113, 118

Poirrier, Philip 14
Pons, Anaclet 18
Poppius, Abraham 159
Porkka, Antti 173, 177
Porrier, Philippe 14
Porthan, H. G. 158–159, 167
Poulsen, Bjørn 13, 90, 99, 131
Pöysä, Jyrki 155
Pressman, Jon F. 170
Prinsloo, Mastin 99
Procacci, Giovanna 26–27
Pulkkinen, Paavo 167
Purcell-Gates, Victori 96, 97, 100

Quey, Delphin 22–23
Quey, Joseph 23
Qvirsfeld, Johann 34

Räisänen, Paavo 173
Rapola, Martti 160, 165, 167
Rasila, Viljo 127
Raumolin-Brunberg, Helena 170
Redfield, Robert 128
Rehumäki, Pekka 77
Renqvist, Henrik 12, 161–162, 166–167
Renvall, Gustaf 159–160, 167
Reutersvärd, Elisabeth 180
Riikonen, H. K. 167
Ringberg, Maja Stina 35, 38
Ringberg, Nils 35, 38
Robin, Jean 22
Roine, Maija-Stiina 118
Roslöf, Kustaa 102, 113, 114, 117, 118
Rossander, Arne 80
Roumiguières, Rosa 23
Rubalcaba Pérez, Carmen 18
Rudé, George 16
Rudéker, George
Runbäck, Jonas 35, 39
Runcis, Maija 38
Runeberg, Johan Ludvig 185
Ruotsalainen, Paavo 12, 111, 161, 163–164, 166–168
Russo, Matteo 18
Ruuth, Martti 77

Saari, Mirja 167
Sæmundur Dúason 66
Sälli, Kaarlo (see Eskola, Kalle)
Salmi-Niklander, Kirsti 10–11, 18, 77, 79, 84, 104, 130
Samuel, Raphael 16
Säteri, Pekka 173
Savander, Anna 83

Savander, Elin 83, 86
Savander, Mikko 83
Saxberg Kolho, Matti 108–109, 118
Schildt, Wolmar 106
Schmidt, W. A. 168
Schofield, R. S. 30
Scott, James C. 21, 127
Scott, Joan 91
Secchi, Luigi 27
Serna, Justo 18, 204
Setälä, E. N. 174
Sigfús Eymundsson 60, 63
Sigfús Jónsson 135
Sighvatur Grímsson Borgfirðingur 10–11, 40–48, 49, 58, 129
Sigurður Árnason 59
Sigurður Gylfi Magnússon 10, 62, 64, 65, 73, 74, 76
Sigurður Lynge 43, 44
Sigurgeir Steingrímsson 55
Silventoinen, Ulla 87
Silverstein, Michael 170, 172, 175, 179, 184, 186, 187
Sinisalo, Hannu 152
Sinnemäki, Maunu 167
Sinor, Jennifer 99
Sjöbring, Pehr 33, 39
Sjögren, A. J. 159
Slay, Desmond 60
Snellman, J. V. 146
Snorri Björnsson 47
Snorri Jakobsson 47
Snorri Sturluson 50
Sokoll, Thomas 16
Springborg, Peter 53
Stark, Laura 117, 129, 132, 146, 149
Stefán Aðalsteinsson 142
Stefán Karlsson 51
Steingrímur Jónsson 52
Stenbäck, Lydia 116
Stenholm, Karl 34, 39
Stephan G. Stephansson 69
Stiaccini, Carlo 25–27
Stoklund, Bjarne 13,
Stolt, Jonas 35, 39
Stone, Lawrence 30
Storå, Nils 89
Strauss, Gerald 38
Street, Brian 40, 87, 100
Strellman, Urpu 189
Sturla Sighvatsson 71
Sumpter, Caroline 87
Sundström, Maria 94, 100
Suodenjoki, Sami 78, 85, 130

213

Suolahti, Gunnar 86
Sutela, Elias 109, 118
Suutarla, Zefanias 110, 118
Svärd, Birgitta 38
Svenske, John 90
Sverrir Tómasson 61

Tanholin, Johan 116
Tanholin, Kaisa 116
Teleman, Ulf 100
Thomas à Kempis 164, 168
Thompson, E. P. 15
Timonen, Senni 155
Tolstoy, Leo 17
Tommila, Päiviö 87, 180
Topelius, Zachris (Sakari) 13, 123
Torfi H. Tulinius 61, 72–73
Traugott, Mark 131
Tunkelo, E. A. 149
Turk, Magnus Persson 34, 39
Turville-Petre, Gabriel 50

Vandenbussche, Wim 8, 170, 171, 177, 188
Varilainen, Mats 174
Västi, Pietari 107, 119
Verschueren, Jef 170

Vésteinn Ólason 61, 65, 66
Viðar Hreinsson 67, 68, 69–70, 75
Villstrand, Nils Erik 180
Vincent, David 131
Virtanen, Maria 131, 132
Vovelle, Michael 17

Warelius, Antti (Anders Varilainen) 174
Weber, Eugen 20
Wenäläinen, Petter 101–102, 115, 119
White, Goodit 170
White, Hayden V. 75
Wiegelmann, Günter 90
Wilson, William A. 150
Winsa, Birger 168
Winter, Jay 26
Woolard, Kathryn A. 170
Wrede, Mathilda 111

Zitzelsberger, Otto J. 60
Zumthor, Paul 60

Þorlákur Skúlason 53
Þorsteinn Guðmundsson 54–55
Þorsteinn M. Jónsson 143
Þorsteinn Þorsteinsson 49, 54, 57, 135, 145
Þórunn Valdimarsdóttir 47

Studia Fennica Ethnologica

Memories of My Town
The Identities of Town Dwellers and Their Places in Three Finnish Towns
Edited by Anna-Maria Åström, Pirjo Korkiakangas & Pia Olsson
Studia Fennica Ethnologica 8
2004

Passages Westward
Edited by Maria Lähteenmäki & Hanna Snellman
Studia Fennica Ethnologica 9
2006

Defining Self
Essays on emergent identities in Russia Seventeenth to Nineteenth Centuries
Edited by Michael Branch
Studia Fennica Ethnologica 10
2009

Touching Things
Ethnological Aspects of Modern Material Culture
Edited by Pirjo Korkiakangas, Tiina-Riitta Lappi & Heli Niskanen
Studia Fennica Ethnologica 11
2008

Gendered Rural Spaces
Edited by Pia Olsson & Helena Ruotsala
Studia Fennica Ethnologica 12
2009

Laura Stark
The Limits of Patriarchy
How Female Networks of Pilfering and Gossip Sparked the First Debates on Rural Gender Rights in the 19th-century Finnish-Language Press
Studia Fennica Ethnologica 13
2011

Where is the Field?
The Experience of Migration Viewed through the Prism of Ethnographic Fieldwork
Edited by Laura Hirvi & Hanna Snellman
Studia Fennica Ethnologica 14
2012

Studia Fennica Folkloristica

Pertti J. Anttonen
Tradition through Modernity
Postmodernism and the Nation-State in Folklore Scholarship
Studia Fennica Folkloristica 15
2005

Narrating, Doing, Experiencing
Nordic Folkloristic Perspectives
Edited by Annikki Kaivola-Bregenhøj, Barbro Klein & Ulf Palmenfelt
Studia Fennica Folkloristica 16
2006

Mícheál Briody
The Irish Folklore Commission 1935–1970
History, ideology, methodology
Studia Fennica Folkloristica 17
2008

Venla Sykäri
Words as Events
Cretan Mantinádes in Performance and Composition
Studia Fennica Folkloristica 18
2011

Hidden Rituals and Public Performances
Traditions and Belonging among the Post-Soviet Khanty, Komi and Udmurts
Edited by Anna-Leena Siikala & Oleg Ulyashev
Studia Fennica Folkloristica 19
2011

Mythic Discourses
Studies in Uralic Traditions
Edited by Frog, Anna-Leena Siikala & Eila Stepanova
Studia Fennica Folkloristica 20
2012

Studia Fennica Historica

Medieval History Writing and Crusading Ideology
Edited by Tuomas M. S. Lehtonen & Kurt Villads Jensen with Janne Malkki and Katja Ritari
Studia Fennica Historica 9
2005

Moving in the USSR
Western anomalies and Northern wilderness
Edited by Pekka Hakamies
Studia Fennica Historica 10
2005

Derek Fewster
Visions of Past Glory
Nationalism and the Construction of Early Finnish History
Studia Fennica Historica 11
2006

Modernisation in Russia since 1900
Edited by Markku Kangaspuro & Jeremy Smith
Studia Fennica Historica 12
2006

Seija-Riitta Laakso
Across the Oceans
Development of Overseas Business Information Transmission 1815–1875
Studia Fennica Historica 13
2007

Industry and Modernism
Companies, Architecture and Identity in the Nordic and Baltic Countries during the High-Industrial Period
Edited by Anja Kervanto Nevanlinna
Studia Fennica Historica 14
2007

CHARLOTTA WOLFF
Noble conceptions of politics in eighteenth-century Sweden (ca 1740–1790)
Studia Fennica Historica 15
2008

Sport, Recreation and Green Space in the European City
Edited by Peter Clark, Marjaana Niemi & Jari Niemelä
Studia Fennica Historica 16
2009

Rhetorics of Nordic Democracy
Edited by Jussi Kurunmäki & Johan Strang
Studia Fennica Historica 17
2010

Studia Fennica Anthropologica

On Foreign Ground
Moving between Countries and Categories
Edited by Minna Ruckenstein & Marie-Louise Karttunen
Studia Fennica Anthropologica 1
2007

Beyond the Horizon
Essays on Myth, History, Travel and Society
Edited by Clifford Sather & Timo Kaartinen
Studia Fennica Anthropologica 2
2008

Studia Fennica Linguistica

Minimal reference
The use of pronouns in Finnish and Estonian discourse
Edited by Ritva Laury
Studia Fennica Linguistica 12
2005

ANTTI LEINO
On Toponymic Constructions as an Alternative to Naming Patterns in Describing Finnish Lake Names
Studia Fennica Linguistica 13
2007

Talk in interaction
Comparative dimensions
Edited by Markku Haakana, Minna Laakso & Jan Lindström
Studia Fennica Linguistica 14
2009

Planning a new standard language
Finnic minority languages meet the new millennium
Edited by Helena Sulkala & Harri Mantila
Studia Fennica Linguistica 15
2010

LOTTA WECKSTRÖM
Representations of Finnishness in Sweden
Studia Fennica Linguistica 16
2011

TERHI AINIALA, MINNA SAARELMA & PAULA SJÖBLOM
Names in Focus
An Introduction to Finnish Onomastics
Studia Fennica Linguistica 17
2012

Studia Fennica Litteraria

Changing Scenes
Encounters between European and Finnish Fin de Siècle
Edited by Pirjo Lyytikäinen
Studia Fennica Litteraria 1
2003

Women's Voices
Female Authors and Feminist Criticism in the Finnish Literary Tradition
Edited by Päivi Lappalainen & Lea Rojola
Studia Fennica Litteraria 2
2007

Metaliterary Layers in Finnish Literature
Edited by Samuli Hägg, Erkki Sevänen & Risto Turunen
Studia Fennica Litteraria 3
2008

Aino Kallas
Negotiations with Modernity
Edited by Leena Kurvet-Käosaar & Lea Rojola
Studia Fennica Litteraria 4
2011

The Emergence of Finnish Book and Reading Culture in the 1700s
Edited by Cecilia af Forselles & Tuija Laine
Studia Fennica Litteraria 5
2011

Nodes of Contemporary Finnish Literature
Edited by Leena Kirstinä
Studia Fennica Litteraria 6
2012

White Field, Black Seeds
Nordic Literacy Practices in the Long Nineteenth Century
Edited by Anna Kuismin & M. J. Driscoll
Studia Fennica Litteraria 7
2013

www.ingramcontent.com/pod-product-compliance
Lightning Source LLC
Chambersburg PA
CBHW080805300426
44114CB00020B/2836